Costa Blanca Lifeline

by
Joanna Styles

SURVIVAL BOOKS • LONDON • ENGLAND

First published 2005

Survival Books Limited, 1st Floor,
60 St James's Street, London SW1A 1ZN, United Kingdom
☎ +44 (0)20-7493 4244, 🖩 +44 (0)20-7491 0605
✉ info@survivalbooks.net
🖥 www.survivalbooks.net
To order books, please refer to page 334.

British Library Cataloguing in Publication Data.
A CIP record for this book is available
from the British Library.
ISBN 1 901130 71 1

Printed and bound in Finland by WS Bookwell Ltd.

ACKNOWLEDGEMENTS

I would like to thank those who contributed to the publication of this book, in particular Katie Styles for her invaluable help, numerous staff at tourist offices and local councils for help with queries, Joe and Kerry Laredo (editing, proofreading and desktop publishing), the Comunitat Valenciana Tourist Board for some of the photographs, and everyone else who provided information or contributed in any way. Also a special thank-you to Jim Watson for the illustrations, maps and cover design.

TITLES BY SURVIVAL BOOKS

Alien's Guides
Britain; France

The Best Places To Buy A Home
France; Spain

Buying A Home
Abroad; Cyprus; Florida;
France; Greece; Ireland; Italy;
Portugal; South Africa; Spain;
Buying, Selling & Letting
Property (UK)

**Foreigners Abroad: Triumphs
& Disasters**
France; Spain

Lifeline Regional Guides
Costa Blanca; Costa del Sol;
Dordogne/Lot; Normandy;
Poitou-Charentes

Living And Working
Abroad; America;
Australia; Britain; Canada;
The European Union;
The Far East; France; Germany;
The Gulf States & Saudi Arabia;
Holland, Belgium & Luxembourg;
Ireland; Italy; London;
New Zealand; Spain;
Switzerland

Making A Living
France; Spain

Other Titles
Renovating & Maintaining
Your French Home;
Retiring Abroad

Order forms are on page 334.

WHAT READERS HAVE SAID ABOUT

Excellent book detailing everything you need to know before you go, as well as when you are there. If like me you are planning on a home in the sun, then this is the book for you before you go.

A revelation! This book tells it like it is – thank you Mr Hampshire, you obviously HAVE lived here, and your advice really hits the spot.

Mr Hampshire's book was invaluable. His research and data was excellent and very timely.

A must for all future ex-pats. Deals with every aspect of moving to Spain. I invested in several books but this is the only one you need. Every issue and concern is covered, every daft question you have on Spain but are frightened to ask is answered honestly without pulling any punches. Highly recommended.

I have been travelling to Spain for more than seven years and thought I knew everything – David has done his homework well. Excellent book and very informative! Buy it!

I am so glad that I chose this book from the others on offer. The author makes it simple to find information and it therefore becomes easier to remember, especially if your getting close to retirement!

We have been living in Marbella for nearly six months now but whenever we have a problem we turn to Living & Working Spain for the solution.

OTHER SURVIVAL BOOKS ON SPAIN

This book tells you the facts straight and simple. What I particularly liked was the way the author gave the advantages and disadvantages in most situations. All aspects are described in complete detail so that you won't miss anything. There is more information in this book than you could possibly hope for.

Everything from legal contracts to local climate. I would highly recommend this book as it gives very sound advice and a lot of facts.

This was a great help for me as I was preparing to move to Spain, and it was an enjoyable read.

The book is up to date and discusses all aspects of day to day life in Spain. I appreciate the book most because it is written in a way that will inform you no matter where you currently live. If you want to read just one book about living in Spain, this one is excellent.

Thank you David Hampshire for putting together such a marvellous book for everyone who wants to live in Sunny Spain! Have a question or concern – about housing, buying, leases, schools, money, even how to sort out your taxes – David gives you the answer.

A must for anyone wanting to travel in the Rioja region of Spain. I am planning a trip soon and this book will be my constant companion.

A very comprehensive guide to buying a place in Spain – presented in a very readable and humorous style – it has become my bible.

THE AUTHOR

Joanna Styles was born in London but has lived and worked for many years on the Costa del Sol, Spain. She is a freelance writer and the author of several books, including *The Best Places to Buy a Home in Spain*, *Buying a Home in Greece*, *Living & Working in the European Union* and *Costa del Sol Lifeline*, all published by Survival Books. She also regularly contributes to and updates many other Survival Books publications. Joanna is married with two daughters.

CONTENTS

11 Sports   243

12 Shopping   261

13 Miscellaneous Matters 281

Appendices 317

Index 327

Order Forms 334

IMPORTANT NOTE

Every effort has been made to ensure that the information contained in this book is accurate and up to date. However, the transient nature of the Costa Blanca – where people and businesses come and go with surprising speed – means that information can quickly change or become outdated. It's therefore advisable to check with an official and reliable source before making major decisions or undertaking an irreversible course of action. If you're planning to travel long-distance to visit somewhere, always phone beforehand to check the opening times, availability of goods and prices, and other relevant information.

Unless specifically stated, a reference to any company, organisation or product doesn't constitute an endorsement or recommendation.

AUTHOR'S NOTES

- In this book the Costa Blanca is also frequently refered to as 'the coast' or 'here'.

- The Costa Blanca has two official languages, Spanish or Castilian (*español* or *castellano*) and Valencian (*valenciano* in Spanish and *valencià* in Valencian – see page 188), a dialect of Catalan, one of Spain's four official languages. Place names throughout the Costa Blanca are often written in both languages or only in Valencian, which can be confusing, especially if the name is very different. This book uses place names in Spanish throughout; Valencian equivalents are shown on page 20.

- Times are shown using am for before noon and pm for after noon. All times are local, and you should check the time difference when making international calls. The Costa Blanca is one hour ahead of GMT.

- Costs and prices – all shown in euros (€) – should be taken as estimates only, although they were mostly correct at the time of publication.

- He/his/him also means she/her/her and is done to make life easier for the reader, and isn't intended to be sexist.

- All spelling is (or should be) British and not American English.

- The Spanish translation of many key words is shown in brackets in italics.

- Frequent references are made to urbanisations, a 'Costa-speak' term translated from the Spanish *urbanización* meaning a purpose-built development of dwellings.

- In some addresses, s/n (*sin número*) is used. This usually means that the location in question is the most important building on the street or at one end of it.

- Warnings and important points are shown in bold type.

- The following symbols are used in this book: ☎ (telephone), 🖳 (internet) and ✉ (email).

- Maps of the different parts of the Costa Blanca can be found in **Chapter 4 (Areas)**, a map of airports in **Chapter 2 (Getting There)** and a map showing the main roads in the area in **Chapter 3 (Getting Around)**.

- Lists of **English-Language Publications**, **Property Exhibitions** and **Useful Websites** are included in **Appendices A, B** and **C** respectively.

Racó de l'Albir,
Alfaz del Pi

INTRODUCTION

If you're thinking of living, working, buying a home or spending an extended holiday on the Costa Blanca, then this is **the book** for you. *Costa Blanca Lifeline* has been written to answer all those important questions about life on the Costa Blanca that aren't answered in other books. Whether you're planning to spend a few months or a lifetime on the coast, to work, retire or buy a holiday home, this book is essential reading.

An abundance of tourist guides and information is available about the Costa Blanca, but until now it has been difficult to find comprehensive information about local costs, facilities and services, particularly in one book. *Costa Blanca Lifeline* fills this gap and contains accurate, up-to-date practical information about the most important aspects of daily life on the Costa Blanca. Its contents include a comprehensive guide to the different areas; accommodation and property prices; employment prospects; health care and education facilities; local transport and communications; getting there; leisure and sport options; plus much more.

Information is derived from a variety of sources, both official and unofficial, not least the experiences of the author, her friends and colleagues. *Costa Blanca Lifeline* is a comprehensive handbook and is designed to make your stay on the Costa Blanca – however long or short – easier and less stressful. **It will also help you save valuable time, trouble and money, and will repay your investment many times over!** (For comprehensive information about living and working in Spain in general and buying a home in Spain, this book's sister publications, *Living and Working in Spain* and *Buying a Home in Spain*, written by David Hampshire, are highly recommended reading.)

The Costa Blanca is one of the world's most popular holiday destinations and a wonderful place to live – few regions can compete with its mild, sunny winters and long, warm summers; its stunning sandy beaches with the Mediterranean sparkling in the background; its vivacious and colourful *fiestas*; the delicious local cuisine and wine; not to mention the captivating Spanish lifestyle, with its emphasis on living life to the full and enjoying every minute of it! I trust *Costa Blanca Lifeline* will help make your life easier and more enjoyable, and smooth the way to a happy and rewarding time on the Costa Blanca.

¡Bienvenidos a la Costa Blanca!

Joanna Styles
February 2005

The church of Santa Maria, Alcoi

1

Introducing the Costa Blanca

The Costa Blanca, one of the world's top tourist destinations (in 2003 nearly 20 million tourists, including 5 million foreigners, visited the region in which it's situated), is widely considered to be one of the world's best retirement locations and is currently one of Europe's fastest growing residential areas.

FAST FACTS

Capital: Alicante
Largest Towns: Benidorm, Denia, Jávea, Orihuela and Torrevieja.
Population: Around 1.3 million (at least double this figure in the summer months).
Foreign Population: Officially around 15 per cent (the highest in Spain), although unofficial figures are considerably higher. Most foreigners are British who make up nearly 50 per cent of foreign residents.
Crime Rate: Generally low, although Alicante and Torrevieja both have higher crime rates than the national average.
GDP Growth in 2003: 1.8 per cent (2.2 per cent nationally)
Inflation in 2003: 2.4 per cent (2.6 per cent nationally)
Average Price of Property: €1,340 per m² (€1,625 per m² nationally).
Unemployment Rate: 3 per cent (10 per cent nationally)

The population currently stands at around 1.3 million and experts predict that if the current growth rate continues, some one million new residents will make the Costa Blanca their home over the next six years. Foreigners who relocate to the coast are mainly British (estimates claim that at least 300,000 British own property there), although the area is popular with Germans and Scandinavians too. Retirees are mainly British (some 44 per cent) who favour the towns of Torrevieja, Jávea and Calpe as retirement locations.

The Costa Blanca lies on the coast of southern Spain and stretches from Denia in the north to Pilar de la Horadada in the south for some 160km (100mi). It's part of the region of Comunidad Valenciana and the Costa Blanca lies in the province of Alicante, where tourism is highly developed and the area's main industry.

Foreigners are attracted to the Costa Blanca for many different reasons, including the following:

● The area's pleasant climate for most of the year (see page 285);

● Very good communications by road and air (see **Chapter 3**) and excellent telecommunications. It's now increasingly popular to 'telecommute' by internet and video conference;

- Accessibility – it's easy to get to and from Europe, particularly the UK, and many other parts of the world. Most European capitals are within three hours flying time of Alicante (see **Chapter 2**);

- Attractive surroundings – the Costa Blanca has very diverse natural and urban landscapes, and is within easy reach of stunning unspoilt scenery;

- Excellent leisure facilities – there's something for everyone (see **Chapter 10**);

- Excellent sports facilities (see **Chapter 11**);

- Good shopping (see **Chapter 12**);

- Friendly environment and cosmopolitan society;

- Good expatriate network.

The Costa Blanca isn't, however, perfect and disadvantages include:

- Overcrowding in the summer months when many resort areas are packed to bursting point;

- Rising property prices (see **Chapter 5**);

- Over-development in some areas of the coast – a high price to pay for the area's popularity;

- Poor infrastructure in some areas where demand hasn't kept up with investment in roads, hospitals and schools;

- The excess of foreigners can make it difficult to integrate with Spaniards and learn Spanish, although there are some areas that have preserved their Spanish identity in the face of tourism.

In spite of the disadvantages, most residents would agree that the Costa Blanca is a very pleasant place to live and judging by the rising population figures, it appears that many newcomers think so too!

FINDING OUT MORE

Essential Reading

- *Buying a Home in Spain 2005*, David Hampshire (Survival Books);

- *Living & Working in Spain 2005*, David Hampshire (Survival Books).

Tourist Guides to the Costa Blanca

- *AA Essential Guide Costa Blanca & Alicante*, Sally Roy (AA Publishing);

- *Berlitz Costa Blanca Guide* (Berlitz Pocket Guides);

- *Costa Blanca*, Mary Ann Gallagher (Dorling Kindersley);

- *Costa Blanca Insight Guide* (Insight Guides);

- *Valencia & the Costa Blanca*, Miles Roddis (Lonely Planet).

For a list of English-language publications available on the Costa Blanca see **Appendix A**.

Websites

The following sites provide tourist and general information in English. For websites about living and working in Spain see **Appendix C**.

- www.comunitatvalenciana.com (official tourist guide to the whole region of the Comunidad Valenciana, including the Costa Blanca);

- www.costablanca.org (the official tourist website for the area);

- www.info-costablanca.com (a general guide to the area);

- www.thisiscostablanca.com (general relocation information plus news and views).

PLACE NAMES

The Costa Blanca has two official languages, Spanish or Castilian (*español* or *castellano*) and Valencian (*valenciano* in Spanish and *valencià* in Valencian - see page 188), a dialect of Catalan, one of Spain's four official languages. Place names throughout the Costa Blanca are often written in both languages or only in Valencian, which can be confusing, especially if the name is very different. This book uses place names in Spanish throughout, but the following is an alphabetical list of major place names in both languages for reference:

Place in Spanish	Place in Valencian
Alfaz del Pi	L'Alfàs del Pi
Alicante	Alacant
Cabo de la Nao	Cap de la Nau
Calpe	Calp
Crevillente	Crevillent
Elche	Elx
Jalón	Xaló
Jávea	Xàbia
Muchamiel	Mutxamel
Peñón de Ifach	Penyal d'Ifac
Playa	Platja
San Juan de Alicante	Sant Joan d'Alacant
Villajoyosa	La Vila Joiosa

Almansa

2

Getting There

One of the Costa Blanca's main advantages is that it's easy and relatively quick to get to from most European countries, particularly the UK. Most visitors fly to Alicante airport, but many travel to Murcia or Valencia airport or by car via ferry to northern Spain or through France. This chapter looks at the different options for getting to the Costa Blanca and includes information on Alicante, Murcia and Valencia airports, flights and car hire, train information and road routes.

AIR

The Costa Blanca is served by three airports: Alicante, the main airport and the most centrally located; Murcia, a handy airport for the southern part of the Costa Blanca but small, with few facilities and no public transport; and Valencia, a good option for the northern parts of the Costa Blanca, but with few budget flight options. A brief guide to each airport follows below. Comprehensive information in English and Spanish about each airport can be found on the Spanish Airport Authorities (AENA) website (💻 www. aena.es) – go to *Elija Aeropuerto* or *Choose airport* on the left-hand side, scroll down the list to the airport you're looking for and click on the arrow.

There have been several attacks on newly arrived passengers at Alicante and Murcia airports by armed gangs. At Alicante airport, the gangs have attacked several people in the hire car parking areas and in the case of Murcia airport, they've followed hire cars or cars that have picked up passengers leaving the airport and attacked the occupants on quiet roads.

> You should be extra vigilant and women in particular are advised to take extra care when travelling to and from Murcia airport on their own at night.

Alicante Airport

Alicante's El Altet airport (general information ☎ 966-919 100, flight information ☎ 966-919 400) is the main entry point for visitors and residents on the Costa Blanca. The airport (11km/7mi to the south-west of Alicante city) is Spain's fourth busiest and handles an annual average of nearly 7 million passengers, the vast majority being from the EU (the UK in particular). The ever increasing number of passengers means the airport has long outgrown its size and construction of a new terminal, which will be divided into two buildings (one for departures and the other for arrivals) will start in the near future and is scheduled for completion by 2008. Meanwhile, expect to find facilities at the airport somewhat cramped!

Check In

The check-in area is situated on the ground floor with 38 check-in desks and seating areas. Numerous flight companies, including Iberia and British Airways have their offices here where last-minute ticket purchases are possible. **Check-in facilities are often over crowded so allow plenty of time for check-in before your flight leaves**, e.g. at least 90 minutes, more in summer. This area also has a post box, a small coffee bar, two cash machines and a bureau de change.

Departures

Once you go through security you go upstairs to the departure area which has a large main restaurant and several small snack-bars. Upstairs you will also find a newsagents, a bureau de change and numerous shops selling cosmetics and perfumes, leather goods, duty-free goods, sportswear and fashion, gifts and music. There are numerous seating areas and VIP lounges for some airlines.

Arrivals

Arrivals are in the basement and currently rather cramped, especially when there are several flights due in at the same time. There's a tourist information office, cash machine, a chemist's (open 7am to 11pm) and a small cafe. If you have long to wait for a flight to arrive, your best bet is to go upstairs to the largest departure facilities.

Banking Facilities

ATMs: Servired, Red 6000 and 4B
Bureau de Change: Offices in departures and arrivals (☎ 966-919 089)

Getting to and from Alicante Airport

By Train

No trains run to Alicante airport, but there are plans to extend the Alicante TRAM to the airport in the future, but not before 2007 at the very earliest. The only public transport option is to travel by bus.

By Bus

Airport to Alicante: This service is operated by the city bus company, SuBús (☎ 965-140 936, 🖳 www.subus.es), who run a daily bus service (C-6) every 40 minutes from the airport to the city centre from around 6.30am to 11pm. A one-way ticket costs €0.90 and the journey takes around 40 minutes.

Other Destinations: ALSA (☎ 902 422 242, 🖳 www.alsa.es) provide a service to and from Benidorm taking one hour and 15 minutes. Buses leave the airport for Benidorm at 10.30am, 2.30pm, 5.30pm and 9.30pm. Services from Benidorm to the airport leave at 8am, noon, 4pm and 8pm. Tickets cost €6 one-way.

By Shuttledirect

Shuttledirect (☎ 902-334 233, 🖳 www.shuttledirect.com) provide a private transport service to Alicante. **Pre-booking is essential** (minimum 24-hours) and prices range from €15 to €50 depending on the time of year and the number of people travelling.

By Taxi

There's a taxi rank outside the departures terminal and taxis are provided by Radio Taxi (☎ 965-910 123) and Unitaxi (☎ 965-252 511) only.

Approximate prices to or from Alicante airport are:

Alicante city centre:	€10
Altea:	€55
Benidorm:	€50
Calpe:	€60
Denia:	€75
Guardamar del Segura:	€20
Jávea:	€75

Orihuela Costa:	€30
Torrevieja:	€30
Villajoyosa:	€40

For information about getting to and from the airport by car see page 33.

Murcia Airport

Murcia's San Javier airport (airport and flight information ☎ 968-172 000) is one of Spain's fastest growing airports – some 1 million passengers used it in 2004 – and an increasingly popular budget-airline destination. The airport, situated on the north-west coast of the Mar Menor and 5km (3mi) from San Javier, is small by international standards and currently only opens when flights are due in or out, although some €16 million has been allocated for its expansion to allow the airport to operate 24-hours a day.

Departures

The departures hall is small with six check-in desks, a cafeteria, some small shops, a Servired cash machine and Ryanair and Iberia offices. **Check-in facilities are often over crowded so allow plenty of time for check-in before your flight leaves**, e.g. at least 90 minutes, more in summer.

Once you've passed security, there are three departure gates and a shop (Merlia) selling souvenirs, duty-free goods and other items.

Arrivals

The arrivals hall is small with car hire offices, an airport information office and tourist information.

There are no currency exchange facilities at the airport.

Getting to & from Murcia Airport

Murcia airport has no public transport services and your only options are by taxi or private car. The taxi rank is located outside the main airport building.

Approximate prices to and from Murcia Airport are:

Alicante:	€80
La Manga:	€30 – €60
Torrevieja:	€42

For information about getting to and from the airport by car see page 33.

Valencia Airport

Valencia's Manisses airport (general information ☎ 961-598 500, flight information ☎ 961-598 515) is the second main entry point for visitors and residents on the Costa Blanca. The airport (10km/6mi to the west of the city) is spacious and caters for more than 2.3 million passengers a year.

Departures

International and domestic flight departures is situated on the first floor where there's also a newsagents and numerous airline offices. Once you pass through security, there are several shops (souvenirs, duty-free, confectionery and gifts) and VIP lounges for some airlines. Upstairs are restaurants, cafes and a chemist's.

Arrivals

Arrivals are on ground level where there's also a newsagents, a bureau de change and an Airport's Authorities office (AENA). There isn't a tourist office, but the AENA office can provide maps of Valencia as well as lists of hotels and restaurants.

Banking Facilities

The bureau de change (☎ 961-598 692) in departures is open from 7am to 10pm Mondays to Fridays and from 9am to 9pm at weekends. The office in arrivals opens from 7am to 10.30pm Mondays to Fridays and from 9.30am to 2.30pm and 4.30am to 8.30pm at weekends.

There are two cash machines (Servired and 4B) in the departures area.

Getting to & from Valencia Airport

By Train

The C-4 local train line connects the airport with the city's mainline station (Estació del Nord), from where you can get regional trains to Alicante, Elche, Orihuela and Murcia (see **Trains** on page 35), or the C-1 local line to Gandía (see page 46). The service runs from 6am to around 11am. Trains for Valencia centre leave at 17 and 47 minutes past the hour and from the centre to the airport at 3 and 33 minutes past the hour. One-way tickets cost €1.15 and the journey takes around 20 minutes.

Information is available from ☎ 902-240 202 and 🖳 www.renfe.es/cercanias/valencia.

When the high-speed AVE trainline from Madrid to Malaga is completed in 2007, the service is expected to run to the airport as well as the city centre.

By Bus

The MetroBús (☎ 962-100 008) service runs from the airport to the city bus station from around 5am to around 11pm and services run approximately every ten minutes. Tickets cost €0.90.

By Taxi

There's a large taxi rank outside the arrivals terminal. Taxis to the city centre cost around €14. For other destinations expect to pay €0.40 per km plus supplements (e.g. €2.50 airport supplement). Taxis operating at the airport are Radio Taxi Valencia (☎ 963-703 333) and Radio Taxi (☎ 963-571 313).

For information about getting to and from the airport by car see page 33.

Flights

Domestic Flights

Daily flights from Alicante and Valencia are available to the following destinations in Spain: Asturias, Bilbao, Barcelona (several flights daily), Ceuta, Gran Canaria, León, Madrid (several flights daily), Malaga, Melilla, Palma de Mallorca, Salamanca, Santiago de Compostela, Tenerife, Valencia and Zaragoza. Domestic flights are operated by:

Air Europa (☎ 902-410 501, 🖳 www.air-europa.com);

Binter Canarias (☎ 928-579 601, 🖳 www.bintercanarias.es);

Iberia (☎ 902-400 500, 🖳 www.iberia.com);

Spanair (☎ 902-131 415, 🖳 www.spanair.com);

One-way flights to most destinations cost from €65 (€95 to the Canaries).

International Flights

Numerous airlines (scheduled, charter and the so-called 'budget' or 'no-frills' companies) fly to the Costa Blanca from destinations all over Europe with the UK and Germany being particularly well-served. Budget airlines are an increasingly popular means of travelling to the Costa Blanca, particularly for those wishing to travel there from smaller airports in the UK.

Prices vary greatly and one-way tickets start from as low as €40 during off-peak season to €250 during the summer months. Shop around (easy to do on the internet) and don't forget to enquire at your local travel agent who may have some good deals, particularly for last-minute flights or those booked well in advance. There are also several specialist flight shops on the Costa Blanca, many of which advertise in the English-language press and offer a good choice of prices and destinations. If you have to travel literally last-minute it may be worth going to the airport where several airlines have offices in the check-in area to see if any tickets are available. This is really only an option outside high season, although British Airways and Iberia often have (expensive) spare seats at any time of year on their scheduled flights. **When consulting prices don't forget to add airport taxes** (sometimes nearly as much or more than the ticket itself) and many airlines charge for payment by credit card (around €7) when you book over the phone or online.

Bear in mind that budget airlines are exactly that and you get nothing on the flight apart from your seat unless you pay for it! Food and drink is expensive on budget flights and the choice is limited. You can save money by taking your own or buying it beforehand in the airport, especially if there are several of you. Other airlines are also following this trend – Iberia no longer provide a newspaper on flights leaving after 10am and you now have to pay for food on its European flights. However, there are still airlines (e.g. British Airways and Monarch) where you get a paper, the chance to watch a video, and drinks and a meal are included in the flight price.

The following airlines fly from the UK and Ireland to airports in the Costa Blanca area.

Flights to Alicante

Company	Flies from	Contact Details
Aer Lingus	Cork, Dublin	☎ Ireland 0818-365 000 🖥 www.aerlingus.com
Air Scotland	Edinburgh, Glasgow	☎ 0141-222 2363 🖥 www.air-scotland.com
Air 2000	Gatwick, Manchester	☎ UK 0870-850 3999 🖥 www.air2000.com
BA	Gatwick, Heathrow	☎ UK 0870-850 9850 ☎ Spain 902-111 333 🖥 www.ba.com).
BMi Baby	Birmingham, Cardiff, East Midlands, Manchester, Teeside	☎ UK 0870-264 2229 ☎ Spain 902-100 737 🖥 www.bmibaby.com

Budgetair	Cork, Dublin, Shannon	☎ Ireland 01-611 4777 💻 www.budgetair.ie
Easy Jet	Belfast, Bristol, East Midlands, Liverpool, Gatwick, Luton, Newcastle, Stansted,	☎ UK 0871-750 0100 ☎ Spain 902-299 992 💻 www.easyjet.com
FlyBe	Birmingham, Exeter (Feb-Oct only), Southampton	☎ UK 0871-700 0535 💻 www2.flybe.com
Flyglobe Span	Edinburgh, Glasgow	☎ UK 08705-561522 💻 www.flyglobespan.com
GB Airways	Gatwick	☎ UK 0870-850 9850 ☎ Spain 902-111 333 💻 www.gbairways.com
Iberia	Heathrow	☎ UK 0845-850 9000 ☎ 902-400 515 💻 www-iberia.com
Jet2	Leeds Bradford	☎ UK 0871-226 1737 ☎ Spain 902-020 051 💻 www.jet2.com
Monarch	Gatwick, Luton, Manchester	☎ UK 0870-040 5040 💻 www.monarch-airlines.com
My Travel Lite	Birmingham	☎ UK 0870-156 4564 ☎ Spain 902-020 191 💻 www.mytravellite.com

Flights to Murcia

Company	Flies from	Contact Details
BMi Baby	East Midlands, Manchester	☎ UK 0870-264 2229 ☎ Spain 902-100 737 💻 www.bmibaby.com
FlyBe	Birmingham, Southampton	☎ UK 0871-700 0535 💻 www2.flybe.com
GB Airways	Gatwick	☎ UK 0870-850 9850 ☎ Spain 902-111 333 💻 www.gbairways.com

Jet2	Leeds Bradford, Manchester	☎ UK 0871-226 1737
		☎ Spain 902-020 051
		🖳 www.jet2.com
Murcia Flights	Birmingham, Gatwick, Manchester	☎ UK 0870-049 3093
		☎ Spain 968-175 150
		🖳 www.murciaflights.com
My Travel Lite	Birmingham, Manchester	☎ UK 0870-156 4564
		☎ Spain 902-020 191
		🖳 www.mytravellite.com
Ryanair	Dublin, East Midlands, Glasgow, Luton, Stansted	☎ UK 0871-246 0000
		🖳 www.ryanair.com

Flights to Valencia

There are (unusually) few charter or budget flights from UK destinations to Valencia.

Company	Flies from	Contact Details
Aer Lingus	Dublin	☎ Ireland 0818-365 000
		🖳 www.aerlingus.com
Easy Jet	Bristol, Gatwick, Stansted	☎ UK 0871-750 0100
		☎ Spain 902-299 992
		🖳 www.easyjet.com
GB Airways	Gatwick	☎ UK 0870-850 9850
		☎ Spain 902-111 333
		🖳 www.gbairways.com
Iberia	Heathrow, Manchester	☎ UK 0845-850 9000
		☎ Spain 902-400 515
		🖳 www-iberia.com
Jet2	Manchester	☎ UK 0871-226 1737
		☎ Spain 902-020 051
		🖳 www.jet2.com

The tour operator Thomson Fly also offer flights from numerous destinations in the UK to the Costa Blanca, although many flights are seasonal (UK only ☎ 08701-900 737, 🖳 www.thomsonfly.com).

Getting to & from the Airports by Car

Car Rental

There are numerous car rental companies based at the airports serving the area and most of those operating on the Costa Blanca offer an airport collection service. If you want to use a car from the airport it's advisable to book it before travelling and to book well in advance if you plan to hire a car in the summer. Out of season it isn't difficult to hire a car once you're here. Local companies are cheaper than national companies, although car hire on the Costa Blanca is generally cheap, mainly due to the intense competition for clients, so it's worth shopping around. When comparing companies **make sure prices include insurance and taxes (VAT at 16 per cent), that insurance cover is adequate and there are no hidden costs**. Note that if you plan to drive anywhere other than the coastal strip it involves mountainous terrain and you need a car with at least a 1.6 litre engine. Air conditioning is a must from June to the end of September.

Approximate starting prices in low season (from mid-November to late March) and in high season are as follows:

Category	Low-season	High-season
Economy/basic	€120	€150
Economy	€175	€225
Small car	€240	€300
Family car	€330	€400
Large family car	€420	€500
People carrier	€540	€630
Luxury car	€1,200	€1,450

Most local and national companies operating on the coast offer the possibility of collecting the car in one location and dropping it off at another.

Some of the main companies (in alphabetical order) operating on the Costa Blanca are:

- **ATESA** (☎ 902-100 101, 💻 www.atesa.es). Offices at Alicante (city and airport) and Murcia;

- **Auriga** (☎ 902-100 101, 💻 www.aurigacar.com). Offices at Alicante (city and airport), Benidorm, Denia, Murcia (city and airport) and Valencia (city and airport);

- **Avis** (☎ 902-135 531). Offices at Alicante airport, Benidorm, Denia, Elche, La Manga, Murcia airport and Valencia (city and airport);

- **Budget** (☎ 901 201 212, 💻 www.budget.es). Offices at Alicante (city and airport);

- **Centauro** (☎ 902-104 103, 💻 www.centauro.net). Offices at Alicante airport, Benidorm, Denia, Jávea, La Cala de Finestrat, Murcia airport, Torrevieja and Valencia airport;

- **Europa Rent a Car** (Alicante: ☎ 961-526 930, Murcia: ☎ 968-336 523, Valencia: ☎ 961-526 143, 💻 www.europa-rentacar.es). Offices at Alicante airport, Benidorm, Denia, Murcia airport, Torrevieja and Valencia airport;

- **Europcar** (☎ 902 405 020, 💻 www.europcar.es). Offices at Alicante (city and airport), Benidorm, Calpe, Denia, Elche, La Manga, Murcia (city and airport) and Valencia (city and airport);

- **Hertz** (☎ 902 402 405, 💻 www.hertz.es). Offices at Alicante (city and airport), Benidorm, Denia, Elche, Murcia (city and airport), Torrevieja and Valencia (city and airport);

- **Record** (☎ 964-343 034, 💻 www.recordrentacar.com). Offices at Alicante airport;

- **Sol-Mar** (Alicante: ☎ 966-461 000, Murcia: ☎ 968-335 542, 💻 www.sol mar.es). Offices at Alicante airport, Benidorm, Denia, Jávea, La Manga, Moraira, Murcia (city and airport), Torrevieja and Valencia (city and airport).

Other companies can be found in the yellow pages under '*Automóviles y furgonetas (alquiler)*'.

There are also rental companies who specialise in the rental of luxury cars (including chauffeur-driven), vans, mini-buses and lorries.

Rental cars are popular targets for thieves and most rental cars are obvious so don't leave valuables on show or easily accessible when you leave your car. Don't leave valuables on the seat with the window open when driving in towns.

Private Cars

Alicante Airport

The airport is easily reached via the A-7 (exit 72) and the N-340 from Elche. Access is well-signposted. The terminal building has a large drop-down area in front of it for drivers leaving passengers. Waiting time is limited to ten minutes after which your car may be towed away by airport authorities. Longer parking is available opposite the terminal building and costs €0.75 an hour up to a maximum of €7.50 a day.

Several private companies offer secure long-term parking facilities, which are considerably cheaper than airport parking, e.g. €3 per day, possibly including an airport collection and drop-off service. These companies are located near the airport and several advertise in newspapers such as *Costa Blanca News*. **Make sure the company you choose has adequate insurance, including fire and flood.**

Murcia Airport

The airport can be reached from the N-332 (via San Javier) and, more quickly, from the AP-7 toll road (exit 784). Access is well-signposted. The airport has free parking for some 177 cars.

Valencia Airport

Access is via the N-220, which can be reached from both the A-3 and N-335. The airport has parking for some 1,250 cars and costs €0.85 per hour or €6.75 a day. Monthly season tickets are also available and cost €101.40.

TRAINS

The Levante region of Spain is well-served by train services and there are various options from Madrid, Barcelona and France to stations in Alicante, Murcia and Valencia. Information on train services is available from RENFE (☎ 902-240 202, 🖳 www.renfe.es). On the website go to the *Quiero Viajar* section, select the arrival and departure stations and then click on *Realizar Consulta*. Note that for most journeys it's cheaper to buy a return ticket than a one-way.

From Madrid

Regular trains connect Madrid with Alicante and Valencia, as detailed below.

Alicante

The journey takes just under four hours in the high-speed TALGO or Altaria train and there are 11 trains a day. One-way tickets cost €31 or €36 in tourist class (*clase turista*) and €51 or €56 in first class (*clase preferente*). The TALGO service (one a day) also serves Bilbao.

Valencia

The journey takes around three and a half hours in the high-speed Alaris train and there are 11 services a day. One-way tickets cost €37 in tourist class and €57.50 in first class.

High-speed AVE lines from Madrid to Alicante and Murcia (via Albacete) and Valencia (via Cuenca) are currently under construction and due to be completed by 2007. The journey time will then be reduced to around one hour 45 minutes to Alicante and to one hour 25 minutes to Valencia.

From Barcelona

There are two train services from Barcelona, as follows:

Euromed

The Euromed train runs from Barcelona to Alicante with stops at Tarragona, Castellón and Valencia. There are five services daily and a one-way ticket to Alicante costs €44 in tourist class and €68.50 in first class. Journey times from Barcelona are two hours 50 minutes hours to Valencia and three hours 35 minutes to Alicante.

Arco

The Arco train runs from Barcelona to Murcia via Valencia, Alicante, Elche and Orihuela as well as numerous other stations on the way. There are two services a day and a one-way ticket to Alicante costs €38 in tourist class and €50 in first class. Journey times from Barcelona are five hours 15 minutes hours to Alicante and six hours 35 minutes to Murcia.

From France

Mare Nostrum

The Mare Nostrum train runs from Montpellier to Cartagena via Barcelona, Valencia, Alicante, Elche and Orihuela. There's one service a day and the journey takes around ten hours.

DRIVING

Many residents prefer to drive to the Costa Blanca from their country of origin, a practical option if you have lots of luggage or wish to have the use of your car while you're on the coast. Bear in mind, however, that the journey is long (the French border is around 650km/ 406mi from Alicante –

at least six hours driving) and you need to take into account the cost of motorway toll fees, the ferry and one overnight stay. (Distances shown below are to Alicante).

Suggested Routes

Via France

The main route to the Costa Blanca (1,780km/1112mi) is generally through central France to Toulouse crossing the Pyrenees at Puigcerdà and then via the north of Barcelona and Valencia. **Note that toll fees via this route cost around €100.**

- **In France** – N-20 (toll) via Toulouse to the Spanish border at Puigcerdà;

- **In Spain** – N-152 and C-146 to Urús (mainly single carriageway);

- C-16 to Berga and Terrassa (some single carriageway);

- A-2B to Matorell;

- AP-7 to Valencia and the Costa Blanca.

Via Bilbao

P&O operate ferries from Portsmouth to Bilbao (UK ☎ 0870-202 020, Spain ☎ 902-020 461, 💻 www.poferries.com) and the best route from Bilbao to the Costa Blanca (826km/516mi) is:

- A-8 to Logroño;

- AP-68 to Zaragoza;

- A-23/N-234 to Daroca, Teruel and then to Valencia (some stretches of single carriageway);

- AP-7 to the Costa Blanca.

Via Santander

The ferry route from Plymouth to Santander is run by Brittany Ferries (☎ UK 0870-536 0360, Spain ☎ 942-360 611, 💻 www.brittany-ferries.com) and the best route from Santander to the Costa Blanca (830km/519mi) is:

- N-623 Santander to Burgos (single carriageway, dual-carriageway under construction);

- A-62, A-1 Burgos to Madrid (take the M-50 and R-3 round Madrid);

- A-3 to Valencia;

- AP-7 to the Costa Blanca.

Roads are generally good and are dual-carriageway throughout most of Spain. Traffic information is available in France from 💻 www.bison-fute.equipment.gouv.fr (in French only) and in Spain from 💻 www.dgt.es (in Spanish only).

Altea

3

Getting Around

This chapter examines the public transport system in different localities on the Costa Blanca, namely trains, buses, ferries and taxis, and different aspects of getting around by car, including information on roads, the toll motorway, driving rules, car maintenance and road tax.

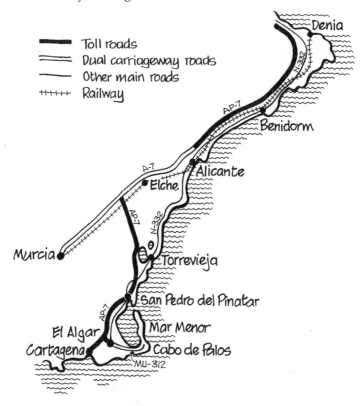

PUBLIC TRANSPORT

Public transport on the coast varies from excellent to poor. In some areas you can use public transport as an efficient means of commuting and in others buses put in a sporadic appearance and are often full so they don't stop. However, public transport is improving and local and regional authorities are making a concerted effort to provide more efficient means of getting around other than by car, e.g. the FGV train line (see **Future Plans** on page 50) is being improved to allow more frequent trains. In general, however, and until this work is completed, unless you live and work in the centre of a town or city, private transport is essential. This section deals with public transport on the coast in general. For information about public transport within each locality see **Chapter 4**.

Buses

Buses are the principal means of public transport on the coast and the main routes are run by several companies, including Alsa (☎ 902-422 242, 💻 www.alsa.es), in the north, and Costa Azul (☎ 965-924 660), Subús (☎ 965-140 936, 💻 www.subus.es) and Vegabús (☎ 965-457 553) in the south. There are also some other local bus operators such as Llorente Bus in Benidorm. Services are generally good, although much reduced at weekends and on public holidays. Frequency increases during the summer months.

The following alphabetical list provides information about bus stations on the Costa Blanca and the services provided.

Alicante

Alicante bus station situated in C/ Portugal 17 (☎ 965-130 700) is the main transport centre for the area. International buses from the UK, France and many European cities stop at this main bus station as well as the main local and regional services. Facilities at the bus station are limited and parking is difficult.

Altea

Altea has no bus station. Most buses stop at the two main bus stops situated by the train station and in the Plaza de Europe. **There are no facilities and parking is difficult.**

Benidorm

The city doesn't have a bus station as such and currently most regional and long-distance buses leave from Avda Europa 8 (Alsa ☎ 902-422 242). Local buses leave from various central points (Llorente Bus ☎ 965-854 322). A large bus station is currently under construction near Terra Mítica and expected to be finished by summer 2005. There's a frequent bus service to Alicante, the airport and localities both in the Marina Baja and Marina Alta. Inland towns and villages also have a regular bus service to Benidorm.

Calpe

Calpe has no bus station and the main bus stop is situated on the west side of the town near the health centre and in C/ Capitán Pérez. Buses run frequently to Alicante and Valencia (via Denia or Jávea). A local bus service with three services in the morning and two in the afternoon connects Calpe with Moraira and Teulada. Information about bus services and times is available from ☎ 965-839 029.

Denia

The bus station (☎ 966-435 045) is situated at the Plaza Archiduque Carlos. There are hourly buses to Las Rotas and Las Marinas, and frequent services to Alicante, Jávea and Valencia. There are also daily bus services to Jalón and Orba as well as Barcelona, Madrid and Malaga. **Note that there is little parking space at the bus station and few facilities.**

Elche

The bus station (☎ 966-615 050) is in Avda del Ferrocarril 4 and there's a good frequent service to Alicante, Murcia, Orihuela and the southern coast.

Guardamar del Segura

The bus station (☎ 965-729 126) is in C/ Molivent. Local services leave frequently for Santa Pola and Torrevieja as well as Alicante and Orihuela.

Orihuela

The bus station (☎ 966-736 089) is situated in the Avda de la Estación s/n and Orihuela is well-connected by bus services to Alicante, Murcia and the coast.

Santa Pola

The town doesn't have a bus station as such and buses stop in the Avda de Elche (near the Red Cross and outdoor market) for Alicante, Elche and the south.

Torrevieja

The bus station (☎ 966-701 068) is situated in Avda del Mar s/n and there are frequent services to Alicante, Orihuela and localities within the southern coastal area.

Villajoyosa

Villajoyosa has no bus station. The main bus stops for Alicante and the south are situated in the Plaza de la Avda del País Valenciá and C/ Cervantes, outside the bank Caja Altea. The bus stop for buses going to Benidorm and the north is also in C/ Cervantes, opposite the bank Caja Altea.

Ferries

To & From Denia

The port at Denia has daily ferry services to Ibiza (Ibiza Town and San Antonio resort) and Palma de Mallorca provided by Balearia (☎ 902-160 180, 🖳 www.balearia.net) and Iscomar (within Spain ☎ 902-119 128, outside Spain ☎ 00 34 971-437 500, 🖳 www.iscomar.com) ferry companies. Crossings to or from Ibiza take two hours or four hours with Balearia depending on the ferry and four and a half hours with Iscomar. The journey to or from Palma takes three and a half hours with Balearia and ten hours with Iscomar. Ferries take passengers and vehicles, and are equipped with restaurants, cabins and shops. Both companies have telephone and internet booking services. It's best to book in advance for all services especially in the summer when ferries get very full.

Bear in mind that ferry crossings may be cancelled in bad weather. Residents on the Balearics are entitled to discount fares.

Balearia runs a daily service to Ibiza Town, Ibiza San Antonio and Palma. The high-speed service to Ibiza taking just two hours runs four times a week. One-way fares cost from €49 for a passenger and €145 for a car.

Iscomar runs services to Ibiza and Palma everyday except Saturday. One-way fares cost from €30 for a passenger and €90 for a car.

To & From Valencia

Spain's main ferry company, Trasmediterranea (☎ 902-454 645, 🖳 www.trasmediterranea.com), runs daily ferry services from Valencia to Ibiza (crossings take three hours) and Majorca (four hours on the high-speed ferry, over seven hours otherwise) throughout the year and a once-weekly service to Minorca (crossing takes 15 hours) during the summer months. Fares vary depending on the time and day of crossing, and time of year.

Taxis

Taxis (white vehicles with a blue or green vertical stripe down the bonnet) are plentiful on the Costa Blanca and aren't expensive, particularly if there are several of you to share the cost. Within urban areas rates are metered and for other journeys there are fixed fees. Taxis charge extra for luggage and after 10pm. You can either take a taxi from an authorised tax rank or telephone for one.

Telephone numbers for taxis in the main towns are listed below:

Alicante	☎ 965-910 591 or ☎ 965-101 611
Altea	☎ 965-845 555
Benidorm	☎ 965-862 626 or ☎ 965-861 818
Benissa	☎ 965-731 513
Calpe	☎ 965-830 038 or ☎ 965-837 878
Denia	☎ 966-424 444 or ☎ 965-786 565
Elche	☎ 965-427 777
Gata de Gorgos	☎ 965-756 366
Guardamar	☎ 965-728 311
Jávea	☎ 966-460 404 or ☎ 965-793 224
La Manga	☎ 968-563 863
Mar Menor	☎ 968-563 039
Moraira	☎ 965-744 281
Orihuela	☎ 966-740 202
Orihuela Costa	☎ 966-761 088
Santa Pola	☎ 965-411 111
Teulada	☎ 965-744 281
Torrevieja	☎ 965-712 277 or ☎ 965-711 026
Villajoyosa	☎ 965-894 545

Trains

The Costa Blanca is served by several train lines: the local narrow gauge *Trenet* and *TRAM* from Alicante to Denia; the local services linking Alicante to Orihuela and Murcia, and Gandía to Valencia; and the Alicante to Valencia service.

Trenet & TRAM

One of the few train services in Spain not run by the state rail company RENFE, is the *Trenet* owned by FGV (Ferrocarriles de la Generalitat Valenciana), a service which is complimented by the *TRAM*, part of the Alicante public transport consortium. The *Trenet/TRAM* service, which runs from Puerta del Mar in Alicante to Denia with stops at El Campello, Creueta, Benidorm, Altea, Calpe, Teulada, Gata and Denia, is efficient and a very popular of commuting into Alicante – some 4,000 passengers use El Campello station a day. The *Trenet/TRAM* involves transport by tram from Alicante to El Campello station where passengers can directly board the *Trenet* train if they wish to travel any further – timetables are co-ordinated.

The trains are comfortable with air conditioning and piped classical music. Tickets can be bought from machines at most stations, or from ticket offices which can be found only at main stations.

TRAM

The *TRAM* (☎ 900-720 472, 🖳 www.tram-alicante.com) runs two services an hour from central Alicante (Puerta del Mar) with stops at La Marina, La Isleta, Albufereta and Condomina within the city, and stops at points along the eastern coastline of Playa de San Juan before reaching El Campello.

The journey from Alicante to El Campello takes 25 minutes and the service is generally very efficient with a high degree of punctuality. The first tram leaves Alicante centre at 5.50am. Subsequent trams leave at 20 and 50 minutes past the hour. The last tram is at 9.50pm. The first tram leaves El Campello at 6.23am. Subsequent trams leave at 53 and 23 minutes past the hour. The last tram leaves at 10.23pm.

Trenet

The *Trenet* service, which follows a very attractive scenic route, stops at some 28 stations between El Campello and Denia, the main ones being Villajoyosa, Benidorm (Terra Mítica theme park), Alfaz del Pi, Altea, Calpe, Benissa, Teulada, Gata and Denia. Ticket prices vary as follows:

- **Alicante to Benidorm** – €3.20 one-way, €5.45 return;

- **Alicante to Calpe** – €4.90 one-way, €8.35 return;

- **Alicante to Denia** – €7.15 one-way and €12.20 return.

The *Trenet* service is divided into two sections:

El Campello to Benidorm/Altea: The *Trenet* service runs from El Campello to Benidorm and Altea hourly with the first at 6.22am and subsequent trains at 50 minutes past the hour. The last train is at 7.50pm. The first train leaves Altea at 6.22am and from Benidorm at 6.36am. Subsequent trains leave at 22 minutes past the hour. The last train leaves Altea at 8.19pm and Benidorm at 8.36pm.

Journey times are as follows (add 25 minutes extra for Alicante to El Campello):

- El Campello to Alfas del Pi (52 minutes);

- El Campello to Altea (58 minutes);

- El Campello to Benidorm (46 minutes);

- El Campello to Villajoyosa (27 minutes).

El Campello to Denia: The *Trenet* service runs from El Campello to Denia around every two hours with the first train at 6.22am and subsequent trains at 8.22am, 10.22am, 1.22pm, 3.22pm, 5.22pm and 7.22pm (the last train). The first train leaves Denia at 6.25am and subsequent trains at 8.25am, 10.25am, 1.25pm, 3.25pm, 5.25pm and 7.25pm.

Journey times are as follows (add 25 minutes extra for Alicante to El Campello):

- El Campello to Benissa (1 hour 29 minutes);

- El Campello to Calpe (1 hour 16 minutes);

- El Campello to Denia (just under two hours);

- El Campello to Gata (1 hour 45 minutes);

- El Campello to Teulada (1 hour 35 minutes).

Note that some stations (Benidorm and Calpe) are to the north of the town itself, but many have parking facilities nearby and local bus services run from the station to the town centre.

Other Local Services

The local train services (*cercanías*) run by RENFE provide two services in the Costa Blanca, the line from Alicante to Murcia and the line from Gandía to Valencia.

Murcia to Alicante

For more information ring ☎ 902-240 202 or visit 💻 www.renfe.es/cercanias/murcia.

This line stops at:

- **Zone 1** – Murcia, Beniaján, Torreagüera, Los Ramos;

- **Zone 2** – Beniel, Orihuela, Callosa del Segura;

- **Zone 3** – Albatera – Catral, Crevillente;

- **Zone 4** – Elche Carrús, Elche Parque;

- **Zone 5** – Torrellano, San Gabriel;

- **Zone 6** – Alicante.

Trains are hourly and the first train leaves Alicante at 6.05am and the last at 10.05pm. From Murcia, the first train leaves at 5.55am and the last at 9.55pm.

Journey times are:

- Alicante to Elche (around 25 minutes);

- Alicante to Orihuela (around an hour);

- Alicante to Murcia (around one hour 20 minutes).

Gandía to Valencia

For more information ring ☎ 902-240 202 or visit 🖥 www.renfe.es/cercanias/valencia.

This line stops at:

- **Zone 1** – Valencia Estació del Nord, Alfar – Benetusser, Massanassa, Catarroja;

- **Zone 2** – Silla, El Romarí;

- **Zone 3** – Sollana;

- **Zone 4** – Sueca, Cullera;

- **Zone 5** – Tavernes de la Valldigna, Xeraco;

- **Zone 6** – Gandía, Playa de Gandía and El Grau.

Trains leave every 15 minutes from Gandía (at 3, 18, 33 and 48 minutes past the hour) and from Valencia (at 8 and 38 minutes past the hour). The first train leaves Gandía at 6.03am and the last at 10.18pm. From Valencia the first train leaves at 7.08am and the last at 10.38pm. The full journey from end to end takes around 55 minutes. A bus service runs from Denia to Gandía station.

Ticket Prices

Murcia to Alicante

Tickets are priced depending on the number of zones you travel through (e.g. Alicante to Elche is three zones and Alicante to Orihuela, five) and prices are as follows:

	Number of Zones					
	1	**2**	**3**	**4**	**5**	**6**
Mondays to Fridays	€1.00	€1.15	€1.65	€2.30	€2.65	€3.70
Return Mondays to Fridays	€1.40	€1.70	€2.65	€3.65	€4.30	€5.65
Return weekends/public holidays	€2.00	€2.30	€3.30	€4.60	€5.30	€7.40

Monthly season tickets are also available and cost €65 for travel over five zones.

Gandía to Valencia

Tickets are priced depending on the number of zones you travel through (e.g. Gandía to Valencia is six zones) and prices are as follows:

	Number of Zones					
	1	**2**	**3**	**4**	**5**	**6**
Mondays to Fridays	€1.00	€1.15	€1.60	€2.20	€2.60	€3.40
Return Mondays to Fridays	€1.40	€1.70	€2.60	€3.65	€4.20	€5.50
Return weekends/public holidays	€2.00	€2.30	€3.20	€4.40	€5.20	€6.80

Monthly season tickets are also available and cost €76 for travel over six zones.

Future Plans

There are advanced ambitious plans for the modernisation of both the *Trenet* and *TRAM* services to provide a more efficient and frequent service for the main localities on the northern section of the Costa Blanca. The *Trenet* line is currently being converted into double-track to allow more services and by 2007 a direct service from Alicante to Denia will be available taking one hour instead of two and a half. There will also be more services between Altea, Benidorm and Alicante. The *TRAM* service is being extended to a total of 40km (25mi) with two lines: Line 1 from Puerta del Mar to El Campello and Line 2 covering central and northern parts of the city. The project is expected to cost in excess of €500 million.

There are also plans to extend the train line from Denia to Gandía where it would join the local RENFE service to Valencia (see page 49), possibly by 2010, although the extension has been put off on numerous occasions by the regional government.

DRIVING

Unless you live in the centre of a town or near a local railway station, private transport is essential on the Costa Blanca. Although road communications have improved enormously in recent years, they haven't kept up with demand and many routes in the Costa Blanca are now extremely busy, a situation that is far worse in the summer months when the population swells.

Basic Driving Rules

● Keep your driving licence, personal ID and car documents (including insurance) with you at all times when driving.

● Seat belts must be worn in the front and back, and children under 12 must sit in a proper child seat. **Note that children under 12 aren't permitted to sit in the front seat.**

● Cars must carry two red warning triangles, a spare set of bulbs and fuses, and a reflective waistcoat (to be worn if you get out of your car on the road or hard shoulder).

● Speed limits are: 40kph or 50kph in built-up areas (*vías urbanas*); 90kph on main roads (*carreteras*); 100kph on dual-carriageways (*autovías*); and 120kph on motorways (*autopistas*).

● Don't drink and drive. Maximum permitted alcohol levels are 0.5mg.

● Don't leave valuables on show when you park your car and don't leave valuables on the seat with the window open when driving in towns.

Note that the police are permitted to impose on-the-spot fines of up to €300, which must be paid immediately unless you're a Spanish resident driving a Spanish-registered vehicle.

Car Dealers

Below is a alphabetical list of the main car dealers on the Costa Blanca. Addresses and telephone numbers can be found in the yellow pages under *Automóviles: concesionarios* or *Automóviles nuevos y de ocasión*.

Alfa Romeo

Alicante	Alimotor, Ctra de Murcia km 73	☎ 965-107 066
Elche	L'Aljub Motor, Avda de Alicante 132 ⌨ www.mundoalfa.com	☎ 966-613 170

Audi

Alfaz del Pi Sala Hermanos Import, Avda Europa 50   ☎ 966-864 056

Alicante Sala Hermanos Import, Ctra N-332, Pol Ind
40, San Juan   ☎ 965-939 040

Elche Serramóvil, C/ Hospitalet Llobregat 3   ☎ 966-613 203

Orihuela Automoción Oleza, Ctra Murcia – Alicante
km 28   ☎ 966-736 902
🖳 www.audi.es

BMW/Mini

Alicante Automóviles Fersan, Ctra Alicante –
Valencia, San Juan   ☎ 965-657 392

Elche Hispamovil, C/ Monovar s/n   ☎ 966-612 052

El Verger Automóviles Fersan, Avda Valencia 27   ☎ 966-439 804

Finestrat Automóviles Fersan, C/ Alicante 4   ☎ 966-889 600
🖳 www.bmw.es

Chrysler

Alicante Sorio y Borja SA, Ctra de Ocaña s/n   ☎ 965-102 231

Denia Sorio y Borja SA, Avda de Valencia 31   ☎ 966-432 189

Elche Sorio y Borja SA, Ctra de Crevillente 53   ☎ 966-671 442
🖳 www.chrysler.es

Citroën

Alicante Cytra SA, Ctra de Madrid km 408, 5,2   ☎ 965-286 000

Benidorm Devesa Móvil, Avda Comunidad
Valenciana s/n   ☎ 965-859 843

Elche Evaristo Vicente SA, Ctra de Alicante km 2   ☎ 966-613 03

Fuengirola Emcasa, Avda Jacinto Benavente   ☎ 952-460 550

**Gata de
Gorgos** Auto Gata, Ctra N-332 km 169   ☎ 965-756 250

| Orihuela | Macauto, Ctra Alicante – Murcia km 28 | ☎ 966-740 786 |
| **San Pedro de Pinatar** | Costamotor, Avda Dr Artero Guirao 228 🖥 www.citroen.es | ☎ 968-180 578 |

Daewoo

Alicante	Plauto SA, Ctra de Ocaña 40-42	☎ 965-165 502
Benidorm	Lilla Móvil, Avda Alfonso Puchades 25	☎ 965-854 066
Denia	Turismos y Posventa, Partida Madrigueras 20A	☎ 965-782 890
Elche	Skei Automóviles, C/ Sor Josefa Alcorta 37B	☎ 966-634 041
Orihuela	Skei Automóviles, Ctra Murcia – Alicante km 27.1 🖥 www.daewoomotor.es	☎ 966-744 154

Fiat/Lancia

Alicante	Alimotor SA, Avda Novelda 100	☎ 965-170 461
Elche	Esthermóvil, C/ Antonio Machado 87	☎ 966-655 661
Orihuela	Esthermóvil, Ctra Orihuela – Bigastro km 27 🖥 www.fiat.es	☎ 966-736 945

Ford

Alicante	Mundicar SA, Ctra de Murcia km 73.6	☎ 965-287 122
	Movilsa, Ctra de Valencia km 88.8, San Juan	☎ 965-657 312
Elche	Automóviles Crespo SA, Avda de Alicante 55 🖥 www.ford.es	☎ 965-453 699

Honda

| Alicante | Hersa Motor, Plaza de la Luna 1 | ☎ 965-100 622 |
| Alfaz del Pi | Hersa Motor, Avda de Europa 179 | ☎ 966-864 681 |

Elche	Ankara Motor, C/ Sor Josefa Alcorta 41	☎ 966-630 606
Orihuela	Ankara Motor, Ctra Murcia – Alicante km 27.1 ▯ www.honda.es	☎ 965-305 531

Hyundai

Alicante	Motrasa Repuestos SA, Avda Aguilera 58	☎ 965-104 118
Altea	Motrasa Repuestos SA, Ctra Altea – Benidorm s/n	☎ 965-845 753
Denia	Motrasa Repuestos SA, Ctra Denia – Ondara s/n	☎ 966-430 066
Elche	Auto Fima, Ctra Murcia – Alicante km 53	☎ 965-431 601
Torrevieja	Auto Fima, C/ Apolo 80 ▯ www.hyundai.es	☎ 966-704 217

Isuzu

Gandía	Martínez y Pastor Autotaller, C/ Marruecos 11 ▯ www.isuzu.es	☎ 962-874 054

Jaguar

Alicante	Automed, Avda de Orihuela 93 ▯ www.jaguar.com	☎ 965-114 333

Jeep

Alicante	Sorio y Borja SA, Ctra de Ocaña s/n	☎ 965-102 231
Denia	Sorio y Borja SA, Avda de Valencia 31	☎ 966-432 189
Elche	Sorio y Borja SA, Ctra de Crevillente 53 ▯ www.jeep.es	☎ 966-671 442

Kia

Alicante	CarTrade, Avda de Orihuela 153	☎ 965-115 600
Elche	Navaliza, Ctra Murcia – Alicante km 53	☎ 956-437 598

| **Finestrat** | Cartrade, Pol Ind Marina Finestrat,
C/ Gandía 1 | ☎ 966-889 874 |
| **Torrevieja** | Navaliza, Avda Cortes Valencianas 46
🖳 www.kia.es | ☎ 965-715 631 |

Land Rover

| **Denia** | Auto Perbo, Ctra Denia – Ondara km 1 | ☎ 966-425 656 |
| **Benidorm** | Auto Perbo, C/ Marbella 1, Edif Mariscal VII
🖳 www.landrover.es | ☎ 965-865 051 |

Lexus

| **Alicante** | Mediterráneo Prestige Car, Ctra
N-332 km 113, Santa Faz
🖳 www.mundolexus.com | ☎ 965-157 807 |

Mazda

Alicante	Novocar Sport, Ctra de Ocaña km 10	☎ 965-107 639
Gandía	Balmoral Sport, Avda de Valencia 62	☎ 962-879 696
Villajoyosa	Aeronáutica Motors, Ctra Alicante – Valencia km 116.7 🖳 www.mazda-es.com	☎ 966-830 492

Mercedes

Altea	Servidauto, C/ Partida Cap Blanch 39	☎ 965-840 732
Denia	Hijos de M. Crespo, Avda Denia 151	☎ 965-266 100
Elche	Vegar Concesiones, Ctra Murcia – Alicante km 53	☎ 965-445 617
Orihuela	Auto-Talleres, Ctra Murcia – Alicante km 28	☎ 966-744 466
Torrevieja	Quesauto, C/ Apolo 103 🖳 www.mercedes-benz.es	☎ 965-714 754

Mitsubishi

| **Alicante** | MMC Alicante, Ctra de Valencia
km 89.5, San Juan | ☎ 965-940 343 |

Altea	MMC Alicante, Partida Cap Blanc 77	☎ 965-843 409
Denia	MMC Alicante, Partida Madrigueres Norte 20	☎ 966-426 206
Elche	MMC Alicante, Ronda Vall D'Uxó 60, Pol Ind Carrús 🖳 www.mitsubishi-motors.es	☎ 966-673 331

Nissan

| **Alicante** | NiuMóvil, C/ Riu Muni 2 | ☎ 965-102 820 |
| **Orihuela** | Francisco Marcos, Ctra Murcia – Alicante km 26 🖳 www.nissan.es | ☎ 965-300 983 |

Opel

Alicante	Borjamotor, Ctra Ocaña s/n	☎ 965-288 800
Benidorm	Pérez Pascual, Avda Alfonso Puchades 25	☎ 965-854 066
Elche	Marcos Motor SA, Ctra Murcia – Alicante km 54.3	☎ 965-463 352
Orihuela	Automoción Vega, Ctra Murcia – Alicante km 22.4 🖳 www.opel.es	☎ 966-740 522

Peugeot

Alfaz del Pi	Alteauto, Avda Europa 55	☎ 966-864 311
Altea	Alteauto, Avda Llano del Castillo 39	☎ 965-840 795
Benidorm	Alteauto, Cala Finestrat km 4	☎ 966-813 520
Callosa d' En Sarrià	Alteauto, Partida Armaig s/n 🖳 www.peugeot.es	☎ 965-882 134

Renault

Alicante	Automóviles Gomis, Avda de Denia s/n	☎ 965-152 510
Altea	Autos L'Olla, Partida La Olla 126	☎ 965-841 036
Elche	Surecar, Ctra de Murcia 32	☎ 966-662 255

Santa Pola	Ctra de Elche 10 🖥 www.renault.es	☎ 965-413 746

Rover

Denia	Auto Perbo, Ctra Denia – Ondara km 1	☎ 966-425 656
Benidorm	Auto Perbo, C/ Marbella 1, Edif Mariscal VII 🖥 www.landrover.es	☎ 965-865 051

SAAB

Alicante	Tuwyncar, Avda Rio Turia 16	☎ 965-110 553
Elche	Marcos Motor, Ctra Murcia – Alicante km 54.3 🖥 www.saab.com	☎ 965-463 352

Seat

Alfaz del Pi	Sayalero, Ctra Alicante – Valencia km 126.8	☎ 966-864 017
Alicante	Automóviles Sala Rodríguez, Avda de Denia 145	☎ 965-263 100
Benissa	José Jorro Such e Hijos SA, Avda de Europa 9	☎ 965-732 115
Elche	Serrauto, Mallorca Pol, Altabaix 1	☎ 966-613 019
Orihuela	Autos Ramón's, Ctra N-340 Km 29.3	☎ 966-754 575
Torrevieja	Rubio Motor, C/ Apolo 97 🖥 www.seat.es	☎ 966-705 287

Skoda

Alicante	Laura Motor, Avda de Aguilera 2-4	☎ 965-926 737
Elche	Serraimport, C/ Hospitalet Llobregat 7	☎ 966-615 371
Torrevieja	Rubio Mar, Avda Estación 1 🖥 www.skoda.es	☎ 965-705 979

Suzuki

Alicante	Motores y Tracción SL, Avda Hospital 8, San Juan	☎ 965-657 747.

Altea	Motores y Tracción SL, Partida Cap Blanc 36	☎ 965-845 753
Denia	Motores y Tracción SL, Partida Madrigueres 20B	☎ 966-430 066
Elche	Motores y Tracción SL, Ctra Murcia – Alicante km 53, 255	☎ 965-437 598
Torrevieja	Avda Cortes Valencianas 46 🖥 www.suzuki.es	☎ 965-715 631

Toyota

Alicante	Medimotors Gestión, Avda de Orihuela 120	☎ 965-106 272
Torrevieja	Lubrocars 99, C/ Apolo 90 🖥 www.toyota.es	☎ 966-709 842

Volkswagen

Alicante	Eurowagen Alicantina, Ctra de Madrid 29	☎ 965-107 007
Elche	Serramóvil, C/ Hospitalet Llobregat 3	☎ 966-613 057
Torrevieja	Rubio Móvil, C/ Gregorio Marañón 62 🖥 www.vw-es.com	☎ 965-710 950

Volvo

Alfaz del Pi	Samar Móvil, Avda Europa 179	☎ 966-864 287
Alicante	Samar Móvil, Ctra de Ocaña 10	☎ 965-115 492
Elche	Samar Móvil, Ctra Murcia – Alicante km 53 🖥 www.volvocars.es	☎ 965-466 501

Car Tax

All vehicles registered in Spain are liable for road tax, payable to the local council annually. Rates vary depending on the fiscal horsepower (*potencia fiscal*) of your car, as calculated for tax purposes. The more powerful your car, the more road tax you pay. Rates also vary greatly from one council to another. Examples of road tax in some towns on the Costa Blanca are shown in the table below:

Locality	Fiscal Horsepower			
	8–11.99	12–15.99	16–19.99	Over 20
Alicante	€49.75	€105.03	€130.83	€163.52
Altea	€34.08	€71.94	€89.61	€112
Benidorm	€36.12	€76.26	€94.99	€118.72
Calpe	€61.34	€129.49	€161.30	€201.60
Denia	€47.71	€100.72	€125.46	€156.80
Elche	€61.49	€129.80	€181.08	€223.99
Guardamar	€42.60	€89.93	€112.02	€140
Jalón	€44.30	€93.52	€116.49	€145.60
Jávea	€40.38	€85.20	€111.13	€139.03
Orihuela	€49	€104.10	€134	€160.60
Rojales	€42.60	€89.93	€112.01	€140
San Fulgencio	€35.70	€75.37	€93.88	€117.33
Torrevieja	€44.30	€93.52	€116.49	€145.60
Villajoyosa	€47.66	€100.67	€125.43	€156.74

Information on road tax in all localities in the province of Alicante can be found on the SUMA (provincial tax collectors) website (⌨ www.suma.es). Go to 'Tarifas IVTM' and scroll down and click on the locality you're looking for. SUMA also have a telephone helpline in English, French and German open from 9am to noon Mondays to Fridays (☎ 965-148 561).

Garages & Repairs

Most localities have several garages offering servicing and repairs. The standard is generally good, although costs can be high (ask for an estimate beforehand). Many car dealers have garages attached to the showrooms where cars are serviced or repaired, and cars of any make can usually be serviced and repaired at any garages. However, for anything more than a minor repair it's advisable to go to the manufacturer's representative.

To find a reputable garage consult a dealer in your area (see below), ask around for a reliable garage or look in the yellow pages under *Talleres mecánicos para automóviles* (for body or paint work, *Talleres de chapa y pintura*).

For most services you need to book – note that garages are generally very busy and it's difficult to get an appointment at short notice. Some garages, e.g. Renault Minuto and Norauto, offer non-appointment services where you just arrive and wait your turn.

Maps

There are numerous good maps of the Costa Blanca, although most of them don't include maps of the towns or urbanisations apart from a map of

Alicante. Guide books usually include a basic map, but if you want more detail it's better to buy a separate one. Maps, which can be bought on the Costa Blanca at bookshops and newsagents, priced from €3, include:

- **Euro Tour** – *Costa Blanca*. Good detail;

- **Firestone** – *Costa Blanca*. Good detail;

- **Michelin** – *123 Zoom Costa Blanca*. An excellent detailed map of the area (including many urbanisations) and an Alicante city-plan;

- **RACE/Everest** – *Costa Blanca, Cálida y del Azahar* (detail of the three coastlines in the area).

Note that maps go out of date, particularly with regard to roads, and many urbanisations aren't marked on maps.

Tourist offices can provide detailed maps of a specific area and maps of towns and urbanisations are included in local telephone directories. Note that most urbanisations are labyrinths and before trying to get somewhere within one you should make sure you have detailed instructions. Many have maps at the entrances to the urbanisation.

Maps of the coast are also available on the internet (🖳 www.costa blanca.org has a route planner, maps of the area and specific towns), but you need good printing quality if you want to use the maps other than on the screen.

Parking

Finding somewhere to park in towns and cities along the coast is a daily challenge and there's a chronic shortage of parking spaces in most localities. Free street parking is extremely difficult to find unless you're prepared to walk some distance to the centre or you can do as many Spanish drivers do and just park anywhere! If you do, however, watch out for tow-away trucks who take illegally parked cars to the car pound (sometimes when the driver's still in it!) where it costs at least €60 to get your car back.

Many councils are investing heavily in car parks and in recent years many new underground car parks have been built. Expect to pay from €0.75 to €1.50 an hour in most municipal and private car parks. Street parking is also available in some areas in the blue zones and must be paid for from around 9am to 2pm and from 4 to 9pm. Parking in blue zones is free on

Sundays and public holidays. Tickets cost from €0.70 to €1 an hour and you can usually park from 30 minutes up to a maximum of two hours.

Some areas have discount parking schemes for frequent users of public car parks and residents in many areas are entitled to reduced rates. Enquire at your local town hall for further information.

Petrol & Service Stations

There are numerous service stations along the main roads throughout the Costa Blanca and many have small shops and a cafe or restaurant attached. Main service stations are 24-hour and those that aren't list the nearest 24-hour station. Some are self-service and others are manned (*servicio atendido*). To stop drivers filling up without paying, some service stations have pumps that require pre-payment. At all 24-hour stations if you want to fill up after 11pm you have to pay at the cash desk beforehand.

Petrol prices vary and if you do a lot of driving it may be worth shopping around to get a cheaper price (petrol stations within Alicante city consistently have some of the lowest prices in the province). Prices per litre in November 2004 were as follows:

Type of Fuel	Price
Unleaded (*sin plomo*)	€0.95
Unleaded premium (*sin plomo extra*)	€1.00
Diesel (*diésel*)	€0.83
Diesel premium (*diésel extra*)	€0.86

> **Beware of thieves operating at service stations, particularly those on the main roads. Always lock your car while you pay for your petrol, especially at self-service stations and be wary of people asking for directions or drawing your attention to a burst tyre or similar – while you're distracted, their accomplice may be helping themselves to your luggage and belongings.**

Roads

The main communications route along the Costa Blanca is the A-7/AP-7, which is also the main route along the entire length of Spain's Mediterranean coast and is known as the *Autovía del Mediterráneo*. The road is divided into two sections: the A-7 running from Murcia to the north side of Alicante and its continuation, the AP-7 toll road running beyond the Costa Blanca to Silla, just south of Valencia.

The A-7

This road is dual-carriageway (*autovías*) in its entirety with a speed limit of 100kph (62mph) or 120kph (75mph) depending on the area, and is well-maintained. Traffic is heavy at peak times and always around Alicante, particularly between exits 67 and 70, and in the San Juan tunnel where speed is limited to 80kph (50mph) – **speed cameras operate here**. There are plenty of exits along the route for the main localities, e.g. Alicante (five exits), Altet airport, Elche and Orihuela.

The AP-7

After exit 67 for El Campello, the A-7 becomes the AP-7 toll road (*autopista de peaje*). From exit 64 the road takes an inland route through several mountain ranges with exceptionally beautiful scenery. The road is dual-carriageway and well-maintained. The speed limit is 120kph (75mph), but beware of cars doing considerably more. Traffic information is broadcast 24-hours a day in Spanish on Radio Vía (96.5FM). The AP-7 has several connections or exits (*salidas*) – listed here from south to north:

Exit	Destination
66	Villajoyosa plus inland villages such as Orxeta and Sella
65A	Finestrat, Benidorm Poniente Beach, La Cala de Finestrat
65	Benidorm. Alfaz del Pi, Albir plus inland villages such as Callosa d'En Sarrià, La Nucia and Polop de la Marina
64	Altea, Calpe
63	Benissa, Gata, Moraira, Teulada and villages in the Jalón Valley
62	Denia, Els Poblets, Jávea, Ondara and Pedreguer

Toll Tariffs

At all points where you join the AP-7 there are unmanned toll booths where you're automatically issued a ticket. When you leave the motorway, you hand in your ticket at the toll booth and pay the following amounts according to the distance travelled:

Journey	Tariff
San Juan to Villajoyosa (exit 66)	€1.80
Villajoyosa to Terra Mítica (exit 65A)	€0.60
Terra Mítica to Benidorm (exit 65)	€0.60
Benidorm to Altea (exit 64)	€1.15
Altea to Benissa (exit 63)	€1.65
Benissa to Ondara (exit 62)	€1.20
San Juan to Villajoyosa	€1.80
San Juan to Terra Mítica	€2.30
San Juan to Benidorm	€2.70

San Juan to Altea	€3.55
San Juan to Benissa	€4.75
San Juan to Ondara	€5.75
San Juan to Silla (Valencia)	€11.75
Benidorm to Silla (Valencia)	€9.35

Discounts

Frequent users of the motorway are entitled to discounts of 15 or 30 per cent if they pay by a credit card or a Spanish debit card. If you use the motorway between four and ten times a month, you receive 15 per cent discount. If you use the motorway 11 or more times a month, the discount rises to 30 per cent. In order to qualify you must always use the same credit or debit card to pay and the discount is automatically credited to the amount deducted for toll fees from your credit card or bank account at the end of the calendar month.

Further information about the AP-7 along the Costa Blanca is available from ☎ 901-307 307 (in English and Spanish) and 🖳 www.aumar.es (in Spanish only).

The N-332

Before the construction of the A-7/AP-7, the N-332 was the sole means of communication along much of the Costa Blanca and even now provides the only means of getting from one place to another in many areas, particularly those along the coastline itself. The N-332 is an extremely busy road and the fact that it's single lane (except for the sections in and out of Alicante and around the Altet airport) means traffic jams are commonplace. The speed limit is generally 100kph (62mph), although the density of traffic often means real speed is slower and in some stretches, e.g. from Santa Pola to Guardamar de Segura, the limit is 70kph (44mph) or 80kph (50mph).

Driving along the N-332 is dangerous and a report issued by the Spanish RACE (see page 60) highlighted the stretch between Gandía and Orihuela (some 128km/80mi) as a 'high-risk' accident zone, with 'black spot' areas at Benidorm, Benissa, Gata de Gorgos and La Marina. It can also be a stressful road as a lot of drivers insist of driving over the speed limit and tailgating the car in front. Added to this are numerous cars turning on and off the road, some of them crossing a lane to do so.

Below is a brief description of the N-332 through the main sections of the Mar Menor and the Costa Blanca (from south to north). Note that in many places it's quicker to use the A-7 or AP-7.

Main Sections

From El Algar to Pilar de la Horadada: One of the quietest sections runs from El Algar up to Los Alcázares from where the road runs through several town centres and hold-ups are commonplace.

From Pilar de la Horadada to Santa Pola: This is one of the busiest stretches, especially from Orihuela Costa to Torrevieja where long hold-ups are the norm. Lots of roundabouts around Torrevieja make progress even slower.

From Santa Pola to Alicante: This stretch is quieter with the exception of the N-332/N-340 intersection south of Alicante where traffic is intense at most times. The road is dual-carriageway near the airport, facilitating access.

Around Alicante to El Campello: In common with all Spanish cities, **Alicante has a chronic traffic congestion problem** and by-passing the city via the N-332 is recommended for patient drivers only! The section from San Juan to El Campello is particularly congested. In spite of the dual-carriageway in the city sections, progress is slow and traffic lights endless!

El Campello to Benidorm: Once you leave El Campello, the road is much quieter in the pleasant stretch along the coast to Villajoyosa. The terrain is mountainous and although there are sections for overtaking, these are few and far between. Villajoyosa presents another bottleneck (one of the worst along the coast), although the by-pass currently under construction is due to be finished by summer 2005, which will bring considerable relief to drivers in the area. Numerous junctions and traffic lights line the road until Benidorm.

Benidorm to Calpe: The N-332 through the north of Benidorm is in poor condition, which together with several sharp bends and junctions, mean **this is one of the most dangerous stretches**. The authorities are currently studying improvements to this stretch, although public funds for the work have yet to be allocated.

North of Benidorm to L'Olla through Altea the road becomes an almost permanent jam and drivers should be prepared for a very slow journey, particularly if you travel at peak times. The speed limit through Altea and immediate surroundings is 50kph (30mph). The long-awaited Altea by-pass is planned, but it's unlikely to be built before 2006.

Calpe to El Vergel: North of Calpe the N-332 offers a scenic ride along its numerous winding hills where there are good overtaking lanes (but going north only). Bottlenecks are common through the towns of Benissa and

Gata de Gorgos, and continuous through Ondara and El Vergel, although a by-pass around these two busy towns should be finished by late 2006.

Other Roads

Area One – Marina Alta

The regionally-maintained roads throughout the Marina Alta are generally good and well-maintained. The stretches near the main towns are usually busy at peak times and very congested in the summer, particularly those with access to popular beaches.

● **CV-700 (Pego to El Vergel)** – An excellent, almost straight route in the heart of the Marina Alta.

● **CV-715 (Orba to Pego)** – A scenic route that is well-maintained, but with several very sharp bends.

● **CV-734 (N-332 to Jávea)** – A good scenic access route to Jávea.

● **CV-737 to CV-740 (Moraira to Jávea via Benitachell)** – An excellent road with good access from Jávea where a new road system has been introduced.

● **CV-746 (Calpe to Moraira)** – Not a road for queasy travellers since it follows all the coastal contours and bends, but it's well-maintained. It's very busy during the summer months.

● **CV-750 (Benissa to Orba and Parcent)** – A good road and the main access to the Jalón Valley.

● **CV-7222 (N-332 to Denia)** – An excellent road with dual-carriageway from around 5km (3mi) outside Denia centre.

Area Two – Marina Baja

● **CV-70 (Benidorm to Alcoy)** – This newly improved road is one of the province's main trunk roads connecting the city of Alcoy and inland with the coast. It's also the main access route for the towns of La Nucia, Polop de la Marina and Callosa d'En Sarrià. The first section from Benidorm to the Montebello development is dual-carriageway with numerous roundabouts and very busy at peak times. Beyond Montebello to the Guadalest exit the road starts to climb and has several sharp bends, although visibility for over-taking is good on many stretches. Expect a lot of coaches travelling to and from Guadalest along this stretch. Beyond Benimantell the road becomes very winding and narrow in places, but the scenic views more than compensate for the difficult driving.

● **CV-755 (Altea to Guadalest)** – This scenic route along the foothills of the Sierra de Bernia and then into Sierra Aitana is a good road, although the section from Callosa d'En Sarrià to Guadalest is extremely winding.

● **CV-767 (La Cala de Finestrat to Finestrat)** – A good road to the village of Finestrat beyond which it joins the winding route to the CV 770 and the villages of Orxeta and Sella.

Area Three – Alicante

● **A-7 (old A-36 and N-340, Alicante to Alcoy via Castalla)** – This road is busy on its city sections, but dual-carriageway and well-maintained, and provides easy access to Alicante from towns such as Castalla and Ibi, both increasingly popular with property buyers.

● **A-31 (old N-330, Alicante to Villena)** – This dual-carriageway is the main gateway to the Costa Blanca from Madrid (the area is one of the *Madrileños* favourite destinations) and is extremely busy during the summer, at Easter and long-weekends throughout the year. Tail backs into Alicante are commonplace. Out of season, the road is busy around the access to Alicante and the junction with the A-7.

● **N-340 (Alicante to Alcoy via Jijona)** – A single carriageway road and busy around Alicante. Beyond Jijona the road is steep and winding, particularly on the ascent to the Puerto de la Carrasqueta at over 1,000m (3,330ft). Access to Alcoy is quicker, but longer distance via the A-7 (see above).

Area Four – Vega Baja

● **CV-855 (Elche to Dolores for San Fulgenio and Urb Marina to Oasis)** – The first stretch of this road from Elche to the roundabout junction with the CV-851 (some 15km/10mi) is currently under conversion to dual-carriageway to facilitate traffic into Elche.

● **CV-865 (Elche to Santa Pola)** – A well-maintained but busy road especially on the approaches to the towns.

● **CV-905 (AP-7 to Torrevieja)** – Dual-carriageway access into Torrevieja from the busy urbanisations of Ciudad Quesada and those just outside the city. Traffic is intense around the approaches to Torrevieja at peak times.

- **CV-91 (Orihuela to Guardamar de Segura)** – A good straight road, but busy around junctions with the AP-7 and Rojales. This road will be converted to dual-carriageway in the near future.

- **CV-95 (Orihuela to Urb Los Balcones/ Torrevieja)** – A good road, but busy at peak times around built-up areas. This road will be converted to dual-carriageway in the near future.

- **N-340 (Elche to El Altet Airport)** – A long straight stretch of road with slow progress through Torrellano and on the approaches to Elche. Speed limited to 80kph (50mph) along most of the road.

Area Five – Mar Menor

- **AP-7 (Alicante to Cartagena)** – This toll motorway runs for 75km (47mi) from Cartagena in the south to the A-7, some 10km (6mi) west of Elche. There are 23 exits along the route, including Los Alcázares, San Javier airport, Campoamor, La Zenia, Torrevieja and Ciudad Quesada, making it a quick and handy (but expensive) route for drivers in the south. Toll rates for cars and motorbikes are €1.50 in low season and €2.65 in high season (June to the of end September and for 17 days over the Easter period). Discounts are available for drivers who use the motorway at least 80 times over four months and who always pay using the same credit card. Discounts range from 5 per cent (for 11 to 15 uses a month) to 50 per cent (for over 36 uses a month) and frequent users pay the low season rate all year. Further information about the AP-7 is available from ☎ 966-730 117 (24-hour) and 🖳 www. autopistasureste.es (both in Spanish only).

- **MU-312 (AP-7 to La Manga)** – Built as a *Vía Rápida* (Fast Route), this dual-carriageway certainly provides quick and easy access out of season along the southern stretch of the Mar Menor and to the entrance to La Manga. But during Easter, the summer months and holiday weekends, hold-ups are common and traffic intense along its 17km (10mi). There are exits to Los Nietos, Los Belones and La Manga Resort.

- **La Manga Road** – The 18km (11mi) stretch of road along La Manga strip is extremely busy during holiday periods and even out of season, the endless traffic lights, sleeping policeman and 50kph (30mph) speed limit mean progress is slow.

Sleeping Policemen

Just about every town and village throughout the Costa Blanca uses sleeping policemen as an effective way of keeping traffic speed down. The humps range from small narrow strips to high raised zebra crossings, which, if driven across at speed, can cause damage to your car's suspension. Most humps are painted in red and white or black and yellow, and are easy to spot. Humps are found every 100m or so.

Technical Inspection

All cars over four years old must have a control test known as *ITV* (short for *Inspección Técnica de Vehículos*) similar to an MOT in the UK, carried out at an authorised test station. You may receive notification of this from the Generalitat Valenciana but the onus is you to remember to take the car for the test. **Note that there are heavy fines for not having a current test certificate.**

The test is valid for two years and then carried out every two years until the car is ten years old, after which time the test is annual. When your car passes the test you receive a sticker (different colours depending on the year) with the month and year of test punched on it. You should display the sticker on the right-hand side of the windscreen and keep the *ITV* paperwork in your car. The *ITV* test costs around €40 for a car. **Note that the stations don't usually accept credit or debit cards and you have to pay in cash.** Note also that employees at the stations may not speak English and if you don't speak enough Spanish to understand their instructions, you should take someone with you who does. Some companies (e.g. garages) provide a service whereby someone takes the car to the *ITV* for you.

ITV stations are always busy and it's best to book an appointment beforehand or to go between 3 and 4pm when it's usually quiet.

ITV stations on the Costa Blanca are situated at:

Area One – Marina Alta

Denia   Ctra Ondara km 6.8   ☎ 966-435 443

Area Two – Marina Baja

Benidorm   Avda Comunidad Valenciana s/n,
               Rincón de Loix   ☎ 966-831 102

Area Three – Alicante

Alicante   Pol Ind Pla de la Vallonga 5, Pla de
               la Vallonga   ☎ 965-107 977

Area Four – Vega Baja

Orihuela	Ctra Orihuela – Almoradí km 8.2, San Bartolomé	☎ 965-367 182
Pilar de la Horadada	C/ Ulises 5	☎ 965-976 068
Torrevieja	C/ San Pascual 103	☎ 966-706 100
	Ctra Crevillente s/n	☎ 965-705 187

There are also stations in Elda and Villena, inland.

Traffic Information

Traffic bulletins are broadcast every hour by SER Alicante, M-80 Alicante and Onda Cero Alicante in Spanish, and in English on expatriate radio stations (see **Radio** on page 309). The national Traffic Department also provides information by phone (☎ 900-123 505 – phonelines are often overloaded) and on the internet (🖳 www.dgt.es).

Benidorm

4

Areas

Where to live is a top priority to consider before you move to the Costa Blanca and a difficult question to answer, especially if you're not familiar with the area. Undoubtedly the best move is to rent a property for a few months when you arrive and take your time to explore the different areas and find out what each one has to offer.

The Costa Blanca from Denia in the north to Orihuela Costa in the south and the Mar Menor offer a huge variety of diverse areas and localities with very different characteristics. You can choose from quiet, tranquil urbanisations or busy town centres; from a quiet village to one of Spain's most up and coming cities; from a country retreat to a high-rise penthouse apartment; from urbanisations with a wealth of services to urbanisations with none; from essentially Spanish areas to ones where English is mainly heard.

When deciding where to live you may wish to bear in mind the following considerations:

- **Distance & Time from an Airport** – This is particularly important if you plan to travel to and from the area regularly. Distances from each town to the airport are included in this chapter, but bear in mind that times vary depending on the traffic and time of year. Journeys in July and August can take considerably longer than at other times.

- **Transport Provisions** – In most places on the Costa Blanca private transport is essential unless you live in a town centre or near a train station. If you have children, particularly adolescents, you may wish to consider living near a town centre or near a regular bus route or train station. Further information on getting around is provided in **Chapter 3**.

- **Price of Property** – A major deciding factor for most people some of whom find themselves priced out of some parts of the coast. This chapter includes a brief guide to property prices within each locality and further information on different types of accommodation, including rental prices can be found in **Chapter 5**.

- **Proximity of Services & Amenities** – Although the Costa Blanca as a whole provides just about any service imaginable, availability varies depending on the locality. Some are very well-serviced with excellent amenities while others have practically none. Most towns have a good range, but many urbanisations have little more than the odd shop. The proximity of a health centre or clinic may be important if you're older or have young children, and you may wish to live near a school or at least a school bus route. This chapter describes services and amenities in each locality. Comprehensive information on health centres is provided in **Chapter 7** and on state and private schools (both Spanish and international) in **Chapter 8**.

● **Spanish or Expatriate?** – In many places the influence of foreigners is so strong, you may be forgiven for thinking you weren't in Spain, while in others the essentially Spanish ambience has been preserved. There are advantages and disadvantages for both environments, and you should consider carefully which you would prefer. Bear in mind that the expatriate world is somewhat artificial and, contrary to popular expatriate myth, isn't problem-free. Your decision may be based on your willingness to learn Spanish and integrate into Spanish society. English is widely spoken on the coast, although you should never assume it will be, but inland and in Alicante it's less widely spoken. Note, however, that wherever you live, you should make a concerted effort to speak Spanish because in an emergency you will need it. Further information for different localities is found in this chapter.

● **Peace or Otherwise?** – Bear in mind that the Costa Blanca is one of the world's top tourist destinations and at peak times (Easter, July and August) the whole coast is packed to bursting point with tourists. Roads are grid-locked, there's only space for one more towel on the beaches and parking is even more impossible than usual. Few places escape the hoards, although undoubtedly inland locations are quieter. Some areas, e.g. Benidorm and Calpe are busy almost all year, whereas Alicante is relatively quiet in the summer. Bear in mind also that Spain is essentially a noisy country (Madrid is the second loudest city in the world after Tokyo) and town and village centres everywhere have more than their fair share of roaring motorbikes, sirens, tooting horns and shouting neighbours. Spaniards are also night owls and noise can continue far into the small hours. If you want total peace and quiet on the coast, choose a small urbanisation or a remote country property.

The only real way to decide where to live is to have a good look round before you commit yourself, particularly before buying a property, **and rent before you buy**.

The following chapter provides a detailed description of the localities on the Costa Blanca together with useful information about facilities and services. Localities are divided into the following five areas (listed alphabetically):

● **Alicante Province** – see page 95;

● **Mar Menor** – see page 111;

● **Marina Alta** – see page 74;

● **Marina Baja** – see page 85;

● **Vega Baja** – see page 100.

Place names are in Spanish, not Valencian. See page 20 for a brief guide to place names in both official languages. Note that the word to describe a development or purpose-built residential area in Spanish is *urbanización*, a term that has been 'translated' by expatriates on the Costa Blanca as 'urbanisation'. The term urbanisation is used in this book.

AREA ONE – MARINA ALTA

The main localities that can be found in the Marina Alta area are listed below in alphabetical order.

On the Coast:

* **Calpe** – see page 80;

* **Denia** – see page 75;

* **Jávea** – see page 77;

* **Teulada & Moraira** – see page 79.

Inland:

* **Benissa** – see page 81;

* **Gata de Gorgos** – see page 81;

* **Jalón Valley** – see page 82.

The northernmost section of the Costa Blanca, known as the Marina Alta, is situated around several capes (Cabo de la Nao and Cabo San Antonio are the most important) where the coastline turns from a south-easterly to a south-westerly direction. This is the least developed section of the Costa Blanca and quieter than resorts further south during high season. Its main geographical feature is the imposing dramatic Montgó mountain range (735m/2,425ft), a highly protected natural park with a wealth of flora and fauna, particularly bird life. Montgó provides the area with a micro-climate, meaning it's warmer in winter and cooler in summer, as well as an impressive backdrop to the towns of Denia and Jávea. The mountain range also conveniently provides an obstacle for major roads and both the AP-7 and N-332 run behind it away from the coast, meaning Denia and Jávea are considerably quieter. The coastline beyond Denia towards the town of Gandía is generally flat with miles of long sandy beaches, while that to the south towards Calpe is characterised by plunging cliffs and rocky coves, some of which have difficult access.

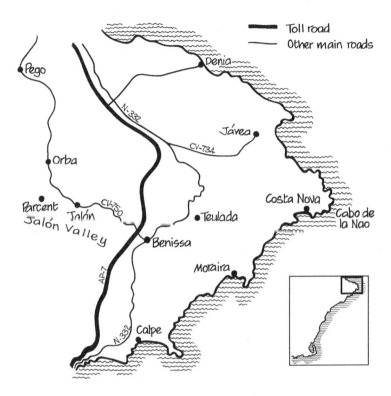

The following section provides information on the places found in this part of the Costa Blanca from north to south.

On the Coast

Denia

Denia (*Dénia*), the 'capital' of the Marina Alta, is backed by the spectacular mound of the Montgó mountain and has almost 20km/12.5mi of coastline with long sandy beaches to the north of the town and small rocky coves to the south. Denia (named after the Roman goddess Diana) is a lively historic town, whose past wealth was based primarily on the raisin trade – during the nineteenth century most of the UK and US's raisins came from here! Historic monuments include the 11th century castle, which dominates the town, and several Baroque churches. The port is one of the busiest in the area and a main departure point for the Balearics.

Some of the Costa Blanca's best sandy beaches are found along the stretch of coastline from Oliva to the north to Denia, where the main localities are Urb Felicidad, Las Bassetes, Els Poblets and Las Marinas. Els Poblets, a small but busy town was recently found to be the richest place on the Costa Blanca, and offers good services and amenities. The nearby larger towns of Vergel and Ondara, both of which have industrial estates, have comprehensive services and communications, although both suffer from chronic traffic congestion as the N-332 runs right through the centre. The long awaited by-pass, due to be finished in late 2006, should alleviate this.

Facts

Population: 39,520
Foreign Population: Around 10,200 (one fifth German and around 1,200 British)
Local Holidays: The main fair is during the first week of July in honour of the town's patron (Santísima Sangre – the Holy Blood). Denia's Moors and Christians festival takes place from 14th to 16th August.
Distance from Alicante Airport: 111km (70mi)
Distance from Valencia Airport: 111km (70mi)
Town Hall: ☎ 965-780 100, 🖥 www.ayto-denia.es
Local Police Station: ☎ 965-780 190

Services

Denia offers an extensive range of facilities and services. Shopping is based around the central Marqués de Campos street where there are also many banks. The town has health centres, a general hospital, primary and secondary schools, and excellent sports facilities. There's an extensive year-round cultural programme, including concerts and a jazz festival.

Communications

Denia has some of the best communications in the area, including direct access by road (dual-carriageway) to the AP-7 and N-332; regular bus services from the town centre to the hospital and to the beaches as well as frequent services to Jávea and the inland villages. The FGV train from Alicante runs to the centre (few towns have central stations) and a regular bus service connects Denia station with Gandía mainline station from where trains run to Valencia.

Property

Property on offer within the town is mainly apartment accommodation. Townhouses and villas are available in Las Marinas and the urbanisations to the east such as Vessanes, La Pedrera and Florida, all of which lie in attractive surroundings at the foot of the Montgó. There's a good choice of both new and resale properties, and over half Denia's properties are used as temporary holiday homes. Property prices are as follows:

- Two bedroom apartment – from €120,000;

- Three bedroom apartment – from €160,000;

- Two bedroom townhouse – from €200,000;

- Three bedroom townhouse – from €270,000;

- Two bedroom villa with communal pool – from €220,000;

- Three bedroom villa with pool – from €300,000.

The well-maintained coast road (CV-736) takes an exceptionally scenic route with lovely views of both the Montgó and the Mediterranean as it climbs up and then down to Jávea, one of the Costa Blanca's most attractive towns. The Cabo de San Antonio en route has spectacular views of the coastline and on a clear day you can see Ibiza in the distance.

Javea

Jávea (*Xàbia*) is one of the Mediterranean's most attractive sea ports and known as the 'Pearl of the Costa Blanca'. Like Denia on the other side to the north, Jávea is backed by the Montgó mountain, which dominates the landscape, and enjoys the same micro-climate – warmer in winter and cooler in summer. The town is divided into three main areas: the old town lies 2km (1.2mi) inland from the coast and is famous for its beautifully preserved traditional architecture, with arched entrances to the narrow streets and large gothic windows; the old fishermen's quarter known as Aduanas del Mar is on the coast where the marina and fishing port are situated; and the main beach and resort area, El Arenal with mainly apartment and townhouse accommodation, which is quiet out of season. The town has a choice of good beaches ranging from the busy El Arenal to the quieter Cala Blanca. Jávea has a thriving expatriate scene, mainly British and a large population of Germans.

Facts

Population: Around 28,800
Foreign Population: Over 40 per cent
Local Holidays: 3rd May and 8th September
Distance from Alicante Airport: 100km (62.5mi)
Distance from Valencia Airport: 119km (74mi)

Town Hall: ☎ 965-790 500
Local Police Station: ☎ 965-790 081

Services

Generally good and the town has good shopping and sports facilities, primary and secondary schools, a health centre, private clinics and a lively cultural scene. Local public transport connects the town centre with El Arenal and the urbanisations on the Cabo de la Nao. Local buses run frequently to Denia, Calpe and Benidorm.

Property

Jávea is one of Costa Blanca's most highly sought after areas and as such has some of the most expensive property, particularly if you want a villa in one of the urbanisations on the Cabo de la Nao. Building has been intense over the last few years, particularly apartments around El Arenal area and villas. Property is among the coast's most expensive, particularly country houses, although there's a wide choice of resale property in the generally buoyant property market (it's claimed that there are more than 80 estate agents serving the Jávea area!). More than half the property in the town is used as temporary holiday homes. Property prices are as follows:

- Two bedroom apartment – from €120,000;

- Three bedroom apartment in beach area – from €125,000;

- Three bedroom bungalow with communal pool – from €300,000;

- Three bedroom villa with private pool – from €400,000.

Jávea to Calpe

Cabo de la Nao

Spain's most easterly point has some of the Costa Blanca's most exclusive property, which generally consists of large luxury houses set in extensive grounds within the three main urbanisations (Tosalet, Tosca and Costa Nova) popular mainly with British and German property buyers. Many properties have exceptional views of the coastline. The urbanisations are well-maintained (but labyrinthine so take a good map!) with reasonable services, including restaurants, banks and small supermarkets situated at different points. Villas start at €400,000, although you can expect to pay in excess of €1 million for many of them.

South of Cabo de la Nao is an area enclosed by three small towns, Benitachell, Moraira and Teulada. This is one of the fastest expanding districts in the northern Costa Blanca and endless cranes testify the numerous construction projects currently underway. The road from Benitachell to Moraira is now a succession of urbanisations, one of the biggest of which is Cumbre del Sol, a huge development of apartments, villas and townhouses, with a small commercial centre on site. Two bedroom apartments here start at €130,000. Benitachell (or *Poble Nou*) is a small town, but with heavy traffic and limited services and amenities.

Teulada & Moraira

For administrative purposes the small towns of Teulada and Moraira share the same council, although Teulada is some 8km (5mi) inland set in a landscape of vineyards and pines and Moraira is on the coast.

Teulada is a small town with a good range of services and amenities, including shops, a chemist's and some sports facilities. There's a good range of restaurants and bars. The council offices are situated here.

Moraira is a pleasant seaside resort with an attractive marina dominated by its large eighteenth century defensive tower. The resort, which is quiet out of season, has numerous shops and restaurants, and a safe sandy bay. Property in the town itself is mainly apartments (two bedroom from €160,000, three bedroom from €180,000), many of which are of new construction. Nearly 60 per cent of property in the area is used as a second or holiday home. Property in outlying urbanisations is mainly townhouses, bungalows and villas. Expect to pay from €205,000 for a small townhouse, from €250,000 for a two bedroom bungalow with communal pool and from €400,000 for a three bedroom villa with private pool.

Facts

Population: Around 12,100
Foreign Population: Approximately 9,000 (around 40 per cent British)
Local Holidays: 19th April and 15th July
Distance from Alicante Airport: 93km (57mi)
Distance from Valencia Airport: 119km (74mi)
Town Hall: ☎ 965-740 158, 🖥 www.teulada-moraira.org
Local Police Station: ☎ 965-740 946

After Moraira the winding coastal road takes you through a succession of pleasant and well-maintained urbanisations with mainly villa accommodation and commercial centres with supermarkets, banks and restaurants. There are a number of pleasant sandy bays. This area is generally quiet out of season, but busy in the summer when traffic congestion on the road is almost permanent.

Calpe

Calpe is one of the coast's most popular resorts and home to numerous foreigners, mainly British and German – the town even celebrates a 'Munich-style' Beer Festival in October. The town boasts the Costa Blanca's emblem, the imposing *Peñon de Ifach*, a rocky outcrop which dominates the coastline and there's also a large salt lagoon, now protected, in the centre. The old quarter remains unspoilt with a typical Spanish fishing village ambience and the many murals and *trompes l'oeil* on buildings pay tribute to the town's popularity with artists. The new town is busy with numerous shops and services. Accommodation within the town is mainly high-rise. Calpe is a year-round resort with no low season and it's very crowded in the summer.

Facts

Population: 24,790
Foreign Population: Approximately 14,385. Calpe is one of the few areas in the Costa Blanca where foreign residents outnumber the Spanish. The town has a large German and Belgian population with around 3,500 British.
Local Holidays: 5th August and 22nd October
Distance from Alicante Airport: 82km (51mi)
Distance from Valencia Airport: 126km (79mi)
Town Hall: ☎ 965-833 600
Local Police Station: ☎ 965-839 000

Services

Generally good with a wide choice of shops in the centre, health centres, a chemist's, primary and secondary schools, and good sports facilities. There's also an excellent choice of restaurants and bars both in the town and on the outskirts.

Communications

Public transport is good with frequent buses connecting Calpe with Alicante and Valencia (via Benidorm or Jávea). A local bus service with three services in the morning and two in the afternoon connects Calpe with Moraira and Teulada. Private transport is essential if you choose to live in one of the outlying urbanisations.

Property

Calpe has seen intense construction in recent years and there's currently a buoyant property market (over half the town's properties are used as temporary holiday homes) with plenty of resale properties. In town, property is mainly apartments in high-rise blocks. Villas are available on the outskirts, particularly in the urbanisations on the south side (e.g. Urb Maryvilla and Calapinets). Property prices are as follows:

- Two bedroom apartment – from €110,000 (from €250,000 for front-line beach);

- Three bedroom apartment – from €150,000;

- Two or three bedroom bungalow with small plot and communal pool – from €200,000;

- Three bedroom villa with private pool – from €325,000.

Inland

Benissa

Benissa is a small town set in attractive surroundings in the foothills of Sierra de Bernia with a well-maintained town centre with numerous fine buildings. The town has a chronic traffic problem as the N-332 runs through the middle and tail-backs are common. Limited shops and services are available.

Facts

Population: Around 11,000
Foreign Population: 4,260 (mostly British)
Local Holidays: 26th April and 28th June
Distance from Alicante Airport: 91km (57mi)
Distance from Valencia Airport: 117km (73mi)
Town Hall: ☎ 965-730 058
Local Police Station: ☎ 965-730 733

Property

Within the town itself, there's little resale property, but outside there's a good choice of villas and bungalows.

- Two bedroom apartments within the town start at €150,000;

- Three bedroom villas start at €300,000.

Gata de Gorgos

This small town set in attractive mountainous surroundings on the banks of the River Gorgos, is well-known for its handicrafts and artisan work, and there are numerous shops in the locality selling hand-made products crafted in wicker, wood and esparto grass. The town has an interesting old quarter and good services, including a health centre, schools and sports facilities. It's one of the few places in the Marina Alta that has preserved its essentially Spanish character in the face of tourism and foreign residents. Traffic congestion is a problem through the town centre along the N-332.

Facts

Population: Around 5,100
Foreign Population: 345
Local Holidays: 6th August and 29th September
Distance from Alicante Airport: 100km (62mi)
Distance from Valencia Airport: 110km (69mi)
Town Hall: ☎ 965-756 089
Local Police Station: ☎ 965-757 432

Property

The property situation is very similar to that in Benissa (see above).

Jalón Valley

The Jalón Valley lies to the west of the Marina Alta set within several mountain ranges, including the spectacular Sierra de Bernia and Sierra de Aixorta, both of which have several peaks over 1,000m (3,300ft). The valley is regionally famous for its beautiful natural surroundings and home to numerous small villages, which are popular with foreign residents and visitors seeking tranquillity and a more-Spanish environment, yet one that's still within easy reach of the services and amenities on the coast via the motorway and N-332. The main villages are Alcalalí, Jalón, Llíber, Orba, Parcent and Pego.

Communications within the valley are generally good with well-maintained roads. Private transport is essential if you choose to live here. Services and amenities vary, but all villages have a small health centre and small shops, and the Marina Alta's larger towns are within easy reach. Numerous foreigners (mainly British, although there's a sizeable population of Germans and Dutch) live in the area and in some villages you hear mainly English spoken.

The Gallinera Valley (Vall de Gallinera), west of Pego, is home to most of the Comunidad Valenciana's thousands of cherry trees and their blossom in mid March is a sight not to be missed.

Facts

Distance from Alicante Airport: 99km (62mi)
Distance from Valencia Airport: 118km (74mi)

Property

Property consists mainly of villas, some townhouse developments (e.g. Urb La Almazara to the west of Jalón) and village houses, and there's a buoyant property market in the area. Construction has been intense in many areas and some councils are considering suspending all further building licence applications in an attempt to preserve the area's natural surroundings. Property prices are as follows:

- Small rural properties in need of restoration – from €100,000;

- Three bedroom village house – from €150,000;

- Large villa with extensive grounds – from €350,000.

Alcalali

A small village with a distinctly English atmosphere and good views of the surrounding valley and the Sierra Bernia.

Facts

Population: 1,180
Foreign Population: 309 (240 from the UK)
Local Holidays: There's a main fair in honour of San Antonio and San Roque (8th to 12th August).
Town Hall: ☎ 966-482 024, 🖳 www.alcalali.es

Jalón

Situated on the banks of the river Jalón, this attractive small market town has good shopping facilities, including a small commercial centre. The local economy is dependent on the wine industry – the town has two wine cellars (*bodegas*).

Facts

Population: 2,800
Foreign Population: Around 660, mainly British and German
Local Holidays: Santo Domingo de Guzmán (2nd to 12th August) and 18th October
Town Hall: ☎ 966-480 101, 🖳 www.xalo.org
Local Police Station: 966-480 101

Lliber

One of the smallest villages in the area with limited services and an interesting and well-preserved centre.

Facts

Population: 880
Foreign Population: Around 200
Local Holidays: There's a main fair in honour of several patron saints (14th to 23rd August).
Town Hall: ☎ 965-730 509

Orba

One of the larger villages with several small shops and services, and a large foreign population.

Facts

Population: 1,720
Foreign Population: Around 500, mainly from the UK
Local Holidays: 20th April and 10th May
Town Hall: ☎ 965-583 001

Parent

One of the highest villages in the valley with commanding views of the surrounding area and situated in one of the greenest parts. The village has an unusual modern church spire and numerous small shops and restaurants.

Facts

Population: 950
Foreign Population: Around 190
Local Holidays: San Antonio Abad (January) and the main fair in honour of San Lorenzo and the Santísimo Cristo de la Fe (9th to 17th August).
Town Hall: ☎ 966-405 301
Local Police Station: ☎ 966-405 301

Pego

The small town of Pego lies to the north of the Jalón Valley among acres of terraces of citrus trees. The town has good services and amenities, and is well-connected to the north of the Marina Alta via the CV-700 road. Pego has maintained its Spanish character and has one of the lowest proportional foreign populations in the area.

Facts

Population: 10,231
Foreign Population: Around 1,280
Local Holidays: 20th April and 1st July
Town Hall: ☎ 965-570 011
Local Police Station: ☎ 965-570 118

AREA TWO – MARINA BAJA

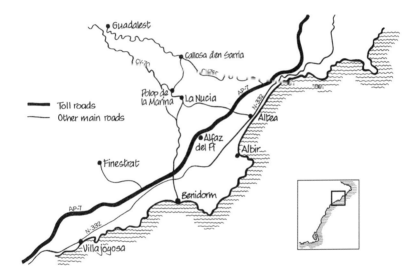

The main localities that can be found in the Marina Baja area are listed below in alphabetical order.

On the Coast:

● **Altea** – see page 86;

● **Alfaz del Pi** – see page 88;

● **Benidorm** – see page 88;

● **La Cala de Finestrat** – see page 90;

● **Villajoyosa** – see page 90.

Inland:

- **Callosa d'En Sarriá** – see page 92;

- **Finestrat** – see page 92;

- **Guadalest** – see page 93;

- **La Nucia** – see page 93;

- **Polop de la Marina** – see page 94;

- **Tarbena** – see page 95.

The Marina Baja is one of the more developed areas of the Costa Blanca and home to the coast's top tourist resort, Benidorm. Geographically, the area has some dramatic mountain scenery, dominated by Puig Campana peak, with some attractive mountain villages.

The following section looks at localities within the Marina Baja from north to south.

On the Coast

Altea

Altea lays claim to one of the Comunidad Valenciana's most attractive towns and its characteristic blue and white tiled church domes on the hillside are a Costa Blanca landmark. The busy town has numerous narrow streets flanked by white houses and a pleasant seafront and fishermen's quarter. Altea is home to a thriving artist community and has many art galleries and craft shops. There's a lot of traffic on the N-332, which runs the length of the town, and queues are long at the traffic lights. Away from the central streets there are no pavements so walking along the road is hazardous.

The north and east sides of Altea are limited by the harsh rocky walls of the Sierra Bernia and Sierra de Toix respectively. The Sierra de Toix cliffs plunge into the sea and the coastline here is abrupt with small rocky coves and spectacular views. Some of the Costa Blanca's most luxurious urbanisations are found here, including the exclusive Altea Hills, a well-maintained complex with golf course, hotel, social club and commercial centre with banks and shops as well as 24-hour onsite security.

Accommodation is mainly villas (from €400,000), but there are some luxury apartments, including those in the innovative Bahía Altea complex. Altea Hills has good access from both the AP-7 and the N-332 with filter lanes. On the coast is Campomanes, which is currently under construction. This vast development includes Urb Mascarat, a striking apartment complex with one of the Costa Blanca's most attractive marinas, and shops and restaurants. The junction at the N-332 to Urb Mascarat is difficult, especially from the north as there are no filter lanes.

Facts

Population: 18,900
Foreign Population: Around 6,000 (predominantly British and German)
Local Holidays: 27th and 28th September (Moors and Christians)
Distance from Alicante Airport: 71 km (44mi)
Distance from Valencia Airport: 136 km (85mi)
Town Hall: ☎ 965-841 300, 💻 www.ayuntamientoaltea.es
Local Police Station: ☎ 965-845 511

Services

Generally very good. Shopping is good and there are numerous decor and furniture shops as well as fashion boutiques along the main street. Altea has good health facilities, primary and secondary schools, sports facilities and a lively cultural scene, which takes place mainly at the modern Palau Arts Centre. Altea has excellent sports facilities and has one of the Costa Blanca's best sailing clubs based at the marina.

Communications

Altea is well connected with towns both to the north and south, and there are regular bus services to Alicante and Valencia. Local buses run between Benidorm and Altea from 7am to 11pm daily, and there's a twice daily bus service from Altea to Guadalest. Altea is also on the train line to Alicante and Denia.

Property

Property prices are as follows:

● Two bedroom apartment – from €170,000 (from €225,000 in Altea Hills or front-line beach);

● Three bedroom apartment – from €200,000 (from €300,000 in Altea Hills);

● Three bedroom townhouse – from €200,000;

● Three bedroom villa – from €350,000 (from €400,000 in Altea Hills).

Alfaz del Pi

Alfaz del Pi (meaning fertile land of pines), further down the coast is divided into two sections, the town itself in the foothills of Sierra Aitana and the coastal section, known as Albir. The town has excellent services and amenities with comprehensive sports facilities, good shops, primary and secondary schools, health centres and a good cultural programme. Alfaz celebrates its annual film festival in July and the seafront has a 'Filmstars' Walk' (*Paseo de las Estrellas*) where the names of participating filmstars are engraved. Frequent local bus services connect Alfaz and Albir with Benidorm and there are two services a day to Guadalest. Alfaz has a train station on the line to Alicante and Denia.

Facts

Population:15,848
Foreign Population: Around 8,750, mainly British, German and Scandinavian
Local Holidays: 7th to 10th October
Distance from Alicante Airport: 69 km (43mi)
Distance from Valencia Airport: 149 km (93mi)
Town Hall: ☎ 965-888 265, www.lalfas.com
Local Police Station: ☎ 965-887 100

Property

Property prices are as follows:

● Two bedroom apartment – from €170,000;

● Three bedroom apartment – from €200,000 (from €300,000 in front-line Albir);

● Three bedroom townhouse – from €200,000;

● Three bedroom villa – from €350,000.

Benidorm

The busiest holiday resort on the Mediterranean and **the** package holiday destination, Benidorm is a mass of high-rise apartment and hotel blocks (at least 20 floors in many cases), which dominate the skyline for miles around topped by the distinctive Hotel Bali with its 45 floors. The city of Benidorm, once a tiny fishing village, has cultivated the art of tourism and prides itself on offering a unique destination for millions of holidaymakers every year. Part of its secret lies in its magnificent sandy beaches which stretch for miles along the western (Playa de Poniente) and eastern (Playa de Levante) sides and are immaculately maintained. The resort is busy all year round and is also home to numerous foreigners. Benidorm's unemployment rate of a mere 1.9 per cent is one of the lowest in Spain.

Facts

Population: 67,573
Foreign Population: Around 18,000 (27 per cent of the population), mainly British and German
Local Holidays: 15th and 16th November
Distance from Alicante Airport: 64 km (40mi)
Distance from Valencia Airport: 144 km (90mi)
Town Hall: ☎ 965-855 500, 🖥 www.benidorm.org
Local Police Station: ☎ 966-807 766

Services

Services are excellent and the city offers a comprehensive range of facilities and amenities. There are primary and secondary schools, good shops, including the new marina shopping centre on the outskirts, public and private health facilities, excellent sports facilities and a wide range of bars and restaurants catering for all tastes (some of the area's best *tapas* are found in the old town). There's a lively expatriate scene and plenty going on culturally all year round. Some of Spain's best nightlife is found in Benidorm.

Communications

Excellent. Benidorm has one of the best bus services in the area and the local bus company, Llorente Bus (☎ 965-854 322), runs efficient and frequent services around the city and surrounding areas. Benidorm is also on the Alicante to Denia train line (half-hourly buses run between the station and centre).

Property

The property market in Benidorm is generally good, although there's little variety in what's for sale apart from high-rise apartments (top-quality front-line beach apartments are in short supply) and there are few villas in the town. Apartment accommodation is, however, among the cheapest on the coast and an apartment in the right location can provide reliable rental return. Property prices are as follows:

● Two bedroom apartment – from €150,000 (from €300,000 for front-line beach);

● Three bedroom apartment – from €175,000;

● Three bedroom townhouse – from €250,000.

La Cala de Finestrat

Around the headland from Poniente Beach lies the small resort of La Cala de Finestrat (known simply as La Cala and part of the municipality of Finestrat – see page 92) with restaurants and cafes around its well-maintained sandy bay. La Cala is currently under intense construction with numerous apartment blocks going up along its northern and western sides. Frequent buses connect the resort with Benidorm. Property prices start at €160,000 for a new two bedroom apartment and at €175,000 for a new three bedroom apartment.

Villajoyosa

Villajoyosa (La Vila Joiosa) is the Marina Baja's historic capital and has one of the area's largest fishing fleets – the auction of freshly caught fish and shellfish takes place every evening at the port. The town is nationally famous for its brightly painted facades and palm trees, which provide a unique multi-coloured sight as you walk along the seafront and round the streets. The town, which has maintained its essentially Spanish character, has a well-maintained sandy bay and is busy in the summer. Villajoyosa's Moors and Christians festival during the last week of July is nationally famous.

The coastline from La Cala de Finestrat to Villajoyosa is abrupt and mountainous with few urbanisations along the N-332 where there are numerous warehouses and factories. This stretch of the Costa Blanca south to Alicante is one of the areas that has best maintained its Spanish character in the face of tourism and foreign residents.

Facts

Population: Around 25,000
Foreign Population: 2,645
Local Holidays: 29th July and 29th September
Distance from Alicante Airport: 55km (34mi)
Distance from Valencia Airport: 155km (97mi)
Town Hall: ☎ 966-851 001
Local Police Station: ☎ 965-890 050

Services

Villajoyosa offers a range of shops, supermarkets, primary and secondary schools, health centres, good sports facilities and a wide range of activities.

Communications

Local buses run frequently to Alicante and Benidorm, and the town is on the Alicante to Denia train line. As far as traffic is concerned, the town has one of the Costa Blanca's worst bottlenecks and queues are long, although this should be solved by summer 2005 when the long-awaited by-pass is finished.

Property

There's plenty of new construction currently underway in the town and the resale market is quite limited. Typical townhouses in the centre come on the market only occasionally and can fetch premium prices. Property prices are as follows:

- Two bedroom apartment – from €160,000;

- Three bedroom apartment – from €200,000.

Inland

In the beautiful countryside and mountains inland from the Marina Baja, there are a number of small towns and villages, popular with foreign residents looking for a more tranquil and Spanish environment than the busy coast yet within easy reach of the amenities and services available in the resorts. The surrounding countryside dominated by the Sierra Aitana with its stunning peaks of Puig Campana (1,410m/4,653ft) and Aitana (1,558m/5,141ft) provide a dramatic backdrop to many of the villages with rich historic roots, whose main protagonists were the Moors who fortified many of the rocky outcrops. The scenery here is a mixture of rocky mountains and fertile valleys housing citrus plantations and olive and almond groves, originally terraced and irrigated by the Moors. Many villages, although small, have sizeable foreign populations, such as Orxeta and the white village of Benimantell, both popular with British residents. The section below provides information (in alphabetical order) on the localities of Callosa d'En Sarriá, Finestrat, Guadalest, La Nucia, Polop de la Marina and Tárbena.

Communications

The towns and villages closer to the coast have relatively easy access, but those further inland are more difficult to reach. Finestrat, Orxeta, Relleu and Sella are north-west of exit 65a from the AP-7 and La Nucia, Polop de la Marina, Callosa d'En Sarriá and Guadalest can be reached from exit 65. The CV-70 road from Benidorm is excellent and dual-carriageway as far as La Nucia, although traffic is often heavy. Beyond Guadalest the road is narrow and winding. The villages and small towns nearer the coast, e.g. Finestrat, La Nucia and Polop have regular daily bus services to both Benidorm and Alicante, although services are much reduced at weekends. **Private transport is essential if you live in this area.**

Property

This part of the Costa Blanca is popular with foreign buyers and there are numerous urbanisations surrounding the villages and towns where many foreigners have holiday homes or permanent residences. There's a good choice of resale property ranging from village or town houses and country homes to luxury villas. Village houses are available from €120,000 to €300,000 depending on size and state of repair, and villas are for sale from €240,000 to more than €1 million.

Callosa d'En Sarria

This busy market town has a stunning location surrounded by vast fruit plantations where mainly tropical fruits such as kiwi, mango and medlars are grown (half of Spain's medlar crop is grown here). Callosa is also well-known for its spectacular waterfalls situated at Fuentes del Algar just outside the town. Services are good and the town has numerous small shops, a health centre and schools. Regular bus services connect Callosa with La Nucia, Polop de la Marina and the coast.

Facts

Population: Around 7,900
Foreign Population: Some 2,000, mainly British
Local Holidays: 26th July (Santiago) and the Friday and Monday around the second weekend in October (Moors and Christians).
Distance from AP-7: 16km (10mi)
Town Hall: ☎ 965-880 050
Local Police Station: ☎ 965-881 405

Finestrat

The attractive village of Finestrat lies just 8km (5mi) west of Benidorm whose skyline is clearly visible down on the coastline and enjoys the stunning backdrop of Puig Campana peak. Finestrat's rocky outcrops are home to some unique 'hanging' houses and narrow winding streets, typical of southern Spanish villages. Services and amenities include shops, supermarkets, schools, a chemist's and a health centre. The town has a lively cultural scene. A frequent bus service connects Finestrat with Benidorm.

Facts

Population: 2,550
Foreign Population: 695 (mainly British)
Local Holidays: The main festivities are around 24th August in honour of the Santísimo Cristo del Remedio and San Bartolomé.

Distance from AP-7: 8km (5mi)
Town Hall: ☎ 965-878 100, 🖥 www.finestrat.org
Local Police Station: ☎ 965-878 000

Property

Accommodation in the village is generally townhouse only, although apartment and villa accommodation is readily available in the immediate neighbourhood, particularly in Sierra Cortina Resort (see below). Property prices are as follows:

● Two bedroom townhouse – from €150,000;

● Three bedroom townhouse – from €175,000.

Sierra Cortina Resort

This huge new development, conceived as part of the Terra Mítica project, is proving popular with both foreign and Spanish buyers, and offers luxury apartment, townhouse and villa accommodation within a typically Mediterranean village setting. The resort will eventually offer sports facilities, shops and two 18-hole golf courses, and has a frequent bus service to Benidorm. Property prices start at €250,000 for a one bedroom apartment and at €420,000 for a three bedroom villa.

Guadalest

Guadalest is widely acclaimed to be the Costa Blanca's prettiest village (as testified by the coach loads of tourists arriving daily!) and is dominated by the San José Castle reached only by a natural rock tunnel and perched on the summit of a rocky outcrop. The village has a maze of narrow streets with a wealth of souvenir and gift shops, and few other services.

Facts

Population: 190
Foreign Population: 19
Local Holidays: 14th to 17th August
Distance from AP-7: 28km (17.5mi)
Town Hall: ☎ 965-885 219

La Nucia

The small town of La Nucia lies 10km (6mi) to the north of Benidorm, and in spite of its proximity to the bustling resort, remains a peaceful

Spanish enclave with an attractive and well-designed centre and magnificent views of the coastline below.

La Nucia has good services, including shops, schools and a sports centre, as well as a new Arts Centre with auditorium. Also, a new health centre is currently under expansion to provide accident and emergency services. The town's Sunday morning second-hand market is one of the most visited on the Costa Blanca. Frequent bus services connect the town with Benidorm.

Facts

Population:11,000
Foreign Population: Around 5,660 (mostly British and German)
Local Holidays: The town's main festivities are in honour of the Immaculate Conception, usually from 15th to 18th August.
Distance from AP-7: 10km (6mi)
Town Hall: ☎ 965-870 700, 💻 www.lanucia.es
Local Police Station: ☎ 965-870 533

Property

The area surrounding the town has many attractive urbanisations, popular with foreign residents. Within the town itself, accommodation is limited mainly to townhouses, although there are some apartments. Property prices are as follows:

● Two bedroom apartment – from €140,000;

● Three bedroom townhouse – from €150,000;

● Three bedroom villa – from €300,000.

Polop de la Marina

This pretty village set on the hilltop whose 12th century castle ruins dominate the surrounding area, has a range of services, a lively cultural scene and good sports facilities. Hourly bus services connect Polop with Alicante, Benidorm and Callosa.

Facts

Population: 2,450
Foreign Population: Around 550

Local Holidays: The village celebrates El Porrat in mid-August in honour of San Roque and the Virgen de la Asunción. The main fair is at the beginning of October in honour of San Francisco de Asis, the patron saint.
Distance from AP-7: 12km (7.5mi)
Town Hall: ☎ 902-303 310, 🖥 www.polop.org
Local Police Station: ☎ 965-880 150

Tarbena

The small village of Tárbena in the heart of the mountains, is home to a sizeable foreign population (there are several foreign bars) and a tepee colony on the outskirts providing an 'alternative' lifestyle. Views from the village are spectacular and it occasionally snows on the nearby mountains.

Facts

Population: 800
Foreign Population: Around 150, mainly British
Local Holidays: 2nd August and 4th December
Distance from AP-7: 28km (17.5mi)
Town Hall: ☎ 965-884 234

AREA THREE – ALICANTE PROVINCE

The main localities that can be found in the Alicante area are listed below in alphabetical order.

- **Alicante City** – see page 98;

- **Los Arenales del Sol** – see page 100;

- **El Campello** – see page 96;

- **Gran Alacant** – see page 100;

- **San Juan de Alicante** – see page 97.

As you would expect, this area of the Costa Blanca is almost totally urbanised, although there are some excellent beaches both north and south of the city. The following section looks at localities from the north to the south.

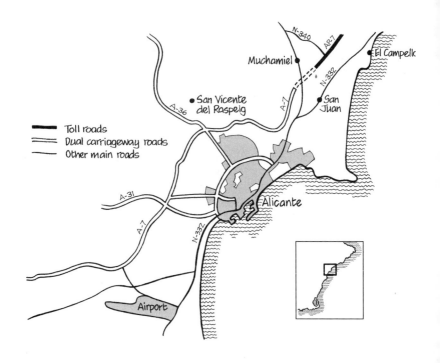

El Campello

This resort, popular with tourists and residents who commute into Alicante, has good services and communications (the *TRAM* train service and buses run every 30 minutes into Alicante), a well-maintained sandy beach and a busy marina. Sports facilities are good and there's a lively cultural scene. El Campello is very Spanish and Valencian (see page 188) is widely spoken here.

The part of the Costa Blanca from Villajoyosa to El Campello, with its abrupt coastline and small rocky coves, is one of the least populated and least popular with foreign residents and property buyers. The N-332 and AP-7 hug the coastline along stretches of yellow sandstone hills. The main urbanisations are (from north to south) Venta Lanuza, Urb Cala d'Or, Urb Coverta Fumá and La Almadraba, where there are some apartment blocks and villa accommodation. Services are few, but this area does have the advantage of being on the Alicante to Denia train line – there are four stops between El Campello and Villajoyosa.

Facts

Population: Around 20,400
Foreign Population: Approximately 3,000
Local Holidays: 16th July (Virgen del Carmen) and the main fair during the first fortnight of October in honour of Santa Teresa.
Distance from Alicante Airport: 25km (15mi)
Town Hall: ☎ 965-637 200, 🖳 http://elcampellodigital.com
Local Police Station: ☎ 965-637 099

Property

There's a good choice of resale property in El Campello, which caters for a mainly Spanish market. Property prices are as follows:

● Two bedroom apartment – from €140,000;

● Three bedroom apartment from €160,000;

● Three bedroom townhouse in beach location – from €275,000.

San Juan de Alicante

San Juan de Alicante (San Joan d'Alacant), situated some 9km (5mi) from the capital, is Alicante's main beach resort boasting one of the best beaches in the area with 6km (4mi) of clean sands with good facilities. Its excellent communications (frequent buses and trains into Alicante) and wide range of services and amenities mean it has become a popular residential area with both Spaniards and foreigners. The European School is situated here (see page 183). The town itself has several fine churches and chapels. San Juan's bonfires celebrating the summer solstice from 21st to 24th June are one of the area's most colourful festivals.

Services and amenities are excellent with health facilities, numerous shops and stores, sports facilities and a good choice of bars and restaurants. Public transport is good with buses to Alicante every 15 minutes and to El Campello every 30 minutes. Traffic congestion between San Juan and Alicante is a major problem, particularly in rush hour and during the summer .

San Juan is a very Spanish town and Valencian is widely spoken here (see page 188).

Facts

Population: 17,478
Foreign Population: 1,862 (mostly of African or South American origin)

Local Holidays: 21st June (San Juan) and 14th September when the main fair takes place in honour of the Santísimo Cristo de la Paz.
Distance from Alicante Airport: 15km (10mi)
Town Hall: ☎ 965-653 245, 🖳 www.santjoandalacant.es
Local Police Station: ☎ 965-942 222

Property

There's a good choice of resale property in the area where apartments and villas area available. Property prices are as follows:

- Two bedroom apartment – from €140,000;

- Three bedroom apartment – from €150,000.

Alicante City

Alicante is the Comunidad Valenciana's second largest city and the capital of the Costa Blanca as well as a major Mediterranean port. The city, which has retained its Spanish character, is compact and dominated by the magnificent Santa Bárbara Castle, rich in military history, and is one of Spain's most up and coming cities,. The old quarter centred round the City Hall and distinctive marble and palm-lined seafront esplanade, has many attractive buildings, small shops and restaurants. The marina with mooring for 748 boats and the port are in the centre of town, near the well-maintained city beach of El Postiguet. Alicante is a lively city with excellent nightlife and its San Juan bonfires and festivities in June are one of the country's most spectacular.

Facts

Population: Around 300,000
Foreign Population: Approximately 21,440 in the capital (some 2,680 from the EU)
Local Holidays: The main festivities take place on 24th June (San Juan), including a smaller version of the *Fallas* held in Valencia in March when *papier mâché* effigies are burnt ceremoniously and fireworks light up the skies. The Virgen del Remedio (patron saint) is honoured on.5th August.
Distance from Alicante Airport: 8km (5mi)
Distance from Murcia Airport: 96km (60mi)
City Hall: ☎ 965-149 100, 🖳 www.alicante-ayto.es
Local Police Station: ☎ 965-107 200

Services

Excellent. Alicante offers everything you would expect from a large city – comprehensive shopping (there are numerous shopping centres), a wide range of public and private health facilities, numerous schools including, several international, excellent communications and sports facilities. There's also a year-round cultural calendar led by the city's recently restored *Teatro Principal* and the recently restored Sala Arniches.

Communications

Generally very good. The city is well-communicated by public transport and this is currently a major investment area for public funds. Local buses are operated by Subús (☎ 965-140 936, 💻 www.subus.es) that runs numerous city lines as well as route connecting the centre with El Campello, San Juan and San Vicente del Raspeig, and the service is generally efficient and reliable. Tickets cost €0.85 one-way and there are season tickets (*bonos*) for ten and 30 journeys. Seniors over 64 and registered as residents are entitled to free bus travel. Local trains run to Campello every 30 minutes and on to Denia, and every hour to Elche and Murcia. Alicante will be connected to the high-speed train (AVE) network in 2007 when the journey to Madrid will take a mere one hour 45 minutes.

Communications in and around Alicante are generally good, and all main roads are dual-carriageway. Traffic congestion is, however, a major problem and at peak times all entrance roads and the A-7 round the city are often jammed.

Property

Alicante has a buoyant property market and there's a good resale market, mainly in apartments. There are also numerous new developments. The city is less popular with foreign property buyers, which is reflected in lower property prices in the city (€1,128 per m²) compared to the Costa Blanca average (€1,385 per m²). Prices are listed below:

Central Alicante:

- Two bedroom apartment – from €100,000;

- Three bedroom apartment – from €120,000.

Expect to pay at least double for a large apartment in a good position.

Alicante North:

Muchamiel (*Mutxamel*) is a popular residential area as it offers good services and amenities, including an English school.

- Two bedroom apartment – from €120,000;

- Three bedroom apartment – from €130,000.

Los Arenales del Sol & Gran Alacant

The residential areas south of Alicante have until recently been overlooked by foreign buyers, but the area's good communications (the airport is literally minutes away), stunning sandy beaches, including the protected Carabassí Dunes and proximity to Alicante with its excellent range of services and amenities means it is fast gaining in popularity. The area is essentially Spanish. **Note that aircraft noise can occasionally be obtrusive.**

Gran Alacant is expanding vastly and home to many new developments and several commercial centres and shops plus excellent sandy beaches. The largest urbanisation is Urb Monte y Mar followed by Urb Novamar and Urb Gran Vista. Several more urbanisations (e.g. Urb Carabasi, Urb Don Pueblo and Urb El Faro) are currently under construction.

Facts

Distance from Alicante Airport: 4km (2.5mi)
Distance from Murcia Airport: 95km (59mi)
Town Hall: This area belongs to the municipality of Santa Pola (see below): ☎ 965-411 100, 🖥 www.santapola.infoville.net
Local Police Station: ☎ 965-411 287

Services

Services are presently somewhat limited, although new construction in the area is improving shops and amenities, and Alicante and Santa Pola are nearby. Gran Alacant offers a health centre, banks and shops, supermarkets as well as restaurants and bars.

Property

This is one of Alicante's fastest expanding areas and there are currently many townhouses and villas under construction. At the moment, property represents good value for money. Property prices are as follows:

● Two bedroom townhouse – from €200,000;

● Three bedroom townhouse – from €250,000;

● Two bedroom bungalow (communal pool) – from €150,000.

AREA FOUR – VEGA BAJA

The main localities that can be found in the Vega Baja area are listed below in alphabetical order.

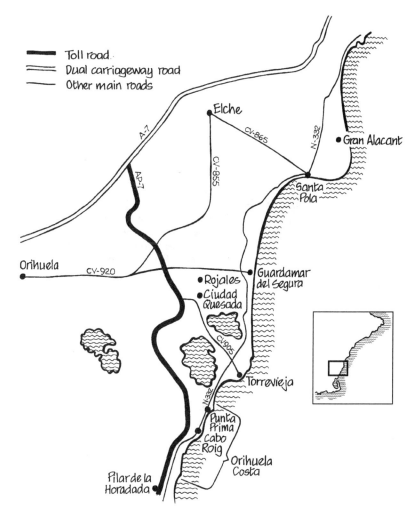

On the Coast:

- **Guardamar del Segura** – see page 104;

- **Orihuela Costa** – see page 107;

- **Santa Pola** – see page 102;

- **Torrevieja** – see page 105.

Inland:

- **Elche** – see page 109;

- **Orihuela** – see page 110.

The Vega Baja is one of the Spain's fastest growing residential areas and several of its towns have seen vast increases in their population over the last ten years. Construction is intense in many parts of the coast here and there's a wide choice of resale property. The landscape is mainly flat and characterised by the many salt-pans and lagoons. This section looks at localities from north to south.

> The vast areas of salt-pans and marsh in this part of the Costa Blanca mean the area is prone to mosquitoes during the warmest part of the year. While they're generally harmless, mosquito bites are itchy and can easily become infected in young children. There are numerous products on the market to prevent mosquitoes biting, including plug-in deterrents, body sprays and candles. An effective way to keep them out of your home is to use fly screens over doors and windows.

On the Coast

Santa Pola

Facing south over the Mediterranean and almost surrounded by salt-pans on its south-west side, Santa Pola is a lively resort and also home to one of Spain's largest Mediterranean fishing fleets. The town is essentially Spanish and quiet out of season when the local fishing and salt industries provide the main sources of income. Its beaches are excellent and well-maintained. There are numerous shops, schools, medical facilities and a chemist's, excellent sports facilities and a good range of bars and restaurants – not surprisingly, fish dishes are exceptionally good! Boats leave Santa Pola for the island of Tabarca, visible in the east. Santa Pola is on local bus routes to Alicante, Elche and localities on the coast further south.

Facts

Population: Around 21,000
Foreign Population: 1,100
Local Holidays: 16th July (Virgen del Carmen) and 8th September (Virgen del Loreto)
Distance from Alicante Airport: 12km (7.5mi)
Distance from Murcia Airport: 85km (53mi)

Town Hall: ☎ 965-411 100, 🖥 www.santapola.infoville.net
Local Police Station: ☎ 965-411 287

Property

Santa Pola's main property interest for foreigners is the area of Gran Alacant (part of the municipality of Santa Pola – see **Gran Alacant** on page 100). Within the town itself, property is mainly bought by Spaniards. Property prices are as follows:

● Two bedroom apartment – from €125,000 (from €160,000 in beach area);

● Three bedroom apartment – from €140,000 (from €175,000 in beach area).

Santa Pola to Guardamar del Segura

Beyond Santa Pola's impressive salt-pans complete with flamingos, is one of the Costa Blanca's most unspoilt stretches of coast and inland, one of its most popular urbanisations. The long sandy stretches at La Marina are well-maintained in season, less so in the winter, but **beware of strong under-currents**. La Marina itself is a small quiet town with some shops and services. Some 4km (2.5mi) inland lies the vast urbanisation of Urb La Marina to Oasis, one of the area's most popular with foreign property buyers and residents.

Urb La Marina to Oasis

This large urbanisation lies in completely flat landscape and is part of the municipality of San Fulgencio, a small village situated several kilometres further south (see below). Urb La Marina is a large sprawl of mainly townhouses, bungalows and villas where the population is almost exclusively foreign, most of whom live here all year.

Services within the urbanisation include two commercial centres with shops, supermarkets, a chemist's, bars and restaurants. San Fulgencio's tourist office is also here and there's a small (and very over-stretched) health centre open in the mornings only. The local primary school is in San Fulgencio and the secondary in Rojales (see below).

Local bus services connect Urb La Marina to Elche, San Fulgencio, Rojales and Guardamar, although services are very limited. In summer only, a bus runs four times day to and from the beach. Private transport is essential if you choose to live here. A good map or directions are also essential for finding your way around the maze of streets.

The property market is buoyant and there's a good choice of reasonably priced townhouses and villas. A small two bedroom bungalow starts at €150,000 and a small villa at €200,000.

San Fulgencio

This small village is the administrative centre for Urb La Marina and is home to several small shops, the local police, the primary school and the town hall.

Facts

Town Hall: ☎ 966-794 201 (it's also a primary school)
Local Police Station: ☎ 966-794 453

Immediately south of San Fulgencio are several small villages, Benijófar, Los Palacios and the largest, Rojales, once a small farming community and now the administrative centre for another of the area's vast urbanisations, Ciudad Quesada. Rojales, on the banks of the River Segura, has several shops, banks, a new cultural centre, primary and secondary schools, a health centre and chemist's, and bars and restaurants.

Ciudad Quesada, although strictly speaking an urbanisation, is almost a town in its own right and its streets stretch for miles. The main access to Ciudad Quesada is via the CV-905 to Torrevieja from exit 745 from the AP-7 toll motorway. Here is the main commercial centre with a good choice of shops, banks and other services. The development has a golf course (La Marquesa Golf & Country Club) and other sports facilities. There's a limited bus service linking various sections with each other and Rojales, but private transport is essential. Orientation isn't easy as there are few landmarks so a good map is a must! Ciudad Quesada is almost exclusively a foreigners' community with the British forming the largest section of the population and many people live here permanently, so it isn't a seasonal resort.

The property market is thriving in Ciudad Quesada and there's a huge selection of resale townhouses, bungalows and villas as well as many new developments currently under construction. Small two bedroom bungalows start at €140,000 and small villas at €175,000.

Guardamar del Segura

Guardamar del Segura on the mouth of the River Segura where an attractive new marina has recently been built, is a thriving small town which boasts some of the best dune areas on the Mediterranean.

Practically the entire coastline forms part of a protected dune area where the long sandy beaches are backed by vast numbers of pines and palm trees, planted a century ago to protect the town from the advancing sands. The town has good services, including shops, medical facilities, schools and bars and restaurants. Communications are good with local bus services to Elche, Orihuela, Santa Pola and Torrevieja. Traffic congestion in and out of the town is problematic and the stretch over the river is particularly busy. A long-awaited by-pass has been budgeted and is expected to be completed in 2008.

Facts

Population: 10,732
Foreign Population: Around 2,400
Distance from Alicante Airport: 31km (19mi)
Distance from Murcia Airport: 44km (27mi)
Town Hall Branch: ☎ 965-729 014, 🖥 www.guardamar.net
Local Police Station: ☎ 965-729 600
Local Holidays: 25th July (Santiago) and 7th October (Virgen del Rosario, patron saint)

Property

Guardamar has a good property market with mainly apartment and townhouse accommodation available, and there are numerous new developments under construction. Apartments are also available on the front-line beach locations at Urb Campoamor and El Moncayo, south of the town itself, but note that **traffic is heavy and it can be difficult to turn off into the urbanisations at peak times**. Property prices are as follows:

● Two bedroom apartment – from €145,000;

● Three bedroom apartment – from €165,000;

● Three bedroom villa (communal pool) – from €250,000.

Torrevieja

Almost directly south of Guardamar del Segura is Torrevieja, one of Spain's fastest growing towns and currently one of the most popular areas in the Costa Blanca for new foreign residents and retirees. The town has around 150 urbanisations based around the main town and the small centre of La Mata with its magnificent sandy beach. Other beaches in the area are well-maintained and most boast blue flags. Torrevieja's main landmark are the two large salt lagoons (Europe's largest and oldest) situated to the north of the town, both of which are natural parks and where salt extraction for export still takes place. The town characterised by its low-level construction and wide avenues, has an attractive centre based around the port and large marina with several museums and monuments such as the old Casino, now a cultural and exhibition centre, and parks.

Torrevieja has one of Spain's lowest unemployment rates (1.9 per cent).

Facts

Population: Around 94,000 (unofficial estimates state around 350,000). Ten years ago the population was a mere 29,900!
Foreign Population: Torrevieja's foreign population is increasing dramatically (up by 12 per cent in 2003) and the British make up the largest group (officially around 42,000, although unofficial estimates push the figure to at least 168,000).
Local Holidays: 16th July (Virgen del Carmen) and the main fair in honour of the Immaculate Conception from 1st to 17th December.
Distance from Alicante Airport: 43km (27mi)
Distance from Murcia Airport: 32km (20mi)
Town Hall: ☎ 965-710 250, 🖳 http://ayto.torrevieja.infoville.net
Local Police Station: ☎ 965-710 154, 🖳 www.pltorrevieja.com (one of the few municipal police forces in Spain with its own website!)

Services

Services are generally very good. Torrevieja offers a range of shops, including a Carrefour hypermarket and a Supercor complex which is under construction (it is due for completion in spring 2005), numerous leisure options; a lively expatriate scene with countless clubs and societies; excellent sports facilities, including an Olympic-sized indoor swimming pool – there are ambitious plans to expand the marina and port area as well as the sports pavilion; good public and private health facilities, although public services are over-stretched in some areas; and primary and secondary schools.

Communications

Good. Public transport consists of frequent bus services to Alicante, Orihuela and locations north and south on the coast. Local buses connect La Mata and outlying urbanisations with Torrevieja centre. Torrevieja has easy access along the CV-905 dual-carriageway and the AP-7 toll motorway is nearby. The N-332, both north and southbound is very busy and often congested.

Property

Torrevieja has one of the fastest growing property markets in the area with numerous new developments currently being built all over the municipality. Prices are generally cheaper than in many parts of the Costa Blanca and there's a good choice of both resale and new properties. Property prices are as follows:

- Two bedroom apartment – from €120,000;

- Three bedroom apartment – from €130,000;

- Three bedroom townhouse – from €180,000;

- Three bedroom villa – from €250,000.

Orihuela Costa

The 16km (10mi) stretch of coastline from Torrevieja to Torre de la Horadada is known as Orihuela Costa. This area is home to the Costa Blanca's biggest concentration of golf courses (there are five here), an attractive marina at Cabo Roig, fine beaches and a good range of services. Orihuela Costa is essentially a foreigners' community with a minority of Spaniards living here and is busy all-year round. The municipality has one of Spain's lowest unemployment rates (1.7 per cent).

The main urbanisations from north to south are Urb Punta Prima, Playa Flamenca, La Zenia, Cabo Roig (Cap Roig) and Dehesa de Campoamor and Mil Palmeras.

Facts

Population: Around 35,000 – one of the fastest growing populations in Spain (up nearly 35 per cent over the last five years).
Foreign Population: Around 13,300 (mostly British and German)
Local Holidays: 17th July (Moors and Christians), 8th September (Virgen del Monserrate)
Distance from Alicante Airport: 51km (32mi)
Distance from Murcia Airport: 22km (14mi)
Town Hall: ☎ 966-760 000 (situated at Plaza del Oriol in Playa Flamenca)
Local Police: ☎ 649-900 304

Services

Generally good, although services are often over-stretched. Most urbanisations have a choice of shops, supermarkets and services. The post office is situated in Cabo Roig. Sports facilities include golf courses, marinas and tennis courts. There are two public health centres (over-stretched at the moment), a chemist's and private clinics. A secondary school opened in September 2004. Beaches are well-maintained all-year round.

Communications

Buses run from Mil Palmeras to Orihuela via the urbanisations three times daily and the journey takes an hour. There are five buses daily from Mil Palmeras to Torrevieja via the urbanisations. Communications are good via local buses which connect the urbanisations with each other, Torrevieja and Orihuela. The nearby AP-7 toll motorway offers quick access to the south and north, and is a good alternative to the very busy N-332 which runs parallel to the coast along Orihuela Costa and is often grid-locked.

Property

In response to keen interest from foreign property buyers and residents, this area is currently under massive expansion and new developments are springing up everywhere, e.g. El Señorío de Punta Prima where some 1,900 apartments are under construction in seven phases. Prices here have risen by around 20 per cent over the last year and there's a buoyant property market. The area is generally more expensive than Torrevieja and Ciudad Quesada, and the most expensive areas are front-line beach and golf properties and the urbanisation of Cabo Roig. Property prices are as follows:

● Two bedroom apartment – from €160,000;

● Three bedroom apartment – from €180,000;

● Three bedroom townhouse – from €200,000;

● Three bedroom villa – from €350,000 up to €800,000.

Pilar de la Horadada

This small town, often considered to the gateway to the Costa Blanca from the south, is dependent on both agriculture (much of the surrounding countryside is under cultivation) and tourism, and offers good services with shops, a health centre and schools. Sports facilities are good with a large marina in Torre de la Horadada and a sports pavilion currently under construction. Public transport consists of a frequent bus service to San Javier and several buses daily to Alicante, Cartagena and Murcia.

The area, particularly the beach side around the resort of Torre de la Horadada (see below) is currently under intense development with several new urbanisations consisting mainly of townhouses.

Torre de la Horadada, named after its imposing sixteenth century watchtower built to defend the coast against pirates, lies on the beach side of the N-340 and AP-7, several kilometres from Pilar de la Horadada itself. It has a pleasant promenade, well-maintained sandy beaches, a marina and shops and restaurants, and is very quiet out of season.

Facts

Population: Around 13,200
Foreign Population: 3,456, mostly British
Local Holidays: 30th July and around 12th October
Distance from Alicante Airport: 67km (42mi)
Distance from Murcia Airport: 15km (10mi)
Town Hall: ☎ 965-352 225, 🖳 www.pilardelahoradada.com
Local Police Station: ☎ 965-352 334

Property

Property is good value in Pilar and Torre de la Horadada, although prices are rising fast.

● Townhouses generally start at €180,000;

● Semi-detached houses start at €225,000.

Inland

Elche

Elche (*Elx*) is Alicante province's second largest city and one of the industrial engines behind its economy. Elche is nationally famous for its shoe and toy industries, both of which have suffered major recession in recent months mainly because of increased competition from Eastern Europe and China, which has resulted in a sharp increase in unemployment and industrial unrest. The city itself is unique in Spain, and seen from afar is a skyline of domes and literally thousands of palm trees. It's estimated there are some 300,000 palms in Elche and a world class selection can be seen in the beautiful botanical gardens, the Huerto del Cura (see page 225). Elche is Alicante's bastion of Valencian (see page 188), which is mainly what you hear on the streets where foreign influence is hardly noticeable, and is also home to the world famous 'Mystery of Elche' (see page 224).

Facts

Population: 201,731
Foreign Population: Approximately 13,000 (only around 900 from the EU)

Local Holidays: 13th to 15th August (in honour of the Virgen de la Ascensión) and 28th December
Distance from Alicante Airport: 14km (9mi)
Distance from Murcia Airport: 75km (47mi)
Town Hall: ☎ 966-658 000, 🖳 www.elche.es
Local Police Station: ☎ 966-658 099

Services

Excellent. Elche offers good shopping, health facilities, primary and secondary schools, sports facilities, and a year-round cultural programme. The city is popular with visitors for shopping. There isn't much of a British expatriate scene in Elche.

Communications

Excellent. Elche has a local bus service linking outlying districts with the centre and there are frequent services to Alicante, Orihuela and the coast. Elche is also on the local train service linking Murcia and Alicante. The local and regional authorities have made substantial investments in the road system and there's a good by-pass and access roads to the city from outlying districts. The CV-855 to San Fulgencio is currently being converted to dual-carriageway. Traffic congestion is, however, a problem and the centre where parking is difficult, is always busy.

Property

Elche is generally of little interest to foreign buyers, most of whom prefer the coast, although the city does offer some of the cheapest property in the area.

● Two bedroom flats start at €100,000;

● Three bedroom flats start at €110,000;

● Villas in the area start at €250,000.

Orihuela

The historic town of Orihuela lies on the banks of the River Segura some 30km (19mi) inland and almost in the region of Murcia (Murcia city itself is a mere 20km/12mi away) and is the administrative centre for the popular and expanding Orihuela Costa. The town boasts numerous well-preserved monuments, including a fine sixteenth century cathedral, several Gothic churches as well as convents and palaces. The town offers excellent services and amenities, including good shops, medical facilities, schools and a year-round cultural calendar – many events take place at the lovely *Teatro Circo*. The municipal area of Orihuela, including its coast is the largest in Alicante province.

Facts

Population: Around 25,550
Foreign Population: Few foreigners live in Orihuela town itself.
Local Holidays: 17th July (Moors and Christians), 8th September (Virgen del Monserrate)
Distance from Alicante Airport: 53km (33mi)
Distance from Murcia Airport: 51km (32mi)
Town Hall: ☎ 966-736 864, 🖳 www.aytoorihuela.com
Local Police Station: ☎ 965-300 204

Communications

Generally good. Frequent local buses run to Alicante, Elche, Murcia and Torrevieja as well as to Orihuela Costa. Orihuela is also on the local train line connecting Murcia and Alicante. Road access to the town is easy via the A-7 from Alicante or the CV-910 from Guardamar del Segura, although this road is usually busy.

Property

Property in the town of Orihuela is of little interest to foreign buyers who tend to buy on Orihuela Costa or in Torrevieja.

AREA FIVE – MAR MENOR

The main localities that can be found in the Mar Menor area are listed below in alphabetical order.

● **La Manga** – page 115;

● **Los Alcázares** – page 114;

● **San Javier** – page 114;

● **San Pedro de Pinatar** – page 113;

● **Santiago de la Ribera** – page 114.

Situated at the far south of the Costa Blanca, the Mar Menor lies in the province of Murcia and officially forms part of the Costa Cálida (Warm Coast), one of the Mediterranean's up and coming coastal areas. This area stretches from San Pedro de Pinatar in the north to La Manga in the south and west where the Mar Menor almost completely closes.

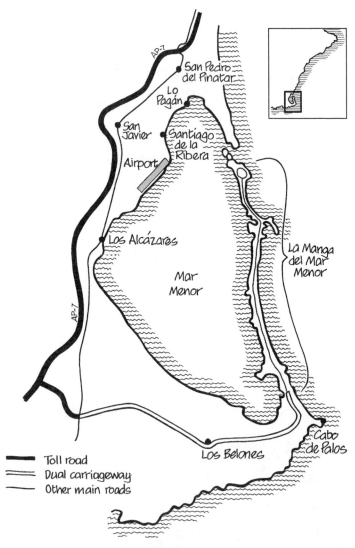

The Mar Menor is the largest salt water lake in Europe, covering an area of 170km² (105mi²) and surrounded on all sides by residential developments, the main one being La Manga, a narrow wedge of land between the Mar Menor and the Mediterranean. The area is known for its excellent beaches, the variety of year-round water sports and the therapeutic benefits of its high salinity (around 45 per cent compared to around 36 per cent in the Mediterranean).

Unlike the Costa Blanca, the Mar Menor is as yet undiscovered by residents from the EU, although there are large numbers of Moroccans and South Americans who live and work in the area.

Communications

The area's proximity to Murcia airport is an advantage. Public transport is limited to bus transport and several services run daily from San Javier and Santiago de la Ribera to Alicante, Cartagena and Murcia. Local services run frequently from San Pedro de Pinatar to San Javier via Lo Pagán and Santiago de la Ribera, and from Santiago de la Ribera up to Campoamor in Orihuela Costa. Buses also run from Santiago de la Ribera to La Manga twice daily.

Property

This is one of Murcia's main development areas and there are vast construction projects currently under way, particularly around Cabo de Palos, Islas Menores, Los Alcázares and Los Narejos. Demand for property is huge at the moment and this is reflected in the fact that prices have doubled over the last four years and show no signs of slowing down. Available property is generally apartments or townhouses, although there are some villa developments. Property prices are as follows:

● Two bedroom apartment – from €140,000;

● Three bedroom apartment – from €170,000;

● Two bedroom bungalow with communal pool – from €150,000;

● Three bedroom villa – from €360,000;

● Three bedroom villa with private pool – from €425,000.

San Pedro de Pinatar

San Pedro de Pinatar (known often as just San Pedro) is the northern most municipality on the Mar Menor and a popular seaside resort with good amenities and services. The district of Lo Pagán is home to the area's famous therapeutic mud baths. San Pedro has numerous shops, sporting facilities, a health centre, schools, a year-round cultural programme and communications by bus with other towns on the Mar Menor and Alicante and Murcia.

Facts

Population: Around 19,800 (quadruples in summer)

Foreign Population: Around 17 per cent (approximately 300 British)
Local Holidays: 28th June (San Pedro, patron saint), 13th August (San Roque). In Lo Pagán: 28th June (San Pedro, patron saint), and 16th July (Virgen del Carmen)
Distance from Alicante Airport: 60km (38mi)
Distance from Murcia Airport: 7km (5mi)
Town Hall: ☎ 968-180 600, 🖳 www.aytosanpedrodepinatar.com
Local Police Station: ☎ 968-183 739

San Javier

San Javier is a small town situated almost in the centre of the eastern coast of the Mar Menor and the main municipality in the area. The municipal area includes San Javier itself, a pleasant busy town with good services and amenities, and an essentially Spanish ambience; Santiago de la Ribera, a smart seaside resort with an attractive palm-lined promenade; and a large section of La Manga (see below or page 115). San Javier is home to Spain's airforce academy.

Facts

Population: Around 17,000
Foreign Population: Around 10 per cent
Local Holidays: 3rd February (San Blas) and 3rd December (San Javier, patron saint). In Santiago de la Ribera: 16th July (Virgen del Carmen) and 28th July (Santiago, patron saint)
Distance from Alicante Airport: 67km (42mi)
Distance from Murcia Airport: 5km (3mi)
Town Hall: ☎ 968-571 401, 🖳 www.sanjavier.com
Local Police Station: ☎ 968-570 880

Services

Generally very good. There are numerous shops, health facilities, including a hospital and health centre, excellent sports facilities, primary and secondary schools, and a good choice of bars and restaurants. San Javier has a lively cultural scene, including an international jazz festival held annually in June and July.

Los Alcázares

Los Alcázares, famous for its thermal baths and spa, is a sprawling municipality where recent investment in infrastructure and town planning is very evident in its pleasant palm-lined avenues and promenade. Los Alcázares is a popular tourist resort with Spaniards and the British. The town has numerous shops, a health centre, primary and secondary schools, excellent sports facilities, including an indoor pool and well-maintained beaches. The nightlife is good and Los Alcázares offers a year-round cultural programme with some of the area's liveliest festivals, including the unique '*Incursiones Berberiscas*', three days commemorating the pirate raids on the area during Medieval times.

Facts

Population: Around 13,500 (increases by as much as 130,000 in the summer)
Foreign Population: Around 17 per cent
Local Holidays: 12th and 13th October
Distance from Alicante Airport: 75km (47mi)
Distance from Murcia Airport: 7km (5mi)
Town Hall: ☎ 968-575 047, 🖳 www.ayto-losalcazares.es
Local Police Station: ☎ 968-171 919

From Los Alcázares to La Manga

Beyond Los Alcázares are several very small resort urbanisations, most of which have new developments under construction and limited services. The resorts are very quiet out of season and generally free of heavy traffic since the main AP-7 and N-332 move inland away from the coast. Urbanisations from north to south are Los Urrutias, Estrella del Mar, Los Nietos, Islas Menores, Mar de Cristal and the larger Los Belones where there are several shops.

La Manga

La Manga (its full name is La Manga del Mar Menor) occupies a narrow strip of land (21km/13mi long, 1.5km/under a mile at its widest and a mere 100m at its narrowest point) is packed to almost bursting point with high-rise hotels and apartment blocks – lending the area an almost Manhattan skyline. Sea front promenades and sandy beaches line both sides of the strip. Plaza Bohemia and Puertobello are La Manga's liveliest areas, which is one of Spain's top tourist destinations: more than half Murcia's hotels and over 75 per cent of its apartment blocks are in La Manga! Not surprisingly, the area is extremely crowded in the summer season, although the winter is quiet.

Administratively, La Manga is divided into two sections at approximately La Cala del Pino: the southern section, including Cabo de Palos belongs to the city of Cartagena, some 32km/20mi away, and the northern section (and most of La Manga) belongs to San Javier, opposite on the other side of the Mar Menor (55km/34mi away).

The town hall (situated in the Gran Vía km2.4) serves as a link between La Manga and the councils of San Javier and Cartagena, meaning that many administrative tasks (e.g. paying taxes, presenting paperwork etc) can be done here. The body also looks after infrastructure on La Manga.

Facts

Distance from Alicante Airport: 122km (76mi)
Distance from Murcia Airport: 55km (34mi)
Town Hall: ☎ 968-145 360, 💻 www.lamangaconsorcio.org
Local Police Station: ☎ 968-570 880 (San Javier), ☎ 968-145 577 (Cabo de Palos)

Services

Generally good and La Manga has numerous shops and supermarkets, banks, a health centre (very over-stretched in the summer), a chemist's, a post office as well as water sports facilities. Restaurants, bars and nightlife spots also line the strip.

Communications

Communications have improved with the MU-312 dual-carriageway linking the southern stretch of the Mar Menor and La Manga, although this road is very busy during the holiday season. The road along La Manga, known as the Gran Vía, itself is often congested, even out of season and its numerous traffic lights, sleeping policeman and 50kph limit (31mph) means progress is slow at the best of times. Public transport is limited to a local bus route along the strip and a twice daily service to Santiago de la Ribera.

Property

Property prices are as follows:

- Two bedroom apartment – from €140,000;

- Three bedroom apartment – from €190,000 (from €250,000 for good position);

- Two bedroom townhouse – from €200,000;

- Two bedroom villa (communal pool) – from €175,000.

Lighthouse at Cabo de Palos,
Mar Menor

5

Accommodation

A major concern for anyone relocating to a new area is somewhere to stay and if possible you should arrange some sort of accommodation before you arrive on the Costa Blanca This chapter looks at accommodation options on the Costa Blanca, including temporary accommodation, rental accommodation, property purchase and retirement and nursing homes.

HOTELS & HOSTELS

There are nearly 300 hotels and numerous hostels in the area to suit all budgets from basic bedrooms with shared bathroom facilities to luxury top of the range suite accommodation. There are also many new hotels currently under construction. Hotel accommodation is officially classified with one to five stars, depending on the facilities they offer, rather than their price. **Note that hotels within the same category can vary considerably in quality and comfort.** A rough guide to room rates is shown below:

Star Rating	Price Range	Class
*****GL	€350++	Great luxury/*Gran Lujo* (none on the coast)
*****	€150-450++	Luxury/*Lujo* (currently seven hotels on the coast)
****	€60-225+	Top class (most hotels are in this category on the coast)
***	€30-150+	Very comfortable
**	€20-80	Comfortable
*	€15-50	Basic

Prices above are for a double room with bathroom for one night. Note that prices in hotels are usually quoted per room and not per person, and that 7 per cent VAT (*IVA*) is added to all bills. You pay your bill at the end of your stay and all but the smaller establishments accept credit cards.

There are also hotel-apartments (*aparthotel*) in many locations on the coast, which offer better rates than standard hotels (although services may be fewer) and usually include cooking facilities, so you can save money on eating out. Some hotels (usually only three-star and below) offer special rates for long stay guests, particularly during the quieter winter months.

Finding a Hotel

If you arrive on the Costa Blanca during low season (e.g. November to the end of February), you will probably be able to find hotel accommodation with little difficulty. For most of the year, however, and particularly during July, August and Christmas, finding a hotel room on spec is virtually impossible. It's advisable to book ahead whenever you plan to come, not least so you don't waste valuable time looking for a room. When you book, you may be asked for your credit card number, particularly if it's a hotel with three stars or more. Booked accommodation is usually held until 6pm on the day of arrival unless you've advised the hotel of a later arrival time. Check-out is usually by noon. Methods of finding a hotel include the following:

● **Costa Blanca Tourism Association** – The Costa Blanca Tourism Association (Patronato de Turismo de la Costa Blanca) publish a list of hotels on the Costa Blanca in English, which can be found on their website (🖳 www.costablanca.org).

● **Guide Books** – Most guide books on Spain contain information about hotel accommodation on the Costa Blanca and there are numerous Spanish hotel guides, including the *Michelin Red Guide España* and *Hoteles y Restaurantes* (El País Aguilar), available from bookshops.

● **Internet** – There's a wealth of information about hotels on the Costa Blanca on the internet (just type in 'hotels Costa Blanca' in any good search engine) and there may be links to the hotels themselves where you can book online or telephone to book your room. Most local council websites also provide information about hotels in the area or links to this information. Council websites are listed in **Chapter 4**.

● **Tourist Offices** – Local tourist offices can provide information about hotels in the area and many also offer information about accommodation on their website. For a full list of tourist offices on the Costa Blanca see **Chapter 10**. Note that tourist offices don't usually provide a booking service.

● **Travel Agents** – When you book your flight to the Costa Blanca you may be offered hotel accommodation as part of the deal or the travel agent may also be able to book your room for you.

● **Yellow Pages** – Look under '*hoteles*'. The Spanish yellow pages are also available on the internet (🖳 www.paginasamarillas.es). You need to type in the category of business you're looking for (i.e. hotel) and the area.

CAMPSITES

This is definitely a cheaper accommodation option especially if you travel
to the coast with a caravan or camper van. The province's 44 campsites are
divided into two categories: first class (*Primera/1ª categoría*) and second
class (*Segunda/2ª categoría*), and there are no luxury or third class campsites
on the coast. Camping costs from €4 to €4.50 per person, per day plus €8
for a caravan or camping space, and around €4 for a car. Most campsites
on the coast are open all year round, and there may be special rates for
long-term stays. Unless it's July or August, it shouldn't be too difficult to
find a campsite with space.

The following is a list of campsites on the Costa Blanca:

Area One – Marina Alta

Benissa	Campina Fanadix (2ª cat)	☎ 965-747 307
Calpe	Camping Ifach (2ª cat)	☎ 965-830 477
	Camping La Merced (2ª cat)	☎ 965-830 097
	Camping Levante (2ª cat)	☎ 965-832 272
Denia	Camping Los Llanos (1ª cat) 🖥 www.losllanos.net	☎ 965-755 188
	Camping Los Patos (1ª cat)	☎ 965-755 293
	Camping Diana (2ª cat)	☎ 965-474 185
	Camping Diana 2 (2ª cat)	☎ 965-784 185
	Camping Los Pinos (2ª cat)	☎ 965-782 698
	Camping Tolosa (2ª cat)	☎ 965-787 294
Jávea	Camping El Naranjal (2ª cat)	☎ 965-792 989
	Camping Jávea (2ª cat)	☎ 965-791 070
Moraira	Camping Moraira (1ª cat)	☎ 965-745 249
	Camping La Cometa (2ª cat)	☎ 965-745 208

Area Two – Marina Baja

Alfaz del Pi	Camping Albir (2ª cat)	☎ 965-888 748
Altea	Camping Cap Blanch (1ª cat)	☎ 965-845 946
	Camping Miami (2ª cat)	☎ 965-840 386
Benidorm	Camping Arena Blanca (2ª cat)	☎ 965-861 889
	Camping Armanello (2ª cat)	☎ 965-853 190
	Camping Don Quijote (2ª cat)	☎ 965-855 065
	Camping El Racó (2ª cat)	☎ 965-868 552
	Camping La Torreta (2ª cat)	☎ 965-854 668
	Camping Villamar (1ª cat)	☎ 966-811 255
	Camping Villasol (1ª cat) 🖥 www.camping-villasol.com	☎ 965-850 422
Villajoyosa	Camping Playa de Torres (2ª cat)	☎ 966-810 031
	Camping El Paraiso (2ª cat)	☎ 966-851 838
	Camping Hércules (2ª cat)	☎ 965-891 343

Area Three – Alicante

El Campello	Camping Bon Sol (2ª cat)	☎ 965-941 383
	Camping Costa Blanca (2ª cat) 🖥 www.campingcostablanca.com	☎ 965-630 670
Muchamiel	Camping Muchamiel (2ª cat)	☎ 965-950 126
San Juan	Camping El Molino (2ª cat), Avda de Elda 35	☎ 965-652 480

Area Four – Vega Baja

Elche	Camping El Pinet (2ª cat)	☎ 965-419 148

	Camping Internacional La Marina (1ª cat)	☎ 965-419 200
	Camping Sombra y Sol (2ª cat)	☎ 965-688 010
Guardamar	Camping Mare Nostrum (2ª cat)	☎ 965-728 073
	Camping Marjal (1ª cat)	☎ 966-727 070
	Camping Pal Mar (2ª cat)	☎ 965-728 856
	Camping Rincón de Luna (2ª cat)	☎ 966-727 400
Santa Pola	Camping Bahía de Santa Pola (2ª cat)	☎ 965-411 012
Torrevieja	Camping La Campana (2ª cat)	☎ 965-712 152
	Camping Florantiles (2ª cat)	☎ 965-720 456

Area Five – Mar Menor

San Javier	Camping Mar Menor (2ª cat)	☎ 968-570 133
	La Encina (3ª cat)	☎ 968-191 080

> **Note that camping is not permitted anywhere outside official campsites on the Costa Blanca or indeed anywhere in Valencia unless you have permission from the owner of the land.**

RURAL ACCOMMODATION

Rural accommodation is currently big business in Spain and heavily promoted on the Costa Blanca where there are numerous options, although some of the accommodation may be rather off the beaten track. You can either rent a room in a house (in which case meals are usually provided) or rent the whole house with self-catering facilities. Several books are published annually on rural tourism, e.g. *Guía de Alojamientos en Casas Rurales* (El País Aguilar) or *Guía de Alojamientos de Turismo Rural* (Anaya Touring), which both include sections on the province of Alicante. The regional tourist board publishes *Guía de Alojamiento Rural*, a comprehensive guide to rural accommodation in the area and available from large tourist offices. Information is also available from their website (🖳 www.comunitatvalenciana.com). There are also numerous national websites, the best of which are 🖳 www.azrural.com and 🖳 www.to

prural.com and several regional websites (e.g. 🖳 www.casasrurales-cv-com and 🖳 www.cederaitana.com, both with information in English). You can usually book accommodation online. Expect to pay from €60 a day for a house for two to four people and from €50 for a room for two people for one night.

RENTAL ACCOMMODATION

In common with the rest of Spain there's a shortage of long-term rental accommodation on the Costa Blanca where it's relatively easy to find somewhere to rent for up to two months, but difficult to find somewhere for longer in spite of the fact that the authorities have nearly 20,000 rental apartments on their official register. Many property owners rent their property for six month periods during the winter and spring, and then for short periods (usually a week) in the summer in order to maximise their rental return. Short-term rentals are very expensive, particularly in the summer when a two bedroom apartment can cost from €500 a week and a villa from €1,000. If you want to rent long-term, then make sure the rental period includes the summer period as well and that you're not required to vacate the property by July.

Some companies specialise in rental accommodation specifically for house-hunters or those waiting for a property to be built and who need somewhere to live for up to three months. Most advertise in the local press.

Finding Rental Accommodation

There are many ways of finding rental accommodation on the Costa Blanca, including the following:

● **Estate Agents** – Many estate agents act as agents for rental property and it may be worth asking to see what they have on their books. **Note, however, that you will have to pay the agent's commission**, so the price could be higher.

● **Local Press** – All the local newspapers carry advertisements for rental accommodation (*Alquileres* in Spanish) in the small advertisements section. If you're interested in a property, it's a good idea to telephone as soon as possible since demand is high, particularly for cheaper properties or those in good locations.

● **Notice Boards** – Some property owners advertise their property on local notice boards or stick notices on lamp posts and inside telephone boxes.

- **Private Advertising** – Many property owners put signs outside the property (*Se Alquila*) with a telephone number.

- **Word of Mouth** – Ask around (particularly in small towns or rural areas) in shops and bars if anyone knows of any rental accommodation.

Rental Costs

The cheapest rental accommodation is found inland and on the outskirts of Alicante city, but prices vary depending on the quality of the accommodation and its location. The following table gives an idea of the minimum monthly rental rate you can expect to pay for a long-term contract in some localities on the Costa Blanca:

Locality	Rental Monthly Rates			
	2-bed. Flat	3-bed. Flat	3-bed. T'house	Villa/ Finca
Alicante Centre	€350	€400	-	-
Alicante North	€400	€450	€600	€800
Altea	€650	€750	€900	€1,100
Benidorm	€600	€700	€900	-
Calpe	€600	€700	€850	€1,000
El Campello	€500	€600	€800	€1,000
Ciudad Quesada	-	-	€650	€800
Denia	€600	€700	€850	€1,000
Elche	€350	€400	-	-
Jalón Valley	-	-	-	€1,000
Jávea	€650	€750	€850	€1,000
La Manga	€500	€600	-	-
Mar Menor	€400	€500	€650	€800
Orihuela Costa	€400	€500	€650	€850
Torrevieja	€400	€500	€650	€800

BUYING PROPERTY

Property prices have risen spectacularly on the Costa Blanca over the last few years (by 19 per cent from October 2003 to October 2004 alone) and Alicante is currently the most popular province in Spain for foreign property buyers. In 2004 the average price per metre (m^2) in the province had risen to €1,341 with prices in many areas on the Marina Alta considerably higher, although some parts of the southern coast have cheaper properties. The America's Cup, which is to be held in Valencia in 2007, is expected to fuel a major price rise with increases of up to 30 per cent in Valencia city itself with a similar effect expected in the northern part of the Costa Blanca.

Some 300,000 properties are owned by foreigners in the province, a figure that is expected to rise by more than 26 per cent over the next four years when it's estimated foreigners will buy nearly 100,000 properties. Foreign property buyers tend to be mainly British – 10 per cent more British bought in 2003 than 2002 – followed by Germans and Scandinavians. On average, foreign buyers have around €200,000 to spend and most favour apartment accommodation. This demand fuels property prices, which rose by between 10 and 15 per cent in 2004.

The Mar Menor area is currently one of Spain's fastest growing residential areas and the property market here is probably one of the most buoyant on the Mediterranean coast. Infrastructure in the area has been improved greatly over the last few years and local councils are continuing to invest in improvements. Experts claim that prices have doubled over the last four years and show no signs of slowing down.

On the northern coastal stretch bargains are now few and far between, and there isn't much available here for under €120,000. Properties with a front-line beach or golf position attract a premium (sometimes as much as 100 per cent). Property inland is generally cheaper, although prices have risen sharply in response to demand from foreigners looking for alternatives to the over development on the coast. Prices are rising fast in villages and small towns as far inland as Castalla (northwest of Alicante) and beyond Guadalest in the Marina Baja.

Property on the Costa Blanca is cheaper than the Costa del Sol – experts calculate that prices are around two-thirds of an equivalent property in Malaga.

Bear in mind that many sellers have jumped on the property bandwagon and prices in general are high. Before you commit yourself to a purchase, consider whether the property is worth the asking price. More importantly, ask yourself if you could resell the property later at the same or higher price. It may be worth making an offer or paying slightly more for a superior property. Cheaper (or less expensive) property on the Costa Blanca can be found in the locations listed below.

Area One – Marina Alta

Calpe	Property in the centre of the town
Denia	Areas popular with Spanish residents

Area Two – Marina Baja

Benidorm   Playa de Levante area, but not front-line beach

Villajoyosa   Property in the town centre, but not front-line beach

Area Three – Alicante

Some of the Costa Blanca's cheapest property can be found in the city, although cheap flats tend to be in poor condition and situated in undesirable areas. Nevertheless, you can still buy a small (80m^2) three bedroom flat for under €100,000.

Area Four – Vega Baja

Property situated to the south of Alicantc is generally considerably cheaper than that in the Marina Baja and Marina Alta, although front-line beach or golf properties anywhere fetch a premium. The popular Spanish resorts of Santa Pola and Guardamar de Segura have cheaper apartments than Benidorm and Calpe.

Area Five – Mar Menor

Property situated away from a front-line beach position or in inland towns, e.g. La Palma and Torre Pacheco, is much cheaper.

Property Prices

The following list gives you an approximate idea of what you can buy within a particular price range. The list is by no means definitive and prices were correct in November 2004. A further guide to property prices in each specific area is included in **Chapter 4**.

Under €150,000

On the Marina Alta there's a shortage of property for sale in this price range except for small apartments in need of renovation. Possibilities are greater inland, particularly if you're prepared to travel beyond villages such as Pego and Benichembla.

Area One – Marina Alta

Calpe   One-bedroom apartment

Inland	New two bedroom apartment or townhouse Small rural properties in need of complete restoration Small village townhouses needing some restoration
Moraira & **Teulada**	New small two bedroom apartment

Area Two – Marina Baja

Benidorm	One-bedroom apartment
Inland	Small rural property in need of restoration
Villajoyosa	Two bedroom apartment

Area Three – Alicante

Alicante	Two or three bedroom apartment in the areas of Carolinas Alta and Pla
Bonalba	Two bedroom apartment or a two bedroom townhouse with no garden
Gran **Alacant**	Two bedroom townhouse

Area Four – Vega Baja

Ciudad Quesada	Two bedroom apartment Small two bedroom bungalow
La Florida	Small two bedroom apartment (not front-line beach)
Torre de **la Horadada**	Three bedroom apartment
Torrevieja	Small two bedroom apartment

Area Five – Mar Menor

Inland	Small townhouse
Los **Alcázares**	Two bedroom apartment
La Manga	Small two bedroom apartment

From €150,000 to €250,000

Area One – Marina Alta

Benitachell   Two bedroom apartment with sea views

Calpe   Two bedroom apartment front-line beach or views of the Peñón
Two bedroom duplex apartment
Three bedroom apartment in town

Denia   Two bedroom apartment on golf course

Jávea   Two bedroom centrally located apartment

Moraira   Two bedroom (small) townhouse
Small two bedroom villa on 500m^2 plot

Teulada   Two bedroom townhouse

Area Two – Marina Baja

Altea   Two bedroom apartment (starting price at around €230,000)

Benidorm   Two bedroom apartment with sea views
Two or three bedroom townhouse
Small villa with no pool

La Cala de Finestrat   New two bedroom apartment

Inland   Three bedroom townhouse

Villajoyosa   Three bedroom apartment

Area Three – Alicante

Alicante   Three bedroom apartment in a good location

Bonalba   Two bedroom apartment front-line golf

El Campello   Large three bedroom apartment

Castalla   Three bedroom villas with 500m^2 plot

Gran Alacant   Three bedroom apartment

San Juan Playa	Two bedroom apartment

Area Four – Vega Baja

Cabo Roig	Two bedroom apartment
Ciudad Quesada	Two bedroom semi-detached villa with communal pool
Dehesa de Campoamor	Two bedroom apartment front-line beach Three bedroom apartment Three bedroom townhouse
Torrevieja	Two bedroom apartment in a good location Small townhouse

Area Five – Mar Menor

Inland	Three bedroom village house.
Los Alcázares	Two bedroom apartment in good location Three bedroom apartment Two bedroom bungalow with communal pool
La Manga	Three bedroom apartment Three bedroom townhouse

From €250,000 to €400,000

Area One – Marina Alta

Benissa Coast	Three bedroom villa with large plot and pool
Calpe	New three bedroom villa
Denia	Luxury two bedroom apartment, front-line golf Three bedroom villa on 650m² plot with pool
Inland	Three bedroom villa with large plot and sea views Large restored townhouses
Jávea	Three bedroom front-line apartment New two bedroom villa with 1,000m² plot
Moraira	Large three bedroom townhouse Small three bedroom villa, small plot, no pool

Area Two – Marina Baja

Albir   Three bedroom apartment front-line beach
              Three bedroom villa

Altea   Luxury two bedroom apartment front-line marina
              Three bedroom townhouse
              Three bedroom apartment front-line beach
              Three bedroom villa

Benidorm   Three bedroom penthouse
              Three or four-bedroom townhouse
              New three bedroom villa with communal pool

Inland   Three bedroom townhouse with communal pool
              Small villa

Area Three – Alicante

Alicante   Large three or four bedroom flat in desirable central location

Alicante   Three bedroom villa with pool
Outskirts

El Campello Three bedroom townhouse in beach location

San Juan   Three bedroom apartment front-line golf
              New four-bedroom villa (no pool)

Area Four – Vega Baja

Most large apartment or small villa property in this area falls into this price bracket.

Ciudad   Three bedroom detached villa on 1,000m^2 plot with pool
Quesada

Dehesa de   Three bedroom apartment front-line beach
Campoamor

La Zenia   Two or three bedroom townhouse near beach

Torre de   Two bedroom semi-detached townhouse
la Horadada

Villamartín Three bedroom detached villa with pool

Area Five – Mar Menor

Most large apartment or small villa property in this area falls into this price bracket.

Los Alcázares   Three bedroom detached villa (new or resale) with no pool

La Manga   Three bedroom apartment in prime position
Three bedroom townhouse

From €400,000 to €600,000

Area One – Marina Alta

Jalón Valley   Large villa with large plot and pool

Jávea   Three bedroom villa with large plot and pool

Moraira   Large three bedroom villa on large plot with pool

Area Two – Marina Baja

Altea   Luxury two or three bedroom apartment in Altea Hills or Urb Mascarat.
Large four bedroom villa with pool

Benidorm   Two bedroom apartment, front-line beach
Large three bedroom apartment in old town

Inland   Three or four-bedroom villa with private pool

Area Three – Alicante

Alicante   Luxury penthouse apartment in top location

San Juan Playa   Luxury three bedroom penthouse apartment

Area Four – Vega Baja

Expect to buy some of the best property this area has to offer in this price bracket.

Ciudad Quesada   Luxury three bedroom villa with large plot and pool

Cabo Roig   Large three-bedroom villa with private pool

Inland   Very large villa on large plot with pool

Area Five – Mar Menor

Expect to buy some of the best property this area has to offer in this price bracket.

Los Alcázares   Three or four bedroom villa with private pool

La Manga   Penthouse apartment in front-line position

From €600,000 to €800,000

Area One – Marina Alta

Benissa   Luxury two bedroom apartment, front-line golf

Jávea   Three bedroom villa front-line beach

La Sella   Five-bedroom country house

Moraira   Luxury villa

Area Two – Marina Baja

Expect to buy the best property this area has to offer in this price bracket.

Alfaz   Luxury three bedroom villa in prime urbanisation

Altea   Three bedroom villa on large plot with sea views
Large country *finca* with large plot

Area Three – Alicante

Expect to buy the best property this area has to offer in this price bracket.

Alicante   Very large villa on large plot near university

Muchamiel   Very large villa with pool

San Juan Playa   Luxury villa with private pool

Area Four – Vega Baja

Expect to buy the very best property this area has to offer in this price bracket.

Cabo Roig   Large luxury villa with pool

Inland   Extensive country property with very large plot of land

La Zenia   Three or four bedroom villa with large plot (at least 900m^2) and private pool

Area Five – Mar Menor

Expect to buy the very best this area has to offer in this price bracket, e.g. an extensive luxury villa.

Over €800,000

The property world becomes your oyster over this price bracket and you can expect to buy the very best the Costa Blanca has to offer, e.g. a large rustic-style villa with extensive plot in a prime inland location in the Marina Alta or a luxury villa with pool and sea views in Jávea.

New Property or Off-plan

Construction is a boom industry at the moment on the Costa Blanca as the endless skyline of cranes testifies, particularly in the municipalities of Calpe, Benidorm, Finestrat, Guardamar de Segura and the area around Orihuela Costa and Torrevieja, which currently has the highest urban growth rate in the country. In Torrevieja alone some 12,700 new properties were sold in 2003 and figures are expected to be similar in 2004 in spite of the rise in house prices. Around 70 per cent of new property is sold to buyers from the UK. In some areas, new construction increased by around 50 per cent and there are no signs that this tendency is starting to slow down and experts calculate that 2005 will see similar levels of new projects. In some areas, building companies are calling on the authorities to release more land for construction in response to demand for new properties.

You can find off-plan properties by calling in at developments themselves (most have onsite offices open from 10am to 2pm and from 4 to 7pm) and from estate agents, most of which have off-plan properties on their books.

There's currently a huge choice of new property for purchase and experts generally agree that new property is a good investment – prices usually rise as soon as the building is finished. The down side to buying off-plan is the waiting – **building work is rarely finished when it's supposed to** (some take a year longer than originally planned) and some promoters don't have the correct paperwork. If you're thinking of buying off-plan, it's especially important that you use the services of a lawyer to check the paperwork, including whether the promoter owns the land he's building on and if he has a bank guarantee to return payments if the company goes bankrupt.

Plots

In the north of the Costa Blanca there's now little building land left (in some areas there are no plots at all available for purchase). Possibilities are greater in the south and inland, although you need to make sure the plot is classed as urban (*urbana*) and not rural (*rústica* or *no urbanizable*) so that you can obtain planning permission to build. You should also check that the plot isn't part of a *LRAU* development now or likely to become one in the future (see below).

Plot Prices

On the Coast

Plots on the coast are expensive and prices start at around €100 per m² for a plot in a poor position and can be as high as €500 or more for land in a prime position possibly with views. A plot on the coast is usually from 500m² to 1,000m². **When inspecting a plot, check the terrain** – the land on the coast is often sloping and it's expensive to dig out terraces and build retaining walls for construction. It's also important to check that a plot has water and electricity supplies nearby.

Inland

Plots inland are considerably cheaper (from €10 per m²) and a plot with a building or small ruin on it costs from €16 per m². Plots tend to be large (usually with a minimum of 2,000m², but often with several thousand more) and often have numerous citrus or almond trees. Such plots need extensive maintenance and before buying a large piece of land make sure you have both the time and inclination to maintain it. **Note that the size of building permitted on a plot is very restricted even though the plot itself may be large**, e.g. a building of up to 120m² on a plot of up to 4,000m², and a building of up to 200m² on a plot of 10,000m². Check there are water and electricity supplies in the vicinity – it's very expensive to connect supplies over a distance. Find out also if a telephone line is feasible. Check the access road – if it's little more than a track, bear in mind that when it pours with rain in the winter, the track may turn into an impassable quagmire suitable for four-wheel drive vehicles only.

Valencian Urbanisation Regulations

The Urban Development Legislation (*Ley Reguladora de Actividad Urbanística/LRAU*) introduced in 1994 in the region of Valencia is currently the centre of a highly-publicised dispute between developers and hundreds of property owners, who are being forced to pay huge sums of money either for infrastructure development or for the repurchase of their own land. If the owners don't (or cannot) pay, developers can legally seize the land and pay owners compensation at a fraction of the market price. Not for nothing is the law known as the 'Land Grab'.

When it was introduced in 1994, the *LRAU*'s objective was to promote urban development in the region where town planning faced continual obstacles mainly from landowners who refused to participate in development projects. As a result, towns and cities could not expand or build low-cost housing or essential public services. Under the *LRAU*, landowners must participate in development projects backed by town councils by paying for contributions towards infrastructure such as roads, mains supplies and street lighting. In the city of Valencia, where there was a chronic shortage of housing, the *LRAU* has worked well and the city and suburbs have benefited hugely from new development for housing, green areas and public services such as hospitals and schools. Control in and around the city has been strict and development highly regulated. However, in other parts of the region, particularly the Costa Blanca, the *LRAU* has been systematically abused by corrupt local authorities and developers who stand to make huge profits by developing rural land for villas. Most of the development plans in this area carried out under the auspices of the *LRAU* provide little or no public benefit.

Many owners, both Spanish and foreign, of semi-rural or rural properties in the area are affected by the *LRAU*, particularly as developers now move further inland where there's a shortage of building land. As a result, many owners are facing large bills (up to €75,000) or are being forced to sell their property. A recent study found Jávea to be the most affected municipality with more than 80 *LRAU*-backed developments in the area.

The *LRAU* has been challenged before the Spanish Constitutional Court as a breach of essential property rights, although a decision by the court is not expected in the near future. A European Commission Report, including findings by three MEPs who visited the area in May 2004, was published last summer and approved by the European Parliament who urged regional authorities to urgently revise the law. Meanwhile, you're advised not to buy rural or semi-rural land in the region of Valencia without taking comprehensive professional advice, preferably from a lawyer who can thoroughly explain all the implications of such a purchase. **Note that the *LRAU* only affects property situated on land that hasn't been developed.**

Further information about the *LRAU* and advice on its consequences for private land owners can be found on ⌨ www.abusos-no.org.

House Hunting

There are many ways of finding homes for sale on the Costa Blanca, including the following:

- Newspapers and magazines such as *Costa Blanca News* (large property section) and *CB Friday*. For a full list of publications see **Appendix A**. Large estate agents also publish in-house property lists.

- Property exhibitions (see **Appendix B** for further details).

- The internet, where there are hundreds of sites dedicated to property on the Costa Blanca. These can be found by typing in 'Costa Blanca property' in a search engine such as Google (🖥 www.google.com). **Most sites belong to or are linked to an estate agent.**

- Visiting an area. Many property owners sell privately to avoid paying the agent's commission and put up 'For Sale' (*Se vende*) signs outside the property.

- Estate agents (see below). Most property owners sell through an agent.

Estate Agents

There are literally hundreds of estate agents on the Costa Blanca – there are more than 80 in the Jávea area alone – some of which are large companies with branches at different locations in the area. The quality of service varies greatly, although the best offer a personalised approach without rushing the client into a purchase and may also provide after-sales services such as finding a school or buying a car. Properties for sale are usually with several agents (sometimes with different prices!) and there are few exclusive sales. Ask around for recommendations for a good estate agent. Reputable estate agents should be registered as a member of a professional association such as Agente de Propiedad Inmobiliaria (API) or Gestor Intermediario en Promociones de Edificios (GIPE). Ask to see an agent's registration number. **Beware of unlicensed, amateur 'cowboy' agents, of which there are many.**

In 2004 there were several scandals involving estate agents on the Costa Blanca, including one where an estate agent closed down owing clients thousands of euros for down payments or stage payments on properties. Clients were left without their savings and their property.

Purchase Procedure

The purchase procedure in Spain isn't especially complicated, but it's different from other countries and there are numerous pitfalls for the unwary. Don't be tempted to buy a property without the conveyancing services of a registered lawyer. Numerous lawyers specialise in conveyancing on the Costa Blanca and many speak good English – ask around for recommendations. You may wish to check with the Alicante Lawyers' Association that a lawyer is registered and has professional insurance cover (Colegio de Abogados de Alicante/ICALI, C/ Gravina 4, 2, Alicante, ☎ 965-145 180, 🖳 www.icali.es). You can find out by telephoning the association or by checking on the website.

Lawyers charge between 1 and 2 per cent of the property price plus 16 per cent VAT for conveyancing. Other taxes and fees associated with property purchase are: transfer tax at 7 per cent, notary and land registry fees and possibly *plus valia* tax (a sort of capital gains tax, which is usually paid by the seller but often passed to the buyer, particularly in the case of new properties). In general you can expect to add around 10 per cent to the price for fees and taxes.

For comprehensive information on the purchase procedure see this book's sister publication *Buying a Home in Spain* by David Hampshire (Survival Books).

PROPERTY RATES

Property rates known as the *Impuesto sobre Bienes Inmuebles* (*IBI*) are payable annually and are calculated as a percentage of the cadastral value of a property, which is based on its fiscal value. Many councils are currently revising cadastral values so you can expect rates to rise in the near future. Most property rates for the Costa Blanca are collected by the provincial tax body (SUMA) on behalf of the councils and rates are usually payable between 26th July and 1st October. If you pay after this date, you may be charged a surcharge for late payment. Payment can be made by direct debit, at SUMA offices (located in most towns) and participating banks (Banco Popular, Banesto, BBVA, BSCH and SabadellAtlántico) and saving banks (CajaMurcia, CAM, La Caixa and some local banks, e.g. Caja de Crédito de Altea). Some councils also charge for refuse collection and disposal (*impuesto sobre residuos urbanos*, known as *basura*) separately. The following table gives examples of *IBI* tax rates in different locations on the Costa Blanca:

Locality	IBI (%)
Alfaz del Pi	0.75
Alicante	0.67
Altea	0.65
Benidorm	0.60
Benissa	0.75
Callosa d'En Sarrià	0.90
Calpe	0.80

Denia	0.85
Elche	0.77
Finestrat	0.70
Gata de Gorgos	0.75
Guardamar	0.60
Jalón	0.65
Jávea	0.85
Los Alcázares	0.77
Orihuela	0.75
Pilar de la Horadada	0.65
Rojales	0.65
San Fulgencio	0.65
Santa Pola	0.64
Teulada	0.65
Torrevieja	0.80
Villajoyosa	0.90

Information on property tax rates for most councils in Alicante province can be found on the SUMA (provincial tax collectors) website (🖥 www. suma.es). SUMA runs a telephone helpline in English, French and German open from 9am to noon Mondays to Fridays (☎ 965-148 561).

RETIREMENT & NURSING HOMES

State and private nursing homes are available on the Costa Blanca where demand has risen spectacularly in recent years. There are still few state nursing homes and places are in very short supply. Any places that are available are usually given to pensioners who have a very low income. Private nursing homes vary in terms of facilities and services, although all must fulfil strict minimum criteria and standards. Prices also vary, with the average being around €1,200 a month for a shared room. Some homes also provide facilities for day care only.

Before committing yourself, look around carefully and compare facilities, levels of care and privacy, staff qualifications and extra services. Social services departments in local councils can provide information on nursing homes in specific areas. **You should also check that the home is registered with the local and regional authorities.**

Private Nursing Homes

Area One – Marina Alta

Benissa	Nuestra Señora de los Dolores,	
	C/ Teulada 6	☎ 965-730 593

Calpe	Colina Club, Urb Colina del Sol 7	☎ 965-835 228

La Saleta   ☎ 961-698 059
💻 www.lasaleta.com
A recently completed residential home offering rooms or double apartments plus 24-hour medical attention, sports facilities, hairdressers and other services.

Residencial Sanyres   ☎ 965-839 990
💻 www.sanyres.es
A newly-completed residential home offering double rooms plus 24-hour medical attention and indoor pool.

Denia	Residencial Santa Lucía, Partida de Santa Lucía s/n	☎ 965-782 912
Jávea	Asilo Hermanos Choli, Avda Puerto 6	☎ 965-791 080

Area Two – Marina Baja

Alfaz del Pi	Forum Mare Nostrum, Camino de Pincho 2	☎ 966-878 400
Altea	Asociación Tercera Edad Verdader, Partida Pla de Castell 110	☎ 966-881 791
Benidorm	Ciudad Patricia, C/ Rumanía 26	☎ 965-868 704
	Residencia Tercera Edad, Partida Foietes 1	☎ 966-807 434
Villajoyosa	Residencia Santa María, C/ Alicante 21	☎ 966-851 421

Area Three – Alicante

Alicante	Analistas Sociales de la Tercera Edad, C/ Reyes Católicos 31	☎ 902-106 020
	Centro Geriátrico Torremar, Avda Ansaldo 12	☎ 965-266 004
	Residencia Nuestra Señora de Lourdes, Plaza San Juan de Dios 2	☎ 965-253 911
	Residencia Tercera Edad Alacant, C/ Cronistas Martínez Morella 1	☎ 965-179 375
	Residencia Tercera Edad Vicent, Balsas del Ebro 14, Ctra Villafranqueza-Tángel	☎ 965-127 226

	Residencia Tercera Edad Vistahermosa, C/ Orgegia 31	☎ 965-263 195
	Residencia Virgen del Remedio, C/ Santa María Mazzarello 2	☎ 965-280 327
El Campello	Centro de Mayores Europa, Rincón de Zogra s/n	☎ 965-941 450
	Grupo Care, C/ Bernat Metge 3 🖥 www.grupo-care.com	☎ 902-200 024
Muchamiel	Cap Blau, C/ Ramón y Cajal 35 🖥 www.capblau.com	☎ 965-951 361
San Juan de Alicante	Cap Blau, Avda de Benidorm 71 🖥 www.capblau.com	☎ 965-942 209

Area Four – Vega Baja

Orihuela	Residencia El Castillo, C/ Las Espeñetas s/n	☎ 966-745 043
Pilar de la Horadada	Residencia Nuestra Señora de las Nieves, C/ Marqués de Peñacerrada 3	☎ 965-352 535
Rojales	Residencial Mediterráneo, C/ Paz 26	☎ 966-715 778
Santa Pola	Residencia Tercera Edad Suecia, C/ Carreteros 76	☎ 965-416 011
Torrevieja	Residencial P. Margalla, Avda de los Marineros 25	☎ 966-704 436
	Residencia Tercera Edad de Torrevieja, C/ Maestro Francisco Casanovas 26	☎ 965-710 708
	Residencia Tercera Edad la Suiza, Santa Rita, Avda Suiza 13, Urb Las Maravillas	☎ 966-920 718

Area Five – Mar Menor

San Pedro de Pinatar	Residencia Nueva Familia, Camino del Churrete s/n	☎ 968-187 346

Retirement Complexes

A few years ago, the Costa Blanca offered nothing specific for retirees other than state or private nursing homes. Over the last two years, however, retirement complexes have started to appear at locations around the coast and there's now a good choice both in facilities and price range. Several large companies have started projects and demand is high and new properties are sold very quickly. The following list provides information about retirement complexes on the Costa Blanca.

Area One – Marina Alta

Benimeli   Benimeli Club Residencial, Carrer
Secanets 12   ☎ 965-587 616
💻 www.benimeliclubresidencial.com
Set in this small village some 6km (4mi) west of Beniarbeig, accommodation consists of 49 double rooms and two singles within the centre, which provides onsite medical care, sports facilities (gym and indoor and outdoor pools), a chapel, rehabilitation services and social activities.

Calpe   La Saleta   ☎ 961-698 059
💻 www.lasaleta.com
A recently completed residential home offering rooms or double apartments plus 24-hour medical attention, sports facilities, hairdressers and other services.

Residencia Costa Blanca, Edif Centro Atlántico,
Avda de los Ejércitos Españoles s/n   ☎ 965-834 604
Accommodation consisting of a central retirement home and sheltered apartments within a self-contained centre, including catering and cleaning services, and 24-hour on call medical service.

Area Two – Marina Baja

Alfaz del Pi Alfaz del Sol   ☎ 902-200 065
💻 www.sanyres.es
This complex, currently under construction, consists of 150 two and three bedroom apartments, guest flats, sports facilities and medical care.

Forum Mare Nostrum, Camino de Pincho 2   ☎ 966-878 400
💻 www.forum-marenostrum.com
A new nearly-completed complex consisting of one and two bedroom sheltered apartments within a self-contained centre, including restaurants, a health and fitness centre and 24-hour on call medical service. Services include catering, cleaning, shopping and laundry. Accommodation is for sale on a 35-year lease and prices start at €52,500 for one-bedroom accommodation. Service charges will cost from €300 a month.

Benidorm   Residencial Sanyres   ☎ 902-200 065
💻 www.sanyres.es
A new complex is planned for the city, due to be finished in 2006.

Area Three – Alicante

Alicante   Paradise Views   *UK* ☎ 0845-658 5065
            🖳 www.kei-homes.com   *Spain* ☎ 968-150 088
            Situated to the west of the city inland, this new project (due to be
            finished by 2007) will consist of one and two bedroom apartments
            within a self-contained complex providing numerous services,
            including medical care and a social centre. Prices start at €180,000
            for a one-bedroom freehold apartment.

            Residencial Zouine   *UK* ☎ 0845-658 5065
            🖳 www.kei-homes.com   *Spain* ☎ 968-150 088
            A new complex (due to be finished by 2007) consisting of one and
            two bedroom apartments within a luxury purpose-built centre
            providing medical care and other services. Prices for a one-
            bedroom apartment start at €90,000 for a life interest lease and at
            €165,000 freehold.

El Campello Residencial Campello   *UK* ☎ 0845-658 5065
            🖳 www.kei-homes.com   *Spain* ☎ 968-150 088
            This complex, currently under construction, will house 98 one and
            two bedroom luxury apartments within a self-contained centre
            providing services such as a medical centre, gym,
            restaurants and hairdressers. Apartments will cost from
            €225,000 freehold.

Hondón de Mi Casa Familie   *UK* ☎ 0845-658 5065
las Nieves 🖳 www.kei-homes.com   *Spain* ☎ 968-150 088
            Situated some 35km (22mi) inland from Alicante near the
            village of Hondón de las Nieves, this complex consists of 440
            detached houses within a self-contained retirement village offering
            numerous services such as property maintenance, shopping and
            medical care. Options include the purchase of plot or ready-built
            home. Prices start at €85,000 for a plot, at €105,000 for
            a one-bedroom property and at €160,000 for a two
            bedroom villa.

Area Four – Vega Baja

Algorfa   Villajardín Residencias, C/ Pablo Picasso
            1, Ctra Algorfa – Montesinos   ☎ 902-106 020
            (situated some 7km/ 4mi west of Rojales and
            Ciudad Quesada)
            🖳 www.grupoaste.com

Santa Pola Residencial Sanyres   ☎ 902-200 065
            🖳 www.sanyres.es
            This huge complex, currently under construction and expected to
            be finished in 2006, will house some 800 sheltered apartments as
            well as numerous services and amenities.

Area Five – Mar Menor

Three large self-contained village complexes are under construction in the Mar Menor area and are expected to be finished towards the end of 2005. The complexes will house their own shops, other amenities and a golf course as well as providing 24-hour security. Information (in Spanish only) about all three complexes is available from the developer, Grupo Polaris World (🖳 www.sainmo.com) or from estate agents in the area.

Mar Menor   Golf Resort
Situated near the town of Torre Pacheco, inland from the Mar Menor, this resort consists of semi or detached villas within a complex housing amenities such as supermarkets and a health clinic. Prices start at €180,000 for a two bedroom semi-detached villa and at €375,000 for a three bedroom villa.

La Torre   Golf Resort
Situated near the town of Torre Pacheco, inland from the Mar Menor, this complex provides two and three bedroom apartment accommodation plus comprehensive services and facilities. Prices start at €130,000 for a two bedroom apartment.

El Valle   Golf Resort
A huge complex with a mixture of apartment and villa accommodation. Prices start at €150,000 for a two bedroom apartment and at €375,000 for a three bedroom villa.

El Peñón de Ifach, Calpe

6

Employment

If you're relocating to the Costa Blanca and need to work, one of your first priorities when you arrive will be to find a job. This chapter looks at the employment market, job opportunities, how to find a job and information about setting up a business.

EMPLOYMENT FIGURES

Unemployment figures on the Costa Blanca are among the best in Spain where the national average is around 10 per cent and in late 2004 some 52,300 people were officially unemployed in the area, around 3 per cent. The figure varies within the province where certain towns such as Elche have rates of nearly 5 per cent due to the problems certain employment sectors are suffering, particularly the shoe manufacturing industry. On the coast, however, employment opportunities are good and there are numerous jobs available, particularly in the construction and services sectors. Tourism and services provide nearly two thirds of employment opportunities in the area and there are comparatively few jobs in industry and agriculture.

WORKING ILLEGALLY

Many businesses on the coast offer casual employment paid in cash, a highly illegal practice, which leaves the employee with no rights whatsoever. Illegal workers employed without a contract and not registered with the social security system have no legal rights (holiday, compensation, unemployment benefit, etc.), no right to health treatment (except in emergencies) and are open to fines from the tax authorities if caught.

> **If you're offered a job without a contract as countless people are on the coast, remember it's illegal for both you and the employer, and you should seriously consider if it's worth working for an employer under those conditions.**

JOB OPPORTUNITIES

Most employment on the Costa Blanca is found within the services sector and in certain jobs related to the tourist industry, the main engine behind the area's economy. Bear in mind that many jobs, particularly those in the restaurant and bar businesses, are seasonal, i.e. from May to November.

If you speak fluent Spanish (and Valencian) you have a better chance of getting a well-paid job and there may be more opportunities as you can look for jobs in Alicante and Valencia where many national and several multi-national companies are based. Many jobs require fluency in several languages (Spanish, English, German and possibly one or more Scandinavian languages).

Jobs are mainly available in the following sectors (listed alphabetically):

- **Administration/Secretarial Work** – Ability in several languages and good working knowledge of computer programmes are generally required. Salary levels depend on experience and responsibility.

- **Beach Bar Staff** – Strictly seasonal employment, although there's a high demand for staff in the summer months. Work is hard (and often physical if you're in charge of the loungers!) and hours long – many beach bars open from noon to the small hours of the morning. Wages are low, but tips can be good.

- **Construction** – The current building boom on the coast means there are plenty of vacancies for anyone with experience from bricklayer to site foremen. Jobs can be found by enquiring at building sites directly or at company offices.

- **Domestic Work** – Wealthy families in the area often require live-in staff to maintain properties, do housework and cooking, gardening or work as a nanny. A driving licence may be a necessity. Wages are often low and hours long, and if you're looking after a remote property while the owner's away, the work can be lonely. Non live-in staff are also in demand, particularly as a nanny or gardener.

- **Education** – Vacancies often arise for qualified teachers at international schools on the coast (many post vacancies on their website) and teachers of English as a foreign language are also in demand for both language schools and private classes. Note that salaries are generally lower than their equivalents in the UK.

- **Holiday Companies** – Foreign holiday companies usually employ staff in their home country to work as holiday representatives (reps) on the coast, but vacancies for on-site representatives are sometimes advertised in the local press. Staff for hotel entertainment, children's representatives and nursery nurses are also required during the summer months. Pay is generally low and hours are long, although you usually receive free board and lodging.

- **Hotel & Catering** – Work is mainly seasonal, although increasing numbers of hotels now open all-year round and require permanent staff. Hotels tend to recruit top posts via adverts in the national newspapers or a recruitment company, but other posts are advertised locally. Shift work is common.

- **Information Technology** – IT experts are always in demand, particularly those with knowledge of website design and programming.

- **Property Sales** – Probably the greatest number of vacancies are available in the property sector. Estate agencies need marketing staff, property finders, administrative personnel and property vendors. Knowledge of English, Spanish and at least one other language plus computer literacy is generally required. Basic salary plus commission is usually offered.

- **Restaurant & Bars** – Work is mainly seasonal, although many restaurants and bars now open all-year round to cater for the resident population. A knowledge of Spanish is usually necessary. Bear in mind that waiting is a respected profession in Spain and you may require previous experience if you wish to be taken on in a Spanish restaurant. Casual waiting is more for beach bars (see above) and nightclubs.

- **Sales** – This is probably the area with the most opportunities for foreigners on the coast at the moment, particularly selling advertising space in the expatriate press or in-house magazines or selling products (often household or health and beauty-related). It's a very competitive area and you need to be good to succeed. You usually need your own transport and must be prepared to cover great distances. Pay is usually based on commission.

  There are several companies based on the coast whose advertising claims their sellers make thousands of euros from part-time work from home. These companies usually market health products (e.g. diet aids, beauty products or body magnets) and their vendors make their commission by finding other people to sell the products, the classic pyramid structure, which is illegal in some countries. Remember that it's only the people at the top who make thousands!

- **Services** – There's a seemingly unlimited demand for household services on the coast, such as cleaners, gardeners, 'odd-job' experts, swimming pool cleaners and child-minders. Work is often piecemeal (intermittent) and poorly paid.

- **Telephone Sales** – Jobs selling holidays or property by telephone are available, usually based in so-called telecentres and worked in shifts, including during the night when sales are made to countries in different time zones. A basic salary plus commission is usually offered.

● **Timeshare/Holiday Schemes** – Vacancies are often available for street vendors of timeshare properties or as on-site vendors. A basic salary plus commission is usually offered.

FINDING A JOB

Your first step should be to register as unemployed with the regionally-run Valencian Employment Service (Servici Valencià d'Ocupació I Formació/SERVEF), which has offices in the main towns on the coast (see list below). If you live in the Mar Menor area you should register with the region of Murcia's Employment Service (Servicio Regional de Empleo y Formación/SEFCARM – see below). Offices are open from 9am to 2pm Monday to Friday. **Note that staff may not speak English**. Once you've registered with SERVEF and/or SEFCARM you have six months in which to find a job, although there are no strict controls on this for EU nationals.

SERVEF Offices on the Costa Blanca

SERVAF has a telephone helpline (☎ 900-100 785) open from 9am to 2pm and 4 to 7pm Mondays to Fridays as well as a website, in Spanish and Valencian only, where you can consult job offers throughout the region (🖥 www.servef.es). Local vacancies are advertised at SERVEF offices, but don't expect staff to notify you of vacancies – the onus is on you to find yourself a job.

Area One – Marina Alta

Calpe	C/ Benissa 2, Edif Atalaya	☎ 965 834 911
Denia	Avda Ramón Ortega 3-B, Edif La Paz	☎ 966-420 610

Area Two – Marina Baja

Benidorm	Avda Comunidad Valenciana 22	☎ 965-850 188
Villajoyosa	C/ Pianista Gonzalo Soriano 1	☎ 965-890 332

Area Three – Alicante

Alicante	C/ Isabel La Católica 1-3	☎ 965-927 940
	C/ Primitivo Pérez 15	☎ 965-250 361
	C/ San Juan Bosco 15	☎ 965-985 267

Area Four – Vega Baja

Elche	C/ José Sánchez Saez 11	☎ 966-613 920
	C/ Pedro Moreno Sastre 20	☎ 965 430 055
	C/ Mariano Benlliure 6	☎ 965-445 312
Orihuela	Prol Ronda Santo Domingo 4	☎ 965-302 647
Torrevieja	C/ Larramendi s/n, Edif Iruña	☎ 966-701 377

SEFCARM Offices

For general information contact ☎ 968-357 563 or visit 🖳 www.sefcarm.es.

Murcia	C/ Jorge Juan 2
	C/ Sagasta 27
	Rda Norte 10
Torre Pacheco	C/ Víctor Pérez s/n

Other Employment Agencies

Spanish Agencies

Spanish employment agencies tend to operate only as temporary employment bureaux (*empresas de trabajo temporal*) and work offered is usually for Spanish-speakers only. Look in the yellow pages under *Trabajo Temporal: Empresas*. Bear in mind that contract conditions and wages are usually poor in temporary employment posts.

Foreign Agencies

In recent months foreign recruitment agencies have started to operate in the area, although they're very much in their infancy (this is a niche market). These companies specialise in the recruitment of English-speakers and offer jobs ranging from waiters to top management posts. You can register online and apply for job vacancies from anywhere, although you're expected to be in the area for a personal interview with prospective employers. According to the companies, successful candidates are able to speak both Spanish and English. The main company offering recruitment services on the Costa Blanca is:

● Job Toaster (☎ 952-053 980, 💻 www.jobtoasterspain.com).

The following companies currently specialise in the Costa del Sol, but may have vacancies for the Costa Blanca:

● Empresolutions (☎ 952-891 328, 💻 www.empresolutions.com);

● Recruit Spain (☎ 952-898 136, ☎ 952-491 842, 💻 www.recruit spain.com);

● Wemploy (☎ 902-021 200, 💻 www.wemploy.com).

Newspapers

Jobs are posted in the Spanish daily local newspapers, *La Verdad* (💻 www.laverdad.es), *Información* (💻 www.diarioinformacion.com) and *El Periódico de Alicante* (💻 www.elperiodicoalicante.com) everyday under '*Empleo*' and in national newspapers on Sundays, usually in the financial supplement. The English-language newspapers also advertise job vacancies – *Costa Blanca News* has the most and this section is probably the one used by most expatriate job hunters on the coast. Adverts are also posted online (💻 www.costablanca-news.com).

You can also post an advert yourself under the '*Situations Wanted*' section, outlining the sort of employment you're looking for and your contact details.

Internet

There are hundreds of sites for job hunters on the internet, an increasingly popular method of finding employment. Most job vacancy websites also offer advice on finding a job and the opportunity to post your CV online. Below is a list of the most popular sites. The sites are for Spain as a whole, although most list vacancies by province, but there are as-yet no Costa Blanca specific sites.

💻 http://jobs.escapeartist.com/Openings/Spain (general with numerous vacancies for the Costa Blanca);

💻 www.laboris.net (general with a good selection for the Costa Blanca);

⌨ www.monster.es (general, good selection);

⌨ www.spanish-living.com/job-offers (general, good selection – click on Valencia);

⌨ www.tecnoempleo.com (job vacancies in IT and telecommunications);

⌨ www.thinkspain.com/services/joboffers (general, good selection – click on Alic/Cast/Val);

⌨ www.trabajos.com (general, good selection).

Notice Boards

Job vacancies are often posted on notice boards outside supermarkets, churches and local businesses. It may be a good idea to post your contact details together with the sort of job you're looking for on the board. Many people include their telephone number in a tear-off section at the bottom to make it easier for the interested party.

Shops

Shops and businesses on the coast requiring staff often don't bother advertising but simply post a notice in the window stating what they're looking for. Notes usually start '*se busca*' or '*se necesita*' followed by the job. A contact number or the words '*información dentro*' or '*razón dentro*' (enquire within) usually follow.

SELF-EMPLOYMENT & STARTING A BUSINESS

A popular option with foreigners on the Costa Blanca is to become self-employed or start their own business. This isn't an option to be taken lightly and you should carefully consider all aspects of such a venture before you commit yourself. Stories of failed businesses and bankruptcy are common on the Costa Blanca and many people fail to realise that behind most self-employed and successful businesses there's a lot of very hard work. There are, however, numerous success stories and many foreigners are self-employed in the province of Alicante. If you're seriously considering this option, the best place to start is at a reputable *gestoría* (a business specialising in advice involving paperwork in Spain) – ask friends or other professionals (e.g. bank managers and lawyers) to recommend one. For a reasonable fee, the *gestoría* will give you comprehensive information on the process involved, guide you through it and take charge of most of the paperwork for you. You can tackle it yourself, but your knowledge of Spanish needs to be good – as well as your stamina for standing in queues!

Self-employment

Income Tax & VAT

The self-employed (*autónomos*) in Spain must register with the tax office both for income tax and for VAT. Income tax is levied at 20 per cent (levied on whatever you earn minus justifiable expenses) and must be paid in quarterly instalments (by 20th January, 20th April, 20th July and 20th October) based on your earnings for the quarter. Once a year (in May/June) you're also required to make an annual tax statement for the previous calendar year when you may be entitled to a refund or required to pay extra tax. Most professions are required to charge (and then pay) 16 per cent VAT, although there are some exceptions. Income tax and VAT information is available from local tax offices listed below (staff may speak little English) or in Spanish only from the telephone helpline (☎ 901-121 224) or website (💻 www.aeat.es). You may find it easier to consult a reputable tax adviser (*asesor fiscal*).

Tax offices on the Costa Blanca can be found at:

Area One – Marina Alta

| Denia | Carrer del Mar 30 | ☎ 965-788 111 |

Area Two – Marina Baja

| Benidorm | Avda Beniardá 2 | ☎ 965-860 411 |

Area Three – Alicante

| Alicante | Plaza de la Montañeta 8 | ☎ 965-149 700 |

Area Four – Vega Baja

| Elche | C/ Gabriel Miró 32 | ☎ 966-665 655 |
| Orihuela | C/ Obispo Rocamora 57 | ☎ 965-305 940 |

Area Five – Mar Menor

| Cartagena | C/ Campos 2 | ☎ 968-333 300 |
| Murcia | C/ Gran Vía Escultor Salzillo 21 | ☎ 968-361 100 |

Social Security

The self-employed must also register with the social security system and make monthly payments. The minimum monthly payment is currently €225.11 and the maximum is around €2,575, which entitles you to sickness and temporary invalidity benefits, maternity benefits, health treatment under the public health system and a retirement pension. Within these limits, you can choose how much you pay but, if you're under 50, there are few advantages in paying more than the minimum amount; if you're over 50, you may consider paying a higher amount in order to qualify for a higher pension.

Information about social security payments and benefits is available from local social security offices listed below (staff may speak little English) or in Spanish only from the telephone helpline (☎ 900-616 200) or website (🖥 www.seg-social.es).

Area One – Marina Alta

Denia   C/ Marqués del Campo 52   ☎ 965-780 022

Area Two – Marina Baja

Benidorm   C/ Tomás Ortuño 69   ☎ 965-855 905

Villajoyosa C/ Constitución 10   ☎ 965-890 194

Area Three – Alicante

Alicante   C/ Churruca 26   ☎ 965-903 133

                     C/ Médico Pascual Pérez 28   ☎ 965-205 910

Area Four – Vega Baja

Elche   C/ Jorge Juan 48   ☎ 965-464 362

Orihuela   C/ San Agustín 20   ☎ 965-300 006

Area Five – Mar Menor

Murcia   Avda Alfonso X El Sabio 15, bajo   ☎ 968-279 458

                     C/ Simón Garás 63   ☎ 968-218 835

Starting a Business

Starting up a business is a complex matter and you should seek professional help with this, particularly in deciding which business option is the best for you. There are several types of company in Spain, all requiring a minimum number of shareholders and minimum investment capital. Some also have accounting and auditing requirements. Tax obligations differ depending on the company, although all are subject to company tax currently levied at 35 per cent. Competent *gestorías* usually have a business advisor and tax advisors can also offer advice on setting up a company.

Buying Premises

Business premises (called a *local*) are often available on the Costa Blanca, although most are bars, restaurants or shops. The majority of premises are sold on a leasehold basis (*traspaso*), which means you pay for the business lease plus rent to the landlord for the use of the premises. Leases may be for any length of time, although they're usually no less than five years and no more than 25. Most leases are renewable. The cost of the rent increases annually by the rate of inflation. **When a lease is renewed, rent may be increased by up to 20 per cent.**

As the leaseholder you're responsible for the payment of local rates, utilities and possibly community fees incurred by the premises. You're permitted to sell the lease to a third party before it expires, although you must offer it to the landlord first and if you sell it to someone else, the landlord is entitled to commission (usually 20 per cent).

Rental payments are usually made monthly in advance and most landlords require two months rent as a security deposit. **If you're considering buying premises, don't undertake the purchase without proper legal advice.**

Business premises for sale on the Costa Blanca may be advertised in estate agents (some of which specialise in the sale of business premises), in the local press or even at the premises (the sign usually says '*Se traspasa local*').

Tourist office, Elche

7

Health

One of the most important aspects of living on the Costa Blanca is maintaining good health and one of expatriates' prime concerns is the standard of the health service and medical staff. All foreigners must have medical insurance cover, public or private, and both systems have an excellent reputation on the Costa Blanca. This chapter looks at the public health system (including how to register) and private health insurance, and in addition provides details and information about health centres and hospitals, dentists and opticians, and chemists'.

PUBLIC HEALTH SYSTEM

The public health system on the Costa Blanca is part of the Valencia Health Department (*Consellería de Sanitat*, ⌨ www.san.gva.es), although in the Mar Menor it's part of the Murcia Health System (*Murcia Salud*, ⌨ www.murciasalud.es). Under the system, residents who are pensioners or contribute to the social security system are entitled to free primary and hospital medical treatment. Pensioners are entitled to free subscriptions; for other residents prescriptions are subsidised. The medical service on the Costa Blanca is generally very good and has an excellent reputation among foreign residents. However, health centres in some areas are overstretched as medical services haven't matched the rapid increase in number of residents over the last few years. Non-urgent operations are also subject to waiting lists, although these have been shortened dramatically in recent months.

You shouldn't expect medical staff to speak English. Some may speak a little, but most don't. If your knowledge of Spanish is poor, you should take someone along with you to translate. Some health centres and hospitals offer translation services, usually provided by a team of volunteer foreigners. The volunteers provide an excellent service, but you shouldn't rely on them in an emergency.

How to Register

EU Pensioners

In order to qualify for free medical treatment European Union (EU) pensioners should take form E-121 (issued in from their home country) to their nearest social security office (INSS – see below) and apply for a Spanish health card (*tarjeta sanitaria*), which is later sent by post. Once you've applied for a card, you're entitled to free medical treatment and prescriptions. Note that if you need treatment before you receive your card, you should show the doctor or health centre the receipt given to you by the social security office.

EU Visitors

Visitors should bring form E-111 with them from their home country. The form must be shown to medical staff if you require any medical treatment. If you don't have the form and need urgent medical treatment, you will be treated but you must pay for treatment. You may get a refund in your home country.

EU Residents

EU residents should bring form E-111 with them, which is valid for three months from the time of arrival. After three months, if you've started work, you should register with the social security system and apply for a Spanish health card. If you don't plan to work, you will need private medical insurance.

European Health Insurance Card

A European health insurance card (EHIC), similar to a credit card, is being introduced in EU countries. The card contains information about the holder (personal and social security details), including the number and length of social security contributions. Holders of the card will no longer need forms E-111 and E-121. The EHIC will be issued in the UK from mid-2005; further information is available from post offices or from 🖳 www. dh.gov.uk/travellers.

Non-EU Residents

Non-EU residents must have proof of medical insurance cover (usually private) before they enter Spain in order to get a visa. If you find employment in Spain you should register with the social security system and apply for a Spanish health card. If you don't plan to work, you must continue with payments towards private medical insurance cover.

Information about your health card is available from ☎ 901-302 020 from 9am to 9pm Mondays to Fridays.

Social Security Offices

Social Security Offices (Instituto Nacional de Seguridad Social/INSS) on the Costa Blanca are listed below. Offices are generally open from 9am to 1.30pm Mondays to Fridays and note that staff may not speak English. Information is also available (in Spanish only) from the INSS telephone helpline (☎ 901-502 050) and website (🖳 www.seg-social.es).

Area One – Marina Alta

Denia   C/ Marqués del Campo 52   ☎ 965-780 022

Area Two – Marina Baja

Benidorm	C/ Tomás Ortuño 69	☎ 965-855 905
Villajoyosa	C/ Constitución 10	☎ 965-890 194

Area Three – Alicante

Alicante	C/ Churruca 26	☎ 965-903 133
	C/ Médico Pascual Pérez 28	☎ 965-205 910

Area Four – Vega Baja

Elche	C/ Jorge Juan 48	☎ 965-464 362
Orihuela	C/ San Agustín 20	☎ 965-300 006

Area Five – Mar Menor

Murcia	Avda Alfonso X El Sabio 15, bajo	☎ 968-279 458
	C/ Simón Garás 63	☎ 968-218 835

Once you have your social security card you should register at your local health centre (see list below). You're entitled to choose your doctor and if you have children (up to 14 or 16 years old), you should choose a paediatrician as well. If you don't choose a doctor the health centre allocates you one.

Most health centres are open all day (e.g. 8am to 8pm), although those in smaller towns and villages have reduced opening hours (e.g. 9am to 3pm). Not all health centres provide emergency treatment and visits to doctors in health centres in small villages may not by appointment, but based on a first-come first-served basis. **For life-threatening emergencies requiring an ambulance dial ☎ 061.**

Public Health Centres

Area One – Marina Alta

Benissa	Avda Ausial March s/n	☎ 965-732 461
Benitachell	Avda Valencia 35	☎ 966-493 481
Calpe	Avda Conde Altea s/n	☎ 965-835 011
Denia	Avda Juan Fuster s/n	☎ 966-425 853

Gata de Gorgos	C/ La Bassa s/n	☎ 965-756 350
Jalón	C/ Lepanto 1	☎ 966-480 543
Jávea	Plaza de la Constitución s/n	☎ 965-795 811
	Jávea-Aduanas: Avda Botanic Cabinilles s/n	☎ 966-460 456
Llíber	Plaza Pública s/n	☎ 965-733 472
Ondara	Avda Marina Alta s/n	☎ 965-767 346
Orba	C/ Lepanto 5	☎ 965-583 011
Pedreguer	C/ Rosal s/n	☎ 965-761 198
Pego	Ctra de Denia 50	☎ 965-571 56
Teulada	C/ Dr Pitarch s/n	☎ 965-741 136
El Verger	C/ de L'Estació s/n	☎ 965-750 303

Area Two – Marina Baja

Alfaz del Pi C/ Príncipes de España s/n
appointments only ☎ 965-889 809
emergencies ☎ 966-880 025

Playa del Albir: Avda Oscar Esplá s/n   ☎ 965-889 809

Altea Partida Galotxa s/n   ☎ 966-880 025

Altea la Vella: C/ Cura Linares s/n   ☎ 965-846 659

Benidorm C/ Tomás Ortuño 69   ☎ 966-803 838

Avda de Venezuela s/n
appointments only ☎ 966-830 061
emergencies ☎ 965-852 683

La Cala de Benidorm Avda Montbenidorm s/n
appointments only ☎ 965-866 858
emergencies ☎ 965-852 683

Callosa d' En Sarrià Partida Mirantbó s/n   ☎ 965-881 563

Finestrat	C/ Fonteta s/n	*appointments only* ☎ 965-878 360
		emergencies ☎ 965-893 490
Guadalest	Casa del Médico	*appointments only* ☎ 965-882 578
		emergencies ☎ 965-881 563
La Nucia	Avda Porvilla s/n	☎ 966-896 490
Polop de la Marina	Avda Sagibarba 24	*appointments only* ☎ 966-895 063
		emergencies ☎ 966-880 025
Sella	Plaza Mayor 8	*appointments only* ☎ 965-879 294
		emergencies ☎ 965-893 490
Tárbena	Plaza Santa Ana s/n	*appointments only* ☎ 965-884 159
		emergencies ☎ 965-881 563
Villajoyosa	C/ Juan Tonda Aragonés s/n	
		appointments only ☎ 965-895 385
		emergencies ☎ 965-893 490

Area Three – Alicante

All health centres in the Alicante district are listed on the following website: 🖥 www2.san.gva.es/area16.

The following centres are in Alicante city itself.

Alicante	C/ Barítono Paco la Torre 35	☎ 965-184 762
	C/ Dr Sapena s/n	*appointments only* ☎ 965-200 232
		emergencies ☎ 965-144 972
	C/ Gerona 24	☎ 965-143 337
	C/ Portugal s/n	*appointments only* ☎ 965-121 843
		emergencies ☎ 965-132 164
	Plaza Santísima Faz 7	*appointments only* ☎ 965-212 266
		emergencies ☎ 965-144 971

The following are centres near Alicante city.

Aguas de Busot	Casa del Médico	☎ 965-690 023

El Campello Avda Germanías s/n   *appointments only* ☎ 965-637 108
                                             emergencies ☎ 965-637 106

Muchamiel C/ del Mar s/n   ☎ 965-952 777

Playa   No address   ☎ 965-941 373
Muchavista

Playa San Avda Bruselas 19   ☎ 965-157 589
Juan

Area Four – Vega Baja

Altet   Avda Dama d'Elx 23   ☎ 965-688 243

Arenales   Avda Bartolomé de Tirajana s/n   ☎ 966-910 518
del Sol

Elche   C/ Vicente Fuentes Sansano 36
                                             appointments only ☎ 965-443 563
                                             emergencies ☎ 965-443 561

               C/ Alfredo Sánchez Torres 8
                                             appointments only ☎ 965-435 180
                                             emergencies ☎ 965-435 205

               C/ Jorge Juan 46
                                             appointments only ☎ 966-679 421
                                             emergencies ☎ 966-679 422

               C/ Vicente Andrés Estellés s/n
                                             appointments only ☎ 966-679 620
                                             emergencies ☎ 966-679 593

               C/ Manuel Alcaraz Mora 13
                                             appointments only ☎966-641 563/4/5
                                             emergencies ☎ 966-641 566

Guardamar C/ Movilent s/n   ☎ 965-729 515

Las Bayas C/ Mutxol 10   ☎ 966-637 311

La Marina Avda de la Alegría s/n   ☎ 965-419 489

Orihuela Plaza de la Salud s/n   ☎ 965-304 343

	Avda Teodomiro 22	☎ 966-742 926
Orihuela Costa	Urb La Zenia, Avda La Playa, Edif Madrid bajo	☎ 966-776 600
	Urb La Regia	☎ 965-322 818
	Torre de la Horadada, C/ Manuel Molino s/n	☎ 966-769 855
Pilar de la Horadada	C/ Vicente Blasco Ibáñez s/n	☎ 966-767 150
Rojales	C/ Constitución s/n	☎ 966-715 750
San Fulgencio	C/ José Antonio 31	☎ 966-794 231
Santa Pola	Avda Albacete s/n *appointments only* *emergencies 24 hours*	☎ 965-412 080 ☎ 965-412 950
Isla de Tabarca	C/ Iglesia s/n	☎ 965-970 595.
Torrevieja	C/ Virgen del Mar s/n	☎ 966-700 702
	C/ Urbano Arregui 6	☎ 966-707 149
Urb La Marina	C/ Amsterdam s/n	☎ 966-796 281

Area Five – Mar Menor

La Manga	Gran Vía s/n, Urb Castillo del Mar	☎ 968-142 125
Los Alcázares	Ctra de Balsicas s/n	☎ 968-575 800
San Javier	C/ Cabo Ras, Esq Cabo Lara s/n	☎ 968-192 333
San Pedro de Pinatar	Avda Salinera Española s/n	☎ 968-182 062

PUBLIC HOSPITALS

All public hospitals provide 24-hour casualty and emergency treatment (*urgencias*). Many hospitals in the area, particularly the Hospital Comarcal

Marina Alta and the Hospital de la Vega Baja are seriously overstretched with overcrowded emergency facilities especially in the summer months when the Costa Blanca's population increases at least three-fold.

Area One – Marina Alta

Denia	Hospital Comarcal Marina Alta, Partida Real de Sta Paula s/n	☎ 965-787 012
Gandía	Hospital Francesc de Borja, Passeig de les Germanies 71 🖳 www2.san.gva.es/hgandia	☎ 962-959 200

Area Two – Marina Baja

Villajoyosa	Comarcal de la Villajoyosa, Partida Galandu 5 Serves the Marina Baja	☎ 966-859 200

Area Three – Alicante

Alicante	Clínico San Juan de Alicante, Ctra Alicante – Valencia s/n 🖳 www2.san.gva.es/hsanjuan	☎ 965-908 700
	Hospital General de Alicante, C/ Maestro Alonso 109 🖳 www2.san.gva.es/hgualicante	☎ 965-908 300

Area Four – Vega Baja

Elche	Hospital General de Elche, Partida Huertos y Molinos s/n 🖳 www2.san.gva.es/area19	☎ 966-606 000
Orihuela	Hospital de la Vega Baja, Ctra Orihuela – Almoradi s/n Serves southern Costa Blanca.	☎ 966-776 166

Area Five – Mar Menor

Santiago de la Ribera	Hospital Los Arcos, Paseo de Colón 54	☎ 968-570 050

USEFUL NUMBERS

AIDS   ☎ 900-850 100
Helpline   Available 10am to 2pm Mondays to Fridays

Alcoholics   ☎ 965-711 162 (Torrevieja) or ☎ 966-421 303 (Denia)
Anonymous   Alicante, Benidorm, Calpe, Denia and Torrevieja have local English-speaking groups. Meeting times and places are listed in the local press.

Alzheimer's   ☎ 965-209 871
Association

Cancer   ☎ 900-100 036
Helpline

Drugs   ☎ 900-200 514
Helpline   Available 8am to 3pm Mondays to Fridays

Helpline for ☎ 900-200 999
Women   Available 24 hours

Sex Advice   ☎ 901-406 969
                  Sex advice for young people available 10am to 2pm and from 5 to 7.30pm Mondays to Fridays

Smokers   ☎ 900-850 300
Helpline

PRIVATE MEDICAL TREATMENT

Private medical treatment is a popular alternative to the public system with both Spaniards and foreign residents. However, private treatment is expensive unless you have private health insurance. There are numerous companies offering a range of private health insurance policies on the coast and a good choice of private clinics and hospitals. Note that most private clinics won't provide free treatment under the conditions of the E-111 form. Note also that most private hospitals don't have the full range of facilities and services provided in public hospitals.

Health Insurance Companies

Spanish Companies

The main companies operating in the area are:

- **Adeslas** – Offices in Alicante, Benidorm, Denia, Elche and Torrevieja (☎ 902-200 200, 🖳 www.adeslas.es);

- **Sanitas** – Offices in Alicante, Denia, Elche and Jávea (☎ 901-100 210, 🖳 www.sanitas.es).

Foreign Companies

- **ASSSA** – Offices in Alfaz del Pi, Denia, Ciudad Quesada/Rojales and Moraira (☎ 965-200 106);

- **AXA PPP Healthcare** – 🖳 www.axappphealthcare.com;

- **BUPA International** – 🖳 www.bupaspain.com. On the Costa Blanca contact Mr Robin Holloway, Apdo de Correos 5.317, Torrevieja or by telephone or email (☎ 965-719 030, ✉ holloway@bupa international.net);

- **Exeter Friendly Society** – 🖳 www.exeterfriendly.co.uk, ☎ in the UK 00 44 1392 353 535 and on the Costa Blanca 966-461 690/278, ✉ jenniferc@teleline.es;

- **International Health Insurance** – ☎ 952-471 204, 🖳 www.ihi.com.

There are also numerous insurance brokers who can give advice on which company and which policy is right for you. Ask around for recommendations or look in the yellow pages under '*Seguros*' or '*Seguros Médicos*'. Many companies also advertise in the local press. Policies and prices vary enormously so it's important to shop around.

Private Clinics

Every town on the Costa Blanca can boast several private clinics and staff usually speak English and sometimes other foreign languages. Some clinics cater for specific nationalities, e.g. British or German. Facilities and services vary greatly: some clinics have only a general practitioner (GP), while others have several specialist doctors and X-ray, testing and scanning facilities. Most clinics provide home doctor services and emergency medical treatment, however, if a clinic doesn't have the facilities you will be referred to or taken to a public hospital. Clinics generally belong to one or more health insurance schemes – your insurance policy should provide a list of participating members in the area. If you don't have a list, consult the yellow pages under '*Clínicas Médicas*'. All private health centres should be registered with the regional authorities who list all legal centres. The list is available from ☎ 965-935 283 or from

🖳 www.san.gva.es (go to *Organizacón Consellería* and then to *Registro de Centros Sanitarios Privados*).

Specialist Private Clinics

There are numerous private clinics specialising in specific areas of medicine, particularly gynaecology, heart complaints and cosmetic surgery.

> There have been several scandals recently on the Costa Blanca concerning clinics offering cosmetic surgery. Irregular practices included unregistered or under-qualified doctors or inadequate facilities. Several cases even involved operations under general anaesthetic without the supervision of an anaesthetist! Check the clinic and doctor you've chosen for cosmetic surgery is properly qualified and registered with the health authorities before committing yourself.

Private Hospitals

Area One – Marina Alta

Denia   Centro Médico Denia: C/ Beniarmut 1   ☎ 965-787 991

Policlínico San Carlos: VP Les Madrigueres Sud A-8 s/n   ☎ 965-781 550

Area Two – Marina Baja

Benidorm   Clínica Benidorm: Avda Alfonso Puchades 8   ☎ 969-658 538
The Hospital de Levante is currently under construction and due to be finished in late 2005.

Area Three – Alicante

Alicante   Clínica Mare Nostrum: C/ La Dorada 16, Cabo Huertas   ☎ 965-160 311

Casa de Reposo: Plaza Dr Gómez Ulla 15   ☎ 965-210 100

Clínica Vistahermosa: Avda Denia 103   ☎ 965-162 200

Hospital Internacional Medimar: Avda Denia 78   ☎ 965-162 200

Muchamiel Les Jardins de Sophia: Partida Almajada s/n   ☎ 965-955 195

Area Four – Vega Baja

Elche   Clínica Ciudad Jardín: C/ Palmerers 2   ☎ 965-452 272

Torrevieja Hospital San Jaime: Partida de la Loma s/n   ☎ 966-921 313

DOCTORS

Many Spanish doctors with private practices speak enough English to understand and explain health problems. Note, however, that the level of English tends to be lower in Alicante city, simply because the doctors there attend far fewer foreign patients than their colleagues in other localities on the coast.

Most private practices hold clinics in the afternoons (e.g. 5pm to 8pm) and few offer morning appointments.

CHEMISTS'

Most localities on the coast have at least one chemist's (*farmacia*) and there are also several located at urbanisations along the coast. Note that chemists' are the only places you can buy medicines in Spain, although supermarkets and *parafarmacias* stock basic first-aid items such as antiseptic cream, plasters and lint. Chemists' also sell a wide range of non-medical wares such as cosmetics, baby food and equipment, toiletries and diet foods. Pharmacists are highly trained and provide free medical advice for treatment of minor ailments. If they cannot help, they will recommend a local doctor or specialist in the area.

Chemists' are generally open from 9.30am to 2pm and from around 4.30 to 8pm Mondays to Saturdays. There are duty-chemists' open 24-hours, from 9.30am to 10pm or from 10pm to 9.30am. **Note that if you visit a duty-chemist's you usually have to ring a bell and are attended to through a hatch.** Lists of duty-chemist's in the locality are posted on chemists' windows, listed in the local press and can be found on the following website: 🖳 www.cofalicente.com – go to *Farmacias de Guardia* on the right and select the locality and day for a list of duty-chemists. Some tourist offices (e.g. Torrevieja) have lists of duty-chemists' with maps showing their location.

Listed below are 24-hour chemists' on the Costa Blanca

Alicante   Avda Alfonso El Sabio 34

              Avda Rosalía de Castro 6

DENTISTS

The only dental treatment currently provided by the public health system are check-ups and decay prevention for all children under 15. Contact your local health centre if you wish your child to be included in the scheme. Otherwise, dental treatment must be included under a private health insurance policy or paid for directly. Many health insurance companies provide policies, including dental treatment, although comprehensive dental policies are usually very expensive!

Numerous dentists, both Spanish and foreign, have practices on the Costa Blanca and many Spanish dentists speak English. Note that a foreign dental practice may be more expensive than a Spanish one. All dentists should be registered and must be able to prove it. Not all dentists provide a full range of treatments, a service provided in large clinics only. Some smaller practices do check-ups, crowns and fillings only, and many don't have in-house X-ray facilities. If you need a tooth extracted, you may have to visit a specialist. **Not all dentists treat children.**

Fees vary greatly and it's worth shopping around before registering with a dental practice. Some surgeries operate a membership scheme (e.g. €100 a year) which includes check-ups, consultations and a scale and polish. Ask around for recommendations or look in the yellow pages under '*Clínicas Dentales*' or '*Dentistas: Odontólogos y estomatólogos*'.

Orthodontic Treatment

Orthodontic treatment tends to be carried out by specialist dentists only and not by general practices. Correction and cosmetic treatment is increasingly popular on the Costa Blanca and there are now numerous clinics operating in the area. If you or your child needs orthodontic treatment, visit several recommended practices and compare the different treatments and prices offered. There's usually a consultation fee (around €30) for which the dentist will offer a diagnosis and treatment plan. Note that prices and treatment vary enormously for children's orthodontic treatment and it's not uncommon for dental practices to carry out unnecessary treatment or start treatment prematurely.

OPTICIANS

There are numerous opticians on the Costa Blanca, some of which cater for specific nationalities and most have English-speaking staff. Ask around for a recommendation or look in the yellow pages under '*Opticas*'. Most opticians provide free eye tests and have a wide range of frames and lenses.

There are several chains of opticians who periodically have special offers on certain types of glasses so it's worth shopping around.

OTHER MEDICAL SERVICES

Spanish and foreign specialists offer a wide range of services on the Costa Blanca such as acupuncture (*acupuncturista*), chiropody (*podólogo*), chiropractic (*quiropráctico*), osteopathy (*osteopatía*), physiotherapy (*fisioterapauta*) and psychology (*psicólogo*). Although most specialists are highly qualified and experts in their field, the odd con-man or 'quack' isn't uncommon on the Costa Blanca and so, before putting your body in anyone's hands you should make sure they're qualified and registered with the local health authorities. Many professionals advertise in the local press, although the best way to find someone good is to ask around for recommendations. A sure sign is if the professional in question has been on the coast for several years – usually only the best last!

Alternative medicine and treatments are also widely available on the coast. A good source of information of what's available is health shops (*herbolisterías*).

Guadalest

8

Education

One of parents' main concerns when considering relocation to the Costa Blanca is their children's education. There are several options available and the one you choose will depend on many factors, such as your finances, short-term plans and whether you wish your child to have a Spanish education. The different options are discussed in this chapter, which also provides a directory of private and international schools on the coast as well as information on after-school and summer activities, and learning Spanish.

The Costa Blanca Kids website (🖳 www.costablancakids.com) has a wealth of information about education and children's activities in many areas of the coast.

> Note that many schools on the Costa Blanca are currently heavily over-subscribed – state schools are over-crowded and private schools have waiting lists for many year groups. If you can, plan ahead and get your child on the waiting list as soon as possible.

SPANISH EDUCATION

Advantages

- Your child has the chance to learn to speak Spanish and Valencian (see page 188) and integrate into a different culture and society.

- Spanish state schools are free and Spanish private schools are considerably cheaper than international schools.

- Entrance to a Spanish university will be easier if your child has gone through the Spanish education system.

Disadvantages

- Learning Spanish can take children time and hold back their learning process.

- You will also need to have good Spanish in order to communicate with teachers (Spanish teachers don't necessarily speak English!).

Education is compulsory for all children between the ages of 6 and 16 in Spain, although places are now available at many schools from the age of three and most children tend to start their schooling early. Education consists of four main phases:

1. *Infantil* (from ages 3 to 6) where the emphasis is on learning social skills;

2. *Primaria* (from 6 to 12) which is divided into three cycles of two years;

3. *Secundaria* (from 12 to 16) which is divided into two cycles of two years, at the end of which students who have achieved set standards receive the School Leaver's Certificate;

4. *Bachiller* (16 to 18), similar to 'A' level or International Baccalaureate (IB) in other countries.

The standard of Spanish education is generally on a par with that in other western countries, although there are major differences in learning methods (the Spanish system favours learning by rote) and there are few extra-curricular activities. The vast majority of Spanish schools are co-educational (mixed sexes).

Valencian

All children in the Spanish education system in the Costa Blanca are required to study Valencian as a first language as well as Spanish. According to the regional education authorities, pupils are expected to have mastered both Spanish and Valencian (see page 188) by the end of their secondary education. Foreign children entering a Spanish school on the Costa Blanca are therefore faced with two new languages.

School Holidays

School holidays consist of around two weeks at Christmas, ten days for Easter and nearly three months in the summer (from around 20th June to 10th September) plus local and national bank holidays.

STATE SCHOOLS

Education in state schools (*colegio público*) is provided free from the ages 3 to 18 for all residents (but you do have to pay for books and materials). As in many countries, places at state schools are determined by catchment areas – to find out which school is in your catchment area ask at the local Town Hall. **Places at state schools in many areas are in short supply and you're unlikely to get a place at a school outside your catchment area.**

Note, however, that your child may be allocated to a state school outside your catchment area if the local authorities have decided to distribute foreign children equally among schools. In September 2004 state schools in Denia (where foreign children account for around 15 per cent of pupils) agreed to distribute foreign children throughout the town's seven schools with a minimum of three foreign pupils per classroom. The measure was introduced to facilitate integration and to discourage children of the same nationality sticking together.

Information about education and state schools is available in Spanish and Valencian from the regional authorities (☎ 900-202 122, 🖳 www.cult-gva.es) who also publish a leaflet (downloadable from the website) in nine languages, including English, French and German. The website also provides a list of all state schools in the province. Information specifically for foreign children is available from the Immigration Reception Centre for School Age Children (*Oficina de Acogida al Alumnado Inmigrante*), C/ Carratalá 47, Alicante (☎ 965-934 000).

Some local councils run specific schemes to help foreign children and their parents integrate into the Spanish school system. Guardamar de Segura council runs a School Office manned by local teachers who provide information on schools and assess pupils to ascertain their linguistic and education levels in order to provide help with language and/or tuition.

Registration

Registration for state schools on the Costa Blanca takes place in the spring (usually in May). Dates and times are advertised in the local press. In practice, however, children can be registered at any time of the year if there are places. To register your child you need the following:

- Your child's passport (original and photocopy);

- Your passport (original and photocopy);

- A family book or equivalent recording the parents' marriage (if applicable) and the child's birth (original and photocopy).

If your child is starting secondary school from the third year upwards you also have to provide proof of their education record and in addition obtain a certificate from the Spanish Education Ministry to confirm this. **Comprehensive information can be obtained from Spanish consulates and embassies in your country of residence.** You're also recommended to refer to *Living and Working in Spain* (Survival Books) for more detailed information – see page 334.

Primary Schools

After-school Activities

Many primary schools now have an after-school activity programme typically running from 5 to 7pm. **Bus travel isn't available after activities.**

Curriculum

Children study Spanish, Valencian, maths, natural and social sciences, English (as a foreign language), music, art and physical education (PE). Catholic religion is optional – the alternative is usually extra reading or studies.

Lunch

Lunch is provided by outside caterers in many schools during the lunch-hour at extra cost (around €3 a day) and the quality is generally excellent.

Parent-teacher Meetings

A time is allocated each week (known as *tutoría*) when parents can meet the teacher. Reports (*notas/evaluación*) are issued at the end of each term.

Timetable

Generally, 9am to noon and 3 to 5pm or from 9am to 2pm. Most primary schools start at 9am and finish at 2pm in June and September. Some schools open earlier in the morning (e.g. at 7.45am) and provide supervision and breakfast before school. A small monthly fee is payable for this service.

Transport

Free buses to and from schools are usually available in large catchment areas (e.g. Orihuela Costa and San Fulgencio/Urb La Marina), but not within towns.

Additional Information

The maximum number of children permitted per class is 25 and children aren't required to wear a uniform.

Secondary Schools

Curriculum

In the first two years students study Spanish, Valencian, maths, natural and social sciences, English (as a foreign language), history and geography,

Information Technology (IT), music, art and PE. In the second two years students may opt for certain subjects, including a second foreign language.

Parent-teacher Meetings

A time is allocated each week (known as *tutoría*) when parents can meet the teacher. Reports (*notas/evaluación*) are issued at the end of each term.

Timetable

Generally, 8.15 or 8.30am to around 2pm depending on the day of the week and time of the year. Students have a 30-minute break when most of them eat a snack.

Transport

Free buses to and from schools are available in large catchment areas (e.g. Orihuela Costa and San Fulgencio/Urb La Marina), but not within towns.

Additional Information

The maximum number of children permitted per class is 30 and children aren't required to wear a uniform. Lunch isn't usually available.

Learning Spanish

If you decide to send your child to a state school, it's vital to give them as much support as possible with their Spanish (and Valencian) AND you should learn to speak the two languages yourself. Some councils provide evening classes for parents in Spanish and Valencian (see page 188) to help them understand school activities, the homework and correspondence from the school.

The region runs special integration schemes for foreign children entering state schools with the aim to helping them to settle in as soon as possible. Many schools have specialist language teachers for foreign children, but there may not be enough help and in any case, some children find it difficult to learn two new languages at the same time and require extra help. If you want your child to make academic and social progress you should make provision for lessons outside school and actively encourage participation in activities with Spanish children.

In Alicante province there were nearly 29,000 foreign children in state schools at the start of the 2004/5 academic year. Some state schools on the coast are currently full of British children who speak little or no Spanish (or Valencian) and they make little academic progress. Teachers don't usually speak English and although they may make an attempt to speak it to help a child they're under no obligation to do so and must teach the rest of the children in the class in Spanish.

Many expatriates on the Costa Blanca are under the false impression that their children will learn Spanish quickly and easily in school. This may be the case for nursery-age children but older children struggle if they have no extra support.

PRIVATE SPANISH SCHOOLS

Around a third of school children in Spain as a whole attend private schools, a figure that's reflected on the Costa Blanca where there are many private schools, although most are situated in Alicante and the majority are of a religious denomination (usually Catholic). Most have long waiting lists (some lists have more children on them than actually attend the school!) and it may be difficult to get a place. **Note also that private Spanish schools tend not to admit children over six who don't speak good Spanish.**

FOREIGN PRIVATE SCHOOLS

There's a reasonable choice of foreign private schools on the Costa Blanca and the majority are so-called international schools offering teaching in English and following a British-based curriculum, sometimes with the International Baccalaureate. Some offer Spanish pupils (and foreign pupils with an exceptional level of Spanish) the possibility of studying a parallel Spanish curriculum. This is advantageous for foreign pupils who wish to study at a Spanish university without having to validate their qualifications.

Advantages

● If you return to your home country, your child's studies won't have been interrupted.

● Children feel more familiar and less isolated if the teaching is in their native tongue.

● Some British schools on the Costa Blanca belong to the National Association of British Schools in Spain/NABSS (🖳 www.nabss.org), whose inspectors visit and approve schools.

Disadvantages

● Fees are high.

- Waiting lists are long.

- Children grow up in a cultural ghetto with little contact with Spanish society. In some schools little progress is made in learning Spanish.

- Foreign private schools are over-subscribed and waiting lists are long in many cases.

English-language Schools

The following is a list of private schools on the Costa Blanca using English as a teaching medium. Schools offering the possibility of studying a parallel Spanish curriculum are denoted *. There are no private schools of any kind in Area Five.

Area One – Marina Alta

Jávea   Firs Independant Primary School,
Ctra la Guardia 125, Costa Nova   ☎ 966-472 929
🖳 www.firsprimary.com
Co-educational, 3 to 11.

*Lady Elizabeth School, Ctra Benissa-Jalón
s/n, Llíber   ☎ 965-731 960
☎ 0871-711 5304

🖳 www.theladyelizabethschool.com
Co-educational, 3 to 18. The primary section is situated in the town of Jávea and the secondary section in Llíber. Buses from Altea, Denia and Jávea.

Xábia International College, Ctra Cabo de la
Nao 21, Apdo Correos 311   ☎ 966-471 785
🖳 www.xabia-international-college.com
Co-educational, 3 to 18. Buses from Altea and Denia via Jávea.

Area Two – Marina Baja

Alfaz de Pi   *Sierra Bernia, La Cañeta s/n, San Rafael   ☎ 966-875 149
Co-educational, 3 to 18. Buses from Benidorm and Calpe.

Benidorm   *Costa Blanca International College,
Partida de Sanz s/n   ☎ 966-803 411
Co-educational, 3 to 18. Buses from Benidorm centre, Calpe and Villajoyosa.

La Nucia   Elian's British   ☎ 902-106 040
🖳 www.elians.com
Co-educational currently for children up to 8.

Area Three – Alicante

Alicante *British School of Alicante, C/ del Reino
Unido 5   ☎ 965-106 351
⌨ www.bsalicante.com
Co-educational, 3 to 16 (up to 18 in the future). Buses from
Alicante, Bonalba and Torrevieja.

The English School, C/ Pintor Gisbert 3,
Muchamiel   ☎ 965-951 097
⌨ www.theenglish-school.com
Co-educational, currently primary only. Bus routes from nearby
localities.

Area Four – Vega Baja

Elche Newton College, Camino Viejo de Elche –
Alicante km 3, Partida de Maitino, Elche   ☎ 96-661 0238
Co-educational, 3 to 14 currently (up to 18 in the future).

Torrevieja El Limonar International School (ELIS),
Avda Orihuela, Urb Los Balcones   ☎ 966-722 821
⌨ http://ellimonarinternational.com
Co-educational, 3 to 9 with an American curriculum. ELIS runs two
other schools in Murcia for children from 3 to 18. Buses run from
Torrevieja to the sites in Murcia.

Mar Azul, Urb Mar Azul, Paseo Central
Bloque K   ☎ 966-701 860
⌨ www.torreviejakids.com
Co-educational and bi-lingual education, up to 12 currently (up to
18 in the future).

Schools Teaching in Other Languages

Alfaz del Pi Norwegian School Costa Blanca (Escuela
Nórdica Costa Blanca), Río Guadiana
14, Urb El Oasis   ☎ 965-887 767
⌨ www.costablancaskole.com.
Co-educational.

Playa de San Juan *European School Alicante, Avda Vicente
Hipólito s/n   ☎ 965-155 610
⌨ www.eursc.org
Co-educational, 3 to 18. Buses from Alicante. Further information
about admittance and entrance criteria to this European School run
by the EU is available from the European Schools' main website
(see above).

Rojales   Norwegian School (Den Norske Skolen),
Avda de Castilla s/n, Rojales – Ciudad
Quesada   ☎ 966-719 684
🖥 www.norskeskolen.com.
Co-educational, 3 to 18.

VOCATIONAL TRAINING

For teenagers aged 16 or over who speak Spanish, there's a wealth of
opportunities in the vocational training (*Formación Profesional/FP*)
programme for students who have completed their compulsory schooling
and gained the School Leaver's Certificate (*Certificado de Graduado en ESO*).
FP includes practical training and academic study depending on the
profession or trade chosen and lasts at least two years. Common choices on
the Costa Blanca include IT, professions within the tourist industry, car
mechanics and gardening. The widest range is offered in Alicante,
although schools along the coast offer different trades and professions as
well. Information about FP is available from Spanish secondary schools
(*institutos*) and education departments of local councils.

AFTER-SCHOOL ACTIVITIES

Parents with children at state schools where the school day finishes around
2pm often want to find something for their children to do during the
afternoon. There's usually a good choice but most activities are based in
towns and if you live in an urbanisation you may have to spend your
afternoon ferrying children from one activity to another.

Information on different activities can be found in schools (who may offer
a variety of after-school activities on the premises), from Town Halls and
municipal sports centres, on local notice boards or in English-language
publications. Bear in mind that places for municipal activities tend to be in
short supply so you should apply early (usually in September). Below is a
brief summary of what's available for children.

The Arts

If your child's artistically inclined, there's a vast choice of activities from
painting and drawing to ceramics, crafts, dance (all forms but Spanish
classical is predominant), drama and music (singing and instruments).
Classes are available privately and in municipal centres (municipal music
schools are known as *conservatorios*).

Information Technology

Many town halls organise courses in IT, including internet and web design for children.

Languages

Language courses are offered all over the Costa Blanca for all ages and levels. If your child is at a Spanish school, it's a good idea to enrol them at extra classes in Spanish after school. Municipal classes are available at subsidised prices, but places are quickly filled so you should enrol your children as soon as possible in September. Some schools offer extra Spanish classes in the afternoons.

Sports

Most towns have good municipal sports facilities (often including an indoor pool) where there's a wealth of sporting activities for all ages. Activities usually take place two or three times a week and charges are low (from €12 to €25 a month depending on the activity). Sport is taken seriously and children who do well are often offered the chance to become a member of the national federation and play at regional and national levels. There are numerous private sports clubs (particularly tennis) where standards are high, but so are the prices. Horse riding and golf classes are available up and down the coast, although they're also expensive.

SCHOOL HOLIDAYS

As anyone with children at school in Spain knows, the summer holidays are **very** long (up to 15 weeks) and by May parents are frantically asking themselves the inevitable question: 'What shall I do with the kids this summer?'.

Summer Camps

Summer camps are available both at municipal and private levels, and many schools also organise camps during the summer. Camps last from one to two weeks depending on the children's ages and activities are usually based around sports, games and craft-type activities with the emphasis on getting out into the countryside – some camps are held in national parks. Camps run by the municipal authorities are good value, but places are always in short supply and residents in the locality are given priority.

Summer Schools

Summer schools are held in many schools and generally run by private companies during July and August. Schools usually run in the mornings only and consist mainly of sport and other leisure activities. Some summer schools offer lunch and slightly longer hours but most are from 9.30 or 10am to 2 or 3pm. Costs vary tremendously and it's worth shopping around to compare both prices and what's on offer. All summer schools should offer an insurance policy for the children and in the case of a private company, the company should be legally registered – ask to see their fiscal number (*CIF*).

Other Activities

Sports centres run special summer courses in most localities and many private sports centres organise intensive courses in tennis or football during the summer.

Otherwise, there's always the beach...

HOME EDUCATION

Some parents prefer to educate their children at home instead of sending them to school and there are many private home tutors operating on the Costa Blanca. Some tutors co-operate with foreign schools in the area, which gives pupils the possibility of taking external exams at the school. Private tutors also offer after-school classes in Spanish, English or extra help in specific subjects. Bear in mind that one-to-one private classes can be expensive but you get what you pay for. Experienced qualified teachers charge from €20 an hour. Ask around for personal recommendations or look in the local press.

LEARNING SPANISH & VALENCIAN

When you first arrive on the Costa Blanca you may be forgiven for thinking you're not in Spain at all because everyone's speaking English and when you try your best evening class Spanish to ask for "*cuatro lonchas de jamón*", the shop assistant replies in English. However, you should make learning Spanish one of your first priorities since not only is it a beautiful language providing an insight into a unique culture, being able to speak Spanish is extremely useful and could be vital in an emergency.

The majority of non-British foreigners on the Costa Blanca make a concerted effort to learn Spanish and many speak it well. Many British, however, make little or no attempt to learn it, and it's common to come across a British expatriate who's been 'here' for years but can hardly manage more than a '*buenos días*'. In some areas of the coast you're more likely to need Spanish than others, but you should never rely on there being someone to speak English or to understand you.

Many expatriates would argue that you don't need to speak Spanish on a daily basis at all and it's true that many Spaniards in the tourist industry on the coast speak and understand enough English to answer basic needs. There are also thousands of fellow Britons providing services in English and some civil servants in councils and public administration speak English. To a certain extent you don't need Spanish and many people live here without speaking a word. However, there are numerous situations where you do need Spanish (unless you're prepared to pay someone to accompany you interpret and translate). Some of these situations include:

● In an emergency – you cannot rely on an interpreter being available.

● For dealings with public administration – correspondence from the tax office, local council, regional government etc., is all in Spanish – staff don't usually speak English.

● If your children are at a Spanish school, you need Spanish to communicate with the teacher and to help your children with homework or problems.

● Communicating with the locals and generally making an effort to integrate into Spanish society.

Like French and Italian, Spanish is a Romance language derived from Latin and Greek. It's not a difficult language to learn the rudiments of and has the huge advantage of being phonetic so once you know how to pronounce each letter, you can pronounce any word correctly (unlike English, for example). Advanced Spanish is, however, more difficult and there are grammatical concepts, particularly tenses, that can tie even the most competent linguist in knots – but mastering a high level of Spanish isn't necessary for everyday life and you really just need a grasp of the basic tenses and vocabulary to express what you want and need.

Many expatriates claim they've tried to learn Spanish, but failed because they're too old or didn't have enough time. Many also claim that it's difficult to practise Spanish on the coast when so many people speak English. Both claims are true and to make a success of learning Spanish you need both time and patience. Usually if you make the effort to speak Spanish to a Spaniard, they will reply in Spanish.

A useful book for expatriates learning Spanish is *Liz Parry's Spanish Phrase Book* by Liz Parry (Santana Books).

Learning Valencian

As part of the Comunidad Valenciana, the Costa Blanca has two official languages, Spanish or Castilian (*español* or *castellano*) and Valencian (*valenciano* in Spanish and *valencià* in Valencian). Valencian is a dialect of Catalan (Europe's seventh most widely-spoken language), although Valencian has its own regional variations of Catalan. Most of the population is bi-lingual and authorities follow the official policy of promoting the use of Valencian. Its use is more common in the northern part of the region, but is widely spoken in many parts of the Costa Blanca, particularly to the north of Alicante, Elche and inland. In the coastal area south of Alicante (with the exception of Santa Pola), however, Valencian is rarely used or heard.

Valencian names of towns and cities are often used in preference to their Spanish equivalents, for example, *Alacant* (Alicante), *Elx* (Elche) and *Xàbia* (Jávea). Road signs are often in Valencian only, which can lead to confusion. Like the Catalans, many inhabitants of the Costa Blanca are 'nationalistic' and fiercely defend their regional language. If you choose to live inland or the northern part of the Costa Blanca you may therefore find integration into the local community easier if you make the effort to learn at least some Valencian.

Methods

There are numerous methods of learning a language from teach-yourself audio tapes or CD-Roms to complete immersion classes in remote rural areas. All methods are available on the Costa Blanca and the most popular are the following:

- **Local Spanish Classes** – Classes for foreigners are offered by most local councils and have the advantages of being cheap (they're usually subsidised) and giving you the chance to meet people in your area. Classes generally run from October to mid-June and there are usually several levels and times available. **Book early, however, because classes tend to be oversubscribed.**

- **Language Schools** – Spanish classes are available at language schools on the coast and a choice of levels is usually available. You may be able to choose how many lessons you want a week, although the minimum is usually three hour-classes. Typical prices are from €130 a week for three hours daily. Language schools advertise in the local press or you can look in the yellow pages under *Centros de Idiomas* or *Escuelas de Idiomas* or ask around.

- **Private Teachers** – Spanish lessons are offered on a one-to-one basis and usually the teacher comes to your home or office. Private classes are usually advertised in the English-language press or on local notice boards. Expect to pay from €15 to €30 an hour for a private class.

- **Intercambio** – An economical and pleasant way to learn Spanish – and often a good way to meet people – is to organise an 'interchange' (*intercambio*) with a Spaniard interested in learning English. Usually you agree to speak Spanish for half the meeting and English for the other half. Notice boards at your local town hall, supermarket or language school are good places to advertise for this.

- **Escuela Oficial de Idiomas (EOI)** – These are official language schools (run by the regional government) which offer Spanish and Valencian classes for foreigners during the academic year. Different levels are available. At the end of the course, successful candidates receive official certificates. **Courses are very popular so subscribe early.** Schools also organise cultural visits throughout the courses, which are offered in Alicante, Benidorm, Elche (no Spanish offered) and Torrevieja. EOI also offers courses in several other languages and summer courses. Courses cost from €40 per language studied plus a subscription fee. Further information can be obtained by contacting a school directly (see below).

Alicante	EOI, C/ Marqués de Molins 56-58 ✉ 0301136@centres.cult.gva.es	☎ 965-144 143
Benidorm	Complejo Escolar del Salt de L'Aigua s/n 🖳 www.eoibenidorm.com	☎ 965-858 161
Elche	C/ Josep Lluís Barceló i Rodríguez 1 🖳 www.eoielx.com	☎ 965-421 907
Torrevieja	C/ Monge y Bielsa s/n 🖳 www.eoitorrevieja.com	☎ 966-700 232

- **Alicante University** – Spanish for foreigners is also offered by the university (the language school is on the San Vicente university campus) at various levels for three or four hours daily over a course of one to three months. Prices for a month's course start at €400 and for three months at €900. Summer courses are also available. Courses are popular, particularly with overseas students. Further information is available from Alicante University, Relaciones Internacionales de la Universidad de Alicante, Apdo de Correos 99, 03080 Alicante (☎ 965-903 793, 🖥 www.ua.es – go to 'International Programs' on the English-language page).

Whichever method you choose, make sure you enjoy it and above all, keep at it – *¡Suerte! or ¡Bona Sort!*

Játiva

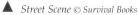
Street Scene © Survival Books

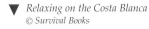
Relaxing on the Costa Blanca
© Survival Books

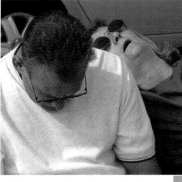

▲ Benitachell Beach
© Agència Valenciana del Turisme

▲ Alicante
© Agència Valenciana del Turisme

▶
Moraira
© Agència Valenciana del Turisme

▲ *Villas, Denia* © *Joanna Styles*

▲ *San Juan Beach*
   © *Agència Valenciana del Turisme*

▼ *Caladela* © *Joanna Styles*

▲ *Benidorm* © *Survival Books*

Guadalest and reservoir © Joanna Styles

Casa Carbonell, Alicante
© Agència Valenciana del Turisme

© Agència Valenciana del Turisme

Costa Blanca chic
© Survival Books

© Survival Books

© Survival Books

▲ Sea view © Survival Books

▲ House in Denia © Joanna Styles

◀ Jávea
© Agència Valenciana del Turisme

▶ Houses in Villajoyosa
© Survival Books

9

<u>Banks</u>

There are numerous banks operating on the Costa Blanca, both Spanish and foreign, and most provide an efficient banking service. There are two main types of bank: clearing banks (*bancos*) and savings banks (*cajas de ahorro*), which are often the only banking facilities in small villages. The banking giants are the BSCH (often referred to as the Santander Hispano) and the BBVA. Other smaller Spanish banks are the Banco Popular, Banesto and SabadellAtlántico. The largest saving banks are La Caixa and Caja Madrid, although Bancaja (which includes the regional Caja de Ahorros de Valencia, Castellón y Alicante) and CAM (originally Alicante's own saving bank) are the ones with the largest presence on the coast. Foreign banks with branches on the coast include Barclays Bank, Deutschebank, Halifax, Lloyds TSB and Solbank. The Royal Bank of Scotland also operates at the main BSCH branches. Note that foreign banks operate in exactly the same way as Spanish banks and you shouldn't expect a branch of a foreign bank to behave in the same way as a branch in the UK. **Note also that bank charges aren't generally lower at a foreign bank, compared to a Spanish one and in some cases may be higher.**

SPANISH & FOREIGN BANKS

Branches of banks are listed in the yellow pages under *Bancos* or *Cajas de Ahorros*. Further information on individual banks can be obtained by contacting the bank directly or by visiting the bank's website (click on *Oficinas* and choose Alicante province for your nearest branch). Telephone numbers and website addresses for banks on the Costa Blanca are provided in the lists below.

Note that there's little difference between the services and types of accounts provided by a clearing bank and a savings bank – so you can choose either type for your personal or business use. For further details on banking in Spain refer to *Living & Working in Spain* (Survival Books) – see page 334.

Clearing Banks

Clearing banks provide similar services to those of savings banks.

● **BBVA** – ☎ 902-224 466, 🖳 www.bbva.es (English language option available);

● **Banco Español de Crédito** – ☎ 902-224 466, 🖳 www.bbva.es (English language option available);

- **Banco Popular** – ☎ 902-301 000, 🖥 www.bancopopular.es (English language option available);

- **BSCH** – ☎ 902-242 424, 🖥 www.gruposantander.es (English language option available);

- **Banco Zaragozano** – ☎ 901-123 321, 🖥 www.bancozaragozano.es;

- **Banesto** – ☎ 902-101 235, 🖥 www.banesto.es (English, French and German language options are available);

- **Bankinter** – ☎ 902-365 563, 🖥 www.bankinter.es (English language option available);

- **SabadellAtlántico** – ☎ 902-365 465, 🖥 www.batlantico.es (English language option available).

Savings Banks

Savings banks provide similar services to those of clearing banks – including current accounts.

- **Bancaja** – ☎ 902-204 020, 🖥 www.bancaja.es;

- **Caja Madrid** – ☎ 902-246 810, 🖥 www.cajamadrid.es (English language option available);

- **CajaMar** – ☎ 952-217 761, 🖥 www.cajamar.es (English language option available);

- **CAM** – ☎ 902-100 112, 🖥 www.cam.es (English language option available);

- **La Caixa** – ☎ 93-404 6000, 🖥 www.lacaixa.es (English language option available).

Foreign Banks

- **Barclays Bank** – ☎ 901-141 414, 🖥 www.barclays.es;

- **Deutsche Bank** – ☎ 902-240 124, 🖥 www.deutsche-bank.es. Note that all post offices are Deutsche Bank agents;

- **Halifax** – ☎ 901-300 900, 🖥 www.halifax.es;

- **Lloyds TSB** – 🖳 www.lloydsbank.es;

- **Solbank** – ☎ 902-343 999, 🖳 www.solbank.es.

Listed below are the foreign banks that can be found on the Costa Blanca.

Area One – Marina Alta

Barclays

Calpe	Avda Gabriel Miró 26
Denia	C/ Marqués de Campos 64
Jávea	Ctra Cabo Nao km 3.2
Moraira	Ctra Teulada – Moraira km 5.7

Deutsche Bank

Benissa	Ctra Calpe – Moraira, Edif La Fustera
Benitachell	Ctra Mar s/n, Urb Cumbres del Sol
Calpe	C/ Corbeta s/n
Denia	C/ Diana 4
Jávea	Ctra Cabo Nao, El Plá 71, local 1/2
Teulada	Ctra Moraira – Calpe, Moravit 200

Halifax

Denia	C/ Diana 1

Solbank

Calpe	Avda Madrid 25
Denia	C/ Marqués de Campo 50 Bis
	Avda Joan Fuster 28
Jávea	El Plá s/n
Moraira	Avda Madrid 7

Area Two – Marina Baja
Barclays

Benidorm   Avda Alcoy, Edif Principado

Villajoyosa   Avda P.Valenciano s/n

Deutsche Bank

Alfaz del Pi   Avda del Albir 8, Edif Capitolio L.25

Altea   Partida Cap Blanc – Planet 117

Altea la Vieja   Ctra de la Callosa 58A

Benidorm   Avda Mediterráneo 17

Via Emilio Ortuño 4

Solbank

Alfaz del Pi   Avda País Valencia 26

C/ Vidalvi 3

Altea   C/ Conde de Altea 66

Benidorm   C/ Del Puente 2, Bis

La Cala Finestrat   Avda Marina Baja 1, Edif Principado 1, Local 5

La Nucia   CC Plaza del Sol, Avda Coloma 1

Area Three – Alicante
Barclays

Alicante   Avda Alfonso X El Sabio 43

Avda Maissonnave 38

Deutsche Bank

Alicante   C/ Pintor Aparicio 32

Esplanada España 21

El Campello Carrer del Metro 10

Lloyds TSB

Alicante   Avda Federico Soto 16

Solbank

El Campello C/ Sant Bartomeu 16

Area Four – Vega Baja

Barclays

Torrevieja   C/ J. Chapaprieta 10

Deutsche Bank

Elche   C/ Reina Victoria 16

Orihuela   Ctra Torrevieja – Cartagena 197

Orihuela   CC Villamartín Local 22
Costa

Pilar de   C/ Mayor 43
la Horadada

               Urb Pinar, Plaza Florida 1

Rojales   Avda de las Naciones 17

San   Urb Marina, C/ Sierra Castilla 29
Fulgencio

Torrevieja   Plaza Waldo Calero 2

               Urb Torre Lomas, Local 10

               Urb La Siesta, Zona Comercial Local 2

Halifax

Torrevieja   Urb Botánico, C/ Orihuela 71, Blq 4A

Solbank

Orihuela   Cabo Roig: Ctra N-332, km 49, CC Costa Marina
Costa

Punta Prima: Ctra N-332, km 53, CC La Campana

Rojales Avda de las Naciones s/n

Santa Pola Urb Gran Alacant, Avda Mediterráneo 72

Torrevieja Paseo Vista Alegre 4

Area Five – Mar Menor

Deutsche Bank

Los Alcázares Ctra Torrevieja – Cartagena, Urb Oasis

Solbank

Los Alcázares Avda Río Nalón s/n

BANKING HOURS

All banks are open from 8.30am to 2pm Mondays to Fridays. In addition clearing banks open on Saturday mornings from 8.30am to 1pm (from 1st October to 1st April) and saving banks are open on Thursday afternoons until 7pm (from 1st October to 1st April).

All banks are closed on national and local holidays, and may close earlier (e.g. at noon) for several days while the local *fiestas* (see page 222) are in progress. Bureaux de change have longer opening hours (usually similar to shops) and some open continuously during the summer.

CHOOSING A BANK

Shop around before you choose a bank and compare bank charges carefully. Bank charges are **very** high in Spain and even the simplest transaction such as a transfer costs at least €2.50. Some banks offer special deals, e.g. fixed monthly charges regardless of the number of transactions or a number of free transactions if you maintain a certain amount in your account. If you're a good client (i.e. one with a healthy bank balance) you should be able to negotiate a reduction in fees.

Most banks have English-speaking staff and many publish leaflets and other information in English. Some will even send you statements in English. Foreign residents and tourists account for a significant part of banking business on the Costa Blanca and competition for clients is fierce. Banking is a very personal affair in Spain and most bank managers know their clients personally.

Most banks now offer online banking, a secure option allowing you to conduct most banking transactions whilst saving considerable time (bank queues are usually very long). ATMs also provide some services as well as cash withdrawal. Servicaixa ATMs (*Servired* networks) are particularly comprehensive: cash and cheques can be paid in; statements and transactions can be printed; tickets for cinema, theatre and concerts can be bought; and you can also recharge your mobile phone.

Opening an Account

It's easier to open an account in person (banks may require credit references if you open an account by post) and all you need is proof of identity and an address in Spain.

Non-residents

Banking regulations are the same for both residents and non-residents, but non-residents can only open a non-resident euro account or a foreign currency account. Charges tend to be higher for non-resident accounts, but there are few differences in services offered.

Residents

Residents need to provide proof of residence in Spain, usually in the form of a residence permit or certificate of residence from the police. It's difficult to open an account without some official proof of residence in spite of the fact that EU nationals employed in Spain no longer require a residence permit – banks still need to see the official stamp! This requirement is expected to be abolished sometime during 2005.

INTERNET BANKING

There are several internet/telephone only banks in Spain, which offer interest on current accounts (around 3 per cent) with immediate access to your money as well as the usual banking services. The most popular is ING Direct (☎ 901-020 901, 🖳 www.ingdirect.es) owned by the European banking giant, ING Nationale-Nedenlanden who have just moved into the mortgage market offering very low interest rates and zero or nominal commission for most transactions. Other internet banks are Patagon (☎ 902-365 366, 🖳 www.patagon.es) owned by BSCH and Uno-e (☎ 901-111 113, 🖳 www.uno-e.es) owned by BBVA and Telefonica.

MORTGAGES

Mortgages are available from most Spanish and foreign banks on the Costa Blanca, and there's currently fierce competition for clients. Banks generally lend up to 80 per cent (90 per cent in some cases) to residents and up to 60 per cent to non-residents. Shop around as rates and commission vary tremendously. **Note that you cannot usually get a mortgage for property on land classed as rural and banks are extremely reluctant to lend to anyone over 65.**

Mortgage Brokers

There are numerous mortgage brokers on the coast who will do the shopping around for you and find you the best mortgage for your circumstances. **Before committing yourself to a broker (and definitely before parting with any money), check his credentials and make sure he's registered with the local authorities as a business.**

CREDIT & DEBIT CARDS

Credit and debit cards are generally accepted in most businesses, although some smaller shops don't take credit cards and you will find that some shops are reluctant to take cards and may offer a discount for cash. Inland and in villages cash may be the only form of payment. Visa and Mastercard are the most accepted credit cards and if you have an American Express or other card you should enquire in advance whether it's acceptable. **Note that most establishments ask for photographic identification (ID — e.g. residence permit, passport or driving licence) if you pay with a card.** Debit cards issued by Spanish banks cannot be used abroad nor can they be used for internet shopping other than with Spanish businesses.

Stolen Cards

If your card is lost or stolen, you should either inform your bank branch or telephone the appropriate number (see below) as soon as possible after you detect the loss or theft. **If your card is stolen, you should report this to the police and obtain a written report from them so that you're not liable for purchases made with the stolen card.**

- 4B (Mastercard, Visa, Visa Electron) – ☎ 913-626 200;

- American Express – ☎ 915-720 303;

- Red 6000 – ☎ 915-965 335;

- Servired – ☎ 915-192 100.

COST OF LIVING

The Costa Blanca is no longer as cheap as it was and the arrival of the euro has pushed prices up spectacularly, with some items going up by more than 50 per cent. It is, however, still possible to live fairly cheaply here and some things such as eating out and alcohol are still very cheap compared to the UK and some other parts of Spain (e.g. the Costa del Sol or Madrid). Prices vary from area to area, with the highest prices in the Marina Alta, and the cheapest in Alicante city and inland. If you want to spend less, shop, have coffee and eat out where the locals do. No sensible resident is going to pay €2 for a coffee when down the road you can enjoy a cup for €1! Imported foods are expensive and it pays to buy Spanish products rather than imported ones (e.g. a packet of imported biscuits costs at least €1.50 whereas a packet of Spanish biscuits costs from €0.60, and a litre of fresh local milk costs around €0.75 compared to a litre of fresh imported milk which costs €1.50).

Although prices vary around the coast, expect to pay from €0.80 to €1.50 for a coffee, from €6 to €8 for a '*menú del día*' and €4 to €5 for a cinema ticket in most localities. Note that beach restaurants are generally expensive and that many businesses (particularly restaurants and bars) put their prices up in high season.

For information on property prices see **Chapter 5**.

Mar Menor

10

Leisure

The Costa Blanca offers numerous leisure possibilities for all ages and tastes, and the fine climate lends itself to a wealth of outdoor activities on the beach, in the country or up in the mountains. This chapter aims to provide a guide to what you can do in your spare time.

> **Information about opening times and prices was correct in late 2004, but they're subject to change and you should double check before making a long journey to visit somewhere.**

FINDING OUT WHAT'S ON

An excellent source of information about activities and what's on is the local tourist office where you will find a wealth of useful information and leaflets about local attractions and events. Tourist offices are usually open from around 9.30am to 2pm and from around 4pm to 7.30 or 8pm Mondays to Saturdays. Hours are longer in the summer when many offices open on Sunday mornings as well.

Tourist Information Offices are listed below in alphabetical order (many of the website addresses are the town council's site, which also include tourist information). The Regional Tourist Board (🖳 www.comunitat valenciana.com) and the Costa Blanca's Tourist Board (🖳 www.costa blanca.org) also provide information on attractions and events. A complete list of tourist offices in Alicante province can also be found on the Costa Blanca's Tourist Board site.

- **Alicante** – Main office, Rambla de Méndez Núñez 23, ☎ 965-200 000, 🖳 www.alicanteturismo.com;

- **Altea** – C/ San Pedro 9, ☎ 965-844 114, 🖳 www.alteadigital.com;

- **Benidorm** – Avda Martínez Alejo 6, ☎ 965-853 224, 🖳 www.benidorm.org;

- **Benissa** – C/ Francisco Sendra 2, ☎ 965-732 991, 🖳 www.benissa.net;

- **Calpe** – Main Office, Plaza del Mosquit, ☎ 965-838 532;

- **Calpe** – Port, ☎ 965-837 413;

- **Calpe** – Avenida Ejércitos Españoles 44, ☎ 965-836 920;

- **Denia** – Glorieta del Oculista Buigues 9, ☎ 966-422 367 (general) or ☎ 902-114 162 (tourists);

- **Finestrat** – Avda Marina Baixa 14, ☎ 966-801 208, 🖳 www.finestrat.org

- **Guardamar del Segura** – Plaza de la Constitución 7, ☎ 965-727 292, 💻 www.guardamar.net

- **Jávea** – Main office, Plaza de la Iglesia, ☎ 965-794 356, 💻 www.xabia.org;

- **Jávea** – Plaza Almirante Bastarreche, ☎ 965-790 736;

- **Jávea** – Ctra Cabo de la Nao s/n, ☎ 966-460 605;

- **La Manga del Mar Menor** – Ctra de La Manga, km 0, ☎ 968-146 136, 💻 www.marmenor.net;

- **Los Alcázares** – Avda Trece de Octubre 13, ☎ 968-171 361, 💻 www.marmenor.net;

- **Orihuela** – C/ Francisco Die 25, ☎ 965-302 747, 💻 www.dip-alicante.es/orihuela;

- **Orihuela Costa** – Urb Playa Flamenca, Plaza del I Oriol 1, Ctra N-332 km 50, ☎ 966-760 000;

- **Pilar de la Horadada** – C/ Carretillas 19, ☎ 966-767 068, 💻 www.pilardelahoradada.org;

- **Santa Pola** – C/ Astilleros 4, ☎ 966-696 052;

- **Teulada – Moraira** – Ctra Moraira-Teulada 51, ☎ 965-745 168, 💻 www.teulada-moraira.org;

- **Torrevieja** – C/ Caballeros de Rodas 27, ☎ 965-706 159;

- **Villajoyosa** – Avda del País Valenciá 10, ☎ 966-851 371, 💻 www.villajoyosa.com.

Most town councils publish a monthly guide to cultural and sports events in the area, which is usually available from tourist offices and town halls. The local press publishes a weekly summary of events and the local Spanish newspapers publish daily events bulletins. Concerts and plays are usually advertised on notice boards and hoardings.

BEACHES

The Costa Blanca boasts some of the finest beaches in the country, some 48 of which were awarded 'blue flag' status in 2004, ranging from long stretches of sand to tiny pebbled coves depending on the area. The tide never really goes out more than a couple of metres except on windy or stormy days. Most municipal beaches are cleaned daily from March to the end of September and some localities (e.g. Benidorm) clean their beaches all year round. Lifeguard services (some with first aid points) are available on many beaches during July, August and part of September, and some localities have teams of beach patrollers walking the beaches as well. Outdoor (cold!) showers are available on many beaches as are taps for washing the sand off your feet. **Note that water in the showers and taps is sea water and therefore not drinkable.** Some beaches have toilets, showers and changing facilities. Beaches in many towns have access for wheelchairs.

Beaches are very busy in the summer months, particularly on Sundays when local families flock to the beach together with plenty of relations, huge tents, food for thousands and tonnes of equipment. It's not uncommon to see tables laid with a tablecloth, cutlery, plates and glasses with a television and/or radio near by. These families arrive at around noon and pack up late in the evening. Unless you enjoy having no more than a square metre to yourself on the beach, it's best to stay at home on Sundays in the summer! On the other hand, many beaches are almost deserted in the autumn and winter months when you can walk for miles and sunbathe in peace.

There are no private beaches on the Costa Blanca and access to the beaches is good and well signposted from the A-7, signs usually say '*Playa*' and/or '*Platja*' (beach in Spanish and *Valenciano*). Parking facilities are limited in some places and in the summer parking attendants operate in some car parks.

A guide to the type of beaches in the different areas of the Costa Blanca follows:

Area One – Marina Alta

Beaches in this area range from long stretches of golden sands in the north to stunning pine-covered cliffs and solitary coves around the Cabo de la Nao with its lovely coves, such as Cala Sarindera and La Granadella. Facilities in the coves range from reasonable to none. Generally speaking the best sandy beaches in the area are in Denia (Marineta Casiana and Les Marines), further north in Playa Devesas, L'Arenal in Jávea and in Calpe. These beaches all have excellent facilities, including disabled access and are very busy during the summer months. South of Denia the coastline becomes more abrupt with plunging cliffs and small secluded coves, usually with pebbles or larger stones, some of which are only accessible on foot.

Area Two – Marina Baja

The Marina Baja includes some of Spain's best beaches, which can be found at Benidorm (home to two long sandy bays), Playa Levante (considered among the eight best in the world – if you ignore the crowds!) and Playa Poniente. Villajoyosa also has a attractive sandy bay. Other beaches in the area tend to be small rocky coves. Beaches are well maintained all year round (Benidorm's beaches are immaculate!) and have excellent facilities.

Area Three – Alicante

Alicante's main beaches are found at San Juan, to the north of the city, where the Playa San Juan and Muchavista are situated. The 7km (over 4mi) of golden sands are well-maintained and clean with excellent facilities and safe bathing. The city beach, Playa del Postiguet, is a blue flag beach with clean water and sands, and has the added advantage of being next to the marina with its many leisure activities.

Area Four – Vega Baja

The Costa Blanca's longest beaches are found here and many of them are still relatively undeveloped and backed by vast areas of protected dunes (pine and palm trees were planted at the end of the nineteenth century to stop the dunes advancing inland). The sands both north and south of Guardamar del Segura are particularly spectacular and the beach at La Marina is also lovely. Facilities near urban areas are good. Beaches are well-maintained during the summer, but less so out of season. Beaches around Torrevieja and Cabo Roig are small coves, often narrow, but clean with good facilities. **Watch out for strong currents in this area.**

Area Five – Mar Menor

The beaches lining the inner shores of the Mar Menor are mainly fine grey sand, with good facilities in urban areas and well-maintained. Bathing is very safe for children as the sea shelves extremely slowly and waters are warm all-year round reaching 30°C (86°F) in summer. The beaches on La Manga facing the Mediterranean are generally extensive with fine sand with good facilities, but **beware of steep shelving**. These beaches can be windy, but if it's unbearable you can always pop over the road to the beaches on the Mar Menor on the other side!

Beaches Further Afield

Beaches along the coastline in the region of Valencia boast nearly 100 blue flag awards and north of the Costa Blanca the majority of beaches are long stretches of golden sands with good facilities and are well worth a visit. Some of the best include those at Les Devesas (along Gandía's coastline), Sagunto and Castellón de la Plana (both north of Valencia city).

The coastline south of the Mar Menor includes Calblanque, a protected regional park with some of Spain's most unspoilt coastline with small isolated coves, but with no facilities.

Nudist Beaches

Nudism is not officially permitted on beaches on the Costa Blanca, except on the ones listed below. On a few other beaches the authorities may turn a blind eye, but bear in mind that if you go nude on a beach where nudism isn't officially permitted, you risk problems with the police if other beach-goers complain. Going topless on beaches is permitted and is quite common, although some beach areas don't allow it. If in doubt, ask.

Official Nudist Beaches

Area One – Marina Alta

Cabo de la Nao   Ambolo

Denia   La Cala

Benitachell   Playa del Moráis

Area Two – Marina Baja

Villajoyosa   Cala Fonda and Torre Conil

Altea   El Metje and Galera de las Palmeras

Area Three – Alicante

San Juan   Cala Palmeras

Area Four – Vega Baja

Guardamar del Segura   Els Vivers

Area Five – Mar Menor

Cartagena   Calblanque/Playa Larga

Beach Bars

Beach bars (*chiringuitos*) are part and parcel of the Costa Blanca's beaches and most beaches have at least one. Beach bars range from little more than a snack bar to full-scale restaurants offering sports equipment hire as well as food and drink. Food ranges from the ubiquitous burger and chips, to paella and fish dishes. Note that beach bars are by no means cheap and a meal for four at some can cost as much as in a good restaurant. Drinks and ice creams can be particularly expensive. If in doubt, ask to see the price list first. In the summer beach bars get very crowded and if you want a table, book early. Popular beach bars are also crowded at weekends and public holidays throughout the year.

Beach bars are open daily during the summer months from around 11am or noon until the small hours. Many close in winter and others open just for lunch and dinner. The ones that remain open all year may close for holidays in the quieter months (e.g. November or January).

Beach Rules

- All litter should be disposed of in bins or taken home;

- Camping is prohibited on all beaches on the Costa Blanca;

- Fishing is permitted only in certain areas;

- Vehicles aren't allowed on the beach;

- Dogs are prohibited on most beaches all year round. If they're allowed it's usually from October to March only;

- Beach bars with sports equipment (pedalos and jet skis) must have an entry and exit lane marked by coloured buoys in the sea. **Swimming is prohibited in this lane.**

Loungers & Sunshades

Unlike some areas of Spain where beach loungers and sunshades are privately owned and managed by beach bars (e.g. on the Costa del Sol), the loungers on beaches on the Costa Blanca are owned by local councils. Staff come round at intervals during the day to issue tickets and collect payment (around €5 a day for lounger and sunshade). You cannot reserve a lounger in advance, so at peak times you need to get to the beach early!

The Sea

Average sea temperatures are around 22°C (72°F) from November to May and at least 26°C (79°F) from June to September and the balmy waters within the Mar Menor never drop below 11°C (52°F) and in summer reach 30°C (86°F). The water is generally clean and in the summer months the water is tested weekly and only rarely in the last few years has bathing been prohibited for health reasons. Occasionally, however, strong currents or storms bring rubbish and sewage to the shore.

The Mediterranean is generally a much calmer sea than the Atlantic, but you should never underestimate the power of the sea. **Every year at least one bather drowns on the Costa Blanca.** On windy days, waves can be extremely strong with powerful undercurrents. Some beaches shelve very quickly from the shore and you can be out of your depth after just two metres. On beaches with lifeguard services a coloured flag is flown indicating the state of the sea:

● Green – good conditions for bathing;

● Yellow – exercise caution;

● Red – bathing is prohibited.

Always respect the lifeguard's decisions and obey all instructions. Keep an eye on children at all times.

Jellyfish

Note that jellyfish are sometimes found near the shore in late summer and autumn, and although their sting isn't fatal, it's painful! If you're stung, wash the sting with fresh water (from a shower on the beach) and apply cream (sun cream is quite effective). If you're badly stung or have an adverse reaction, go to the nearest lifeguard station or doctor.

Sea Urchins

Some beaches on the Costa Blanca are home to colonies of sea urchins (particularly beaches with rocky areas). Sea urchin spines are poisonous and extremely painful to humans, although they're not fatal. In areas where you see sea urchins, you shouldn't go barefoot. If you do tread on one, try not to walk on that foot and bathe it in warm water and vinegar, either at home or at a lifeguard post. Then wipe the affected area with antiseptic lotion before trying to take out as many spines as possible. You won't be able to remove all the spines (most break before you can get them out), but if they're not painful you can leave them to come out on their own rather like splinters.

Parking

Most beaches have parking facilities nearby and these are for public use unless the parking area is part of a hotel or complex. In the summer at some car parks there may be a car park attendant who guides you to a parking space and probably expects a fee for this (around €1). The fee should be paid at your discretion and **you're under no obligation to pay for parking in a public area near the beach** unless you're in a blue zone in a town.

BOAT TRIPS

Several companies offer boat trips leaving from the various marinas or ports on the coast (mainly Altea, Calpe, Denia, Jávea and the Mar Menor) to another location on the coast. Before you get on, make sure the company (and boat) have comprehensive insurance and are legally registered.

Benidorm to Benidorm Island	Excursiones Marítimas 🖳 www.excursionesmaritimasbenidorm.com Hourly return trips to the island on a glass-bottomed boat. Adults €10, children €8.	☎ 965-850 052
Benidorm to Altea	Excursiones Marítimas 🖳 www.excursionesmaritimasbenidorm.com Weekly trips (Tuesdays) to Altea and its outdoor market. Adults €15, children €11.	☎ 965-850 052
Benidorm to Calpe	Excursiones Marítimas 🖳 www.excursionesmaritimasbenidorm.com Twice daily return trips to Calpe (trip takes around an hour). Adults €16, children €11.	☎ 965-850 052
Benidorm to Villajoyosa	Excursiones Marítimas 🖳 www.excursionesmaritimasbenidorm.com Weekly trips (Thursdays) to Villajoyosa and its outdoor market. Adults €15, children €11.	☎ 965-850 052
Denia to Jávea and	Mundo Marino 🖳 www.mundomarino.es)	☎ 966-423 066

Calpe   Several trips daily (trips take around one hour). Adults €25, children
                €12.50.

Denia to   Mundo Marino   ☎ 966-423 066
Jávea, Calpe 💻 www.mundomarino.es
and Altea   Two trips daily on Tuesdays, Thursdays and Sundays (trips take
                around 75 minutes). Adults €30, children €15.

Torrevieja to Marítimas Torrevieja   ☎ 966-702 122
Tabarca   Trips are available once a day from Torrevieja port to Tabarca
Island   Island (see page 227) on a glass-bottomed catamaran (trip takes 40
                minutes).

Mar Menor Islands

Boat trips to the Mar Menor's two islands, Isla Mayor and Isla Pedriguera
are offered by several companies during most of the year, including:

Mar Menor   La Gaviota   ☎ 968-181 718
                Trips from Lo Pagán to the islands

Mar Menor   Solaz Lines   ☎ 968-564 074
                Trips from La Manga or Los Nietos to the islands

Marine Life Spotting

As well as boat trips from one port to another, you can also go on a marine
life spotting trip. The Mediterranean along the Costa Blanca, particularly
around the rocky coastlines and the Cabos de la Nao and San Antonio in
the north, is home to a rich variety of marine life. **Before getting on a boat,
check the company (and boat) are registered and has adequate insurance.**

Benidorm   Excursiones Marítimas   ☎ 965-850 052
                💻 www.excursionesmaritimasbenidorm.com
                Hourly return trips to the island on a glass-bottomed boat. Adults
                €10, children €8

CASINOS

Casinos that can be found on the Costa Blanca are detailed below.

Torrevieja Casino Mediterráneo, Torrevieja Casino,
                Ozone Leisure Centre   ☎ 902-332 141
                This casino opened in May 2004. Offers buffet lunch or dinner plus
                entrance to the casino. **Entrance is for over 18s only, passports**

must be shown and formal dress worn. Open all year from 1pm to 5am (the restaurant) and from 6pm to 5am (the casino).

Villajoyosa   Casino Mediterráneo, Ctra Villajoyosa-
Benidorm km 3.5   ☎ 965-890 700
The Costa Blanca's oldest gambling establishment, offering buffet dinner with live music and entertainment on Friday and Saturday nights, as well as entrance to the casino. €62 dinner and entertainment, €30 entertainment only. **Entrance is for over 18s only, passports must be shown and formal dress worn.** Open all year from 6pm to 5am.

CINEMAS

Films in Spanish

The Costa Blanca has a good selection of cinemas, although many of the multi-screen complexes tend to show blockbuster films only and it can be difficult to see an alternative or minority film. Tickets cost around €5 and many cinemas offer a discount on Wednesdays. Tickets can be bought in advance from many cinemas by phone or internet. Note that there's a surcharge for this service (around €0.60 per ticket). The following locations have cinemas showing films in Spanish:

Area One – Marina Alta

Denia   Cine Condado, C/ Marqués de Campo 42
(one screen)   ☎ 965-780 177

Autocine Drive In, Playa de las Marinas 5
(one screen)   ☎ 965-755 042

Area Two – Marina Baja

Alfaz del Pi   Cine Roma, C/ El Hort s/n (one screen)   ☎ 965-888 266

Benidorm   Cines Colci, Avda Almendros 35
(seven screens)   ☎ 965-865 060

Cines Colci-Rincón, C/ Zamora s/n
(seven screens)   ☎ 902-221 622
💻 www.entradas.com

IMF, CC Finestrat (nine screens)   ☎ 902-221 622
💻 www.entradas.com

Villajoyosa   Cines La Vila, C/ Constitución s/n
(four screens)   ☎ 966-851 884

Area Three – Alicante

Alicante   Aana, C/ Pascual Pérez 44 (three screens)   ☎ 965-143 920

ABC Gran Vía, C/ García Sellés
(ten screens)   ☎ 902-260 262
🖳 www.serviticket.com

CineBox, CC Plaza Mar 2 (13 screens)   ☎ 902-221 636
🖳 www.cinebox.es

CineBox, CC Vistahermosa (12 screens)   ☎ 902-221 636
🖳 www.entradas.com

Navas, C/ Navas 37 (one screen)   ☎ 965-213 084

Panoramis Multicines, Centro Panoramis
(ten screens)   ☎ 902-233 343
🖳 www.serviticket.com

Yelmo Cineplex, Puerta de Alicante
(13 screens)   ☎ 902-220 922
🖳 www.cinentradas.com

Area Four – Vega Baja

Elche   ABC Elche, CC L'Aljub (ten screens)
🖳 www.cinesabc.com

Torrevieja   IMF, Polígono San José S/10 (eight screens)   ☎ 902-221 622
🖳 www.entradas.com

Films in English

The following cinemas show films in English, usually with Spanish sub-titles. Films in English are usually indicated by a V.O. (*versión original*) next to the title and may be recent films. Note that few new releases are shown (and different cinemas may show the same one) and if you want to see a particular film, you may have to see it in Spanish or wait until it comes out on video and DVD.

Area One – Marina Alta

Denia   Cine Club Pessic (based at IES Roc Chabàs secondary school)
             🖳 www.cine-clubpessic.com
             Shows one foreign film a week, often in English.

Jávea   Cine Jayan, C/ Puerto de Jávea s/n
             One film a week, usually in the afternoon (around 5pm)

Area Two – Marina Baja

Benidorm   Cine Colci Rincón, C/ Zamora s/n   ☎ 902-221 622
             🖳 www.entradas.com
             One film a week

Area Three – Alicante

Alicante   Yelmo Cineplex, Puerta de Alicante   ☎ 902-220 922
             🖳 www.cinentradas.com
             One film a week, several showings daily.

Area Four – Vega Baja

Pilar de   Near C/ Mayor (☎ 696-632 098
la Horadada 🖳 www.cinemapilar.com
             One film, two showings on Saturdays and Sundays. **This is an
             independent enterprise and relies on local support.**

EATING OUT

With over 4,000 restaurants and nearly 800 cafes, the Costa Blanca offers a
wide variety of places to eat out and there's something to suit all budgets
and tastes from €6 for a *menú del día* in a local bar to a gourmet meal costing
more than €100 a head in a top restaurant. Eating out is a popular pastime
on the coast, both with locals and foreigners, mainly because it's a
relatively cheap option – a family can eat out for as little as €35 in a
restaurant. Weekends and public holidays are generally very busy and
Sundays are particularly busy from 2pm. Unless you arrive early (e.g.
before 2pm for lunch and before 8.30pm for dinner) you should book in
advance. Bear in mind that the Spanish generally eat late – lunch is from
2pm (3pm in the summer) and dinner from 9pm (10pm in the summer).

Where to Eat

There's a huge choice of eateries on the Costa Blanca and below is a
summary. The best way to find a good meal is to ask friends for

recommendations or try out local restaurants. The quality of food is generally good at most places and it's difficult to go wrong, although not impossible, but if you have a poor meal the chances are it won't break the bank and you needn't go back!

Local Bars

Some people claim there are more bars in Spain than people – this may be an exaggeration, but there are certainly bars everywhere. Most offer breakfast (rolls and pastries) and lunch, usually a *menú del día* consisting of two home cooked courses plus bread, a drink and fruit, which costs from €6 depending on the food and venue. Some bars offer *tapas* in the evening. Most bars are cheap and cheerful, and the best are usually packed during opening hours and if you want lunch, you should arrive before 2pm to get a table. The best bars offer good food and value for money. To find the best, look around a town centre at lunchtime and see which ones are full.

There are also many bars run by foreigners (usually British) where you can get the ubiquitous all-day English breakfast, snacks and other meals.

Restaurants

Restaurants are obviously more up market and expensive than bars, although the food isn't always better quality! Food tends to cost from €3 for a starter, from €5 for a main course and from €3 for a dessert, although many have special offers for two-course lunches or set-menus. All have wine lists, but the majority include Spanish wine only or a very limited choice of foreign wine. Some restaurants specialise in seafood and fish, or a Spanish regional gastronomy such as Basque, Catalan or Galician or local specialities such as Valencian rice dishes.

Beach Restaurants

Beach restaurants (often known as *chiringuitos*) are an essential part of Costa Blanca living and are found on most beaches in the area. Many specialise in fresh fish and seafood as well as rice dishes. Beach restaurants are popular and get very crowded at weekends and in July and August. Prices have gone up in recent years at beach restaurants where it's generally no longer cheap to eat, but most are in pleasant locations and have 'beach' terraces.

Ventas

Typically Spanish venues, *ventas* are found in the country, usually outside a main town and often in the middle of nowhere. They offer country food, usually home cooked and often of excellent quality, at reasonable prices in rustic surroundings. Most have tables outside as well as inside and are extremely popular especially at weekends. Saturdays in May and June are particularly busy with large parties of locals celebrating first communions or christenings. Some *ventas* also do wedding banquets.

Fast Food

For those in a hurry, take-away options on the Costa Blanca include:

- **Burgers & Chips** – Burger King, KFC and McDonalds offer take-away purchases. Several McDonalds have a drive-in facility (McAuto) for the 'ultimate' in take-away convenience.

- **Chinese & Indian Food** – The majority of Chinese and Indian restaurants (there are lots) do take-away as well as in-house meals.

- **Fish & Chips** – No British expatriate scene could be without its fish and chips, and the coast has plenty of 'frying tonight' venues, most of which claim to offer 'the real thing' – complete with mushy peas!

- **Jacket Potatoes** – In the evenings, it's common to see a take-away jacket potato stall on sea-fronts or in busy squares. Potatoes are usually served with just salt and butter (no baked beans!).

- **Pizza** – Most pizza restaurants on the coast offer take-away (pizza, pasta and drinks) and you can phone most of them to order in advance. Some companies offer home-delivery (e.g. TelePizza).

- **Sandwiches & Baguettes** – Available from most cafes and bars. The specialist baguette company, Pans & Company, has several branches on the Costa Blanca, where you can eat in or take-away.

- **Tapas** – *Tapas* can be found at most bars or at specialist venues such as Gambrinus, Lizarrán and Cañas y Tapas, all of which have branches round the coast.

Local Food

The Costa Blanca offers many local specialities, although by far the most famous are made with locally-grown rice and include:

- **Paella** – The king of rice dishes and possibly Spain's best-known dish. Paella originated in Valencia and there are two main versions: one with meat (usually chicken and/or rabbit) and green beans, and the other with seafood, although paella often includes other ingredients such as fish and pork. Paella may be served as a *tapa* from a large communal *paellera* pan or as an individual dish – most restaurants require a minimum order from two people.

● ***Arròs amb Fesols i Naps*** – A rice dish with beans and turnips.

● ***Arroz a Banda*** – A rice dish cooked in fish stock

● ***Arroz al Horno*** – A baked rice dish.

● ***Arroz Negro*** – A black rice dish whose main ingredient is squid (the ink turns the dish black).

Rice dishes are often served with garlic mayonnaise (*alioli*). If you order a rice dish expect to wait at least 30 minutes for it to cook. If you fancy a change from rice, try another local speciality, *fideuá*, a variant of seafood paella but made with noodles or short pasta instead of rice.

The Costa Blanca is also famous for its fish and seafood, such as squid rings (*calamares*), sardines (often cooked on an open fire on the beach) and anchovies (*boquerones*). Larger fish are also available and fish baked encased in sea salt crystals (*pescado a la sal*) is a local delicacy – surprisingly the fish doesn't taste at all salty. Salted cod and roasted pepper, known as *escarrat*, is a popular starter. Freshwater fish is also popular, particularly eels, caught locally usually on the Albufera lake near Valencia and served with a pepper sauce.

Inland, fish is also on offer, although meat dishes tend to predominate. Local lamb, pork and kid goat are excellent and most restaurants in season also offer game such as venison (*venado*), wild boar (*jabalí*) and partridge (*codorniz*). Nourishing stews and soups are also popular inland such as *gazpacho manchego* (hot, thick with pasta and meat – a million recipes away from the chilled tomato Andalusian version) and *tombet* stew with pork and lamb. Pork products such as *chorizo* and black pudding (*morcilla*) are popular fried and may be served with chips, fried eggs and fried green peppers.

Locally-grown vegetables and fruits, particularly citrus, form part of many restaurants' menus. Valencian salad (*ensalada valenciana*) is made with lettuce, tomato, onion, olives and tuna dressed with olive oil.

Local desserts include almond pastries, *arnadí* (a rich cake made with pumpkin, almonds and pine-nuts), fresh fruit and locally-made ice cream – the area's ice cream is reputedly the best in Spain.

Turrón

Alicante's top sweetmeat is *turrón*, traditionally served only at Christmas when every Spanish family ends their Christmas Eve meal with a huge platter of *turrón* and sugared nuts. *Turrón* made from almonds, honey, egg whites and sugar, comes in two varieties: *turrón de jijona* (or *turrón blando*), soft, creamy and the colour of fudge because the almonds are ground to a powder, and *turrón de Alicante* (or *turrón duro*), hard (avoid if you have delicate teeth!) and white with pieces of roughly chopped almond. The best *turrón* is hand-made and costs from €10 for a 250g packet. Manufactured *turrón* costs from €4 per packet.

Foreign Food

Cuisine from just about every country is represented on the Costa Blanca where there are Chinese, Indian, Italian, Japanese, Moroccan and Thai restaurants in most large localities. Other countries such as Colombian, French, Greek, Indonesian and Russian are also represented, although you may have to travel further afield to sample the food.

Eating Out with Children

Children are generally welcome at most restaurants and bars along the coast, although it's probably best to avoid 'posh' restaurants if there are children in your party. Many restaurants have children's menus (usually for those under 12) or you can order half-portions of a main course. Most restaurants and bars will heat up baby food or a bottle if you ask. Some restaurants provide colouring pencils and paper for their child guests and a few have outdoor swings or climbing frames.

¡Qué aproveche! or *Bon Profit!*

EVENING & DAY CLASSES

There are plenty of opportunities to learn new skills and activities on the coast during the afternoons and evenings. Local councils run numerous courses such as Spanish and other languages, sporting activities, art and crafts, cookery, computing and internet skills, and dance. Courses are offered to all ages and generally run twice or three times a week from October to June. Advantages of courses offered by local councils include subsidised prices and the chance to integrate with the local community and speak Spanish. Courses are usually very popular and you need to book early to get a place. Information is available from town halls, sports centres and tourist information offices.

Courses are also run privately by professionals and local clubs. Check the local press and notice boards for information.

FAIRS & FESTIVALS

Festivals (*fiestas*) and fairs (*ferias*) form an essential part of cultural and social life in the whole of Spain, but the Comunidad Valenciana is world-famous for its particularly colourful and lively celebrations, most of which involve plenty of bonfires and fireworks as well as several bulls. Every village and town has its annual fair lasting from one or two days to a whole week. They're usually held on the local saint's day (*patrón* or *patrona*) when the saint is usually paraded through the streets or a pilgrimage (*romería*) is organised to the local shrine.

All localities have two local holidays a year (for dates see **Local Holidays** in **Chapter 4**) as well as the national holidays. Festivals are a great occasion for all the family (tourists and foreigners are usually welcome), when celebrating goes on for hours and often until the next day. Bullfights, fireworks, bonfires, recitals and competitions are all part of most fairs. There's rarely any violence or serious crime, although **pickpockets and bag snatchers are common at the fairgrounds of the main fairs.**

The main fairs and festivals on the Costa Blanca are listed below.

Fairs

- **Alfaz del Pi** – Santísimo Cristo del Buen Acierto (7th to 10th November);

- **Alicante** – Santa Faz (22nd April) and San Juan (24th June);

- **Altea** – Autumn fair (27th and 28th September);

- **Benidorm** – Patron saint (15th and 16th November);

- **Benissa** – Día des Riberers (26th April) and Moor and Christians (28th June);

- **Calpe** – Santísimo Cristo del Sudor and Moor and Christians (end of October);

- **Denia** – Santísima Sangre (first half of June) and San Roque (mid-August);

- **Elche** – San Crispín (24th October);

- **Finestrat** – Santísimo Cristo del Remedio and San Bartolomé (around 24th August);

- **Guardamar de Segura** – San Vicente (19th April) and Nuestra Señora del Rosario (7th October);

- **Jalón** – Santo Domingo de Guzmán, patron saint (beginning of August) and Virgen de la Consolación (3rd Monday in October);

- **Jávea** – Moor and Christians (second half of July).

- **La Nucia** – Purísima Concepción (15th to 18th August);

- **Orihuela** – Fiesta de la Reconquista (17th July) and Nuestra Señora de Monserrate (8th September);

- **Rojales** – San Pedro (second half of June);

- **San Fulgencio** – Virgen del Remedio (4th to 13th October);

- **Santa Pola** – Virgen del Carmen (16th July) and Virgen del Loreto (8th September);

- **Teulada** – San Vicente (19th April) and Virgen de los Desamparados (15th July);

- **Torrevieja** – San Vicente (13th April) and Virgen del Carmen (16th July);

- **Villajoyosa** – Santa Marta and San Jaime, Moor and Christians (end July).

Festivals

Las Fallas

One of Spain's most colourful (and loudest) festivities, Las Fallas, takes place in the city of Valencia from 15th to 19th March in honour of San José and is a unique experience that shouldn't be missed. Different neighbourhoods in the city spend months constructing huge papier-mâché structures (known as *fallas*) depicting local or current affairs, which are erected at different spots throughout the city a week before 19th March. On the night of 19th March all the *fallas* except for one small 'pardoned' one are burnt amid huge celebrations and tonnes of fireworks. Weekly celebrations include a daily *mascletà* (a ear splitting ricochet of rockets), paella making competitions, bullfights, concerts and recitals as well as plenty of round the clock eating and drinking. Information about the celebrations can be found on the official website (💻 www.fallas.com).

Misterio de Elche

The *Misterio de Elche* (the Mystery of Elche) is one of Spain's finest Medieval dramas and the two-act lyrical drama is performed annually in Elche's main church by local people on 14th and 15th August. The mystery, which tells of the Virgin's death and subsequent rise to heaven, has been narrated through song and rhyme since the late 15th century.

Moors & Christians

Many towns and villages commemorate the time of the 'Reconquest' when parts of the Comunidad Valenciana were freed from Arab rule during the twelfth and thirteenth centuries. Celebrations are extremely colourful and usually involve half the population dressing up as Christians and the other half as Moors – costumes are extremely elaborate. The two sides parade through the streets and often engage in mock battles (which, needless to say, the Moors always lose) accompanied by fireworks and general celebrations. The most famous battle is held in Alcoy (22nd to 24th April), but numerous other places in the Costa Blanca also fight out the Reconquest annually. The celebrations in Villajoyosa at the end of July include the disembarkation (known locally as *El Desembarco*), at first light, of the conquering Turks. Further information is available from the *Desembarco*'s website (💻 www.desembarco.com).

San Juan

With its long tradition of fire and fireworks, it's not surprising that one of the Comunidad Valenciana's key celebrations is the summer solstice, which falls on St John's (San Juan) day on 21st June. Parties and purifying bonfires are held on most beaches, but it's in Alicante where *Las Hogueras* (The Bonfires), the biggest celebrations, take place. Huge wooden effigies are erected at every corner (similar to the Fallas in Valencia (see above) and are burnt to the ground amid huge celebrations at midnight on 21st June. San Juan celebrations also take place in Altea (where the tallest available tree is burnt in the main square), Benidorm, Jávea and Torrevieja.

Virgen del Carmen

This saint is the patron of fishermen and on 16th July most coastal localities celebrate a safe year's fishing by parading the saint's image in a procession of boats along the coast. Celebrations then continue with fireworks and merry-making.

FUN PARKS & ATTRACTIONS

Benidorm   Festilandia Park, Avda Mediterráneo 20   ☎ 966-854 196
Open from 5pm to 1.30am, from April to September and at weekends only from 5 to 9pm, from October to March. The park offers funfair rides and attractions suitable for younger children. Entrance is free, rides cost from €1.50 to €3.

Terra Mítica ☎ 902-020 220
(situated to the north of Benidorm, AP-7 exit 65A)
💻 www.terramiticapark.com)
Terra Mítica is one of Spain's biggest theme parks which is divided into 'mythical' areas such as Ancient Egypt, Greece, Iberia, Rome and the Spanish islands. The park offers plenty of sedate and hair-raising rides (wet and dry) catering for a wide range of ages. There are also shows and concerts in the summer. Restaurants, bars and snacks are available onsite. Open everyday from 10am to midnight in June, July and August, and from 10am to 8pm in April, May and September. In October, November and December the park is open at weekends and public holidays only from 10am to 8pm. One-day ticket: adults €32, children (aged 5 to 10) and seniors over 60 €24. Two-day ticket: adults €45, children (aged 5 to 10) and seniors over 60 €32. Children under five enter free. Season tickets are also available.

Santa Pola   Pola Park, Avda Zaragoza s/n   ☎ 965-417 060
More than 50 rides and attractions suitable for all the family. Catering facilities are available. Currently under refurbishment. Entrance is free and rides cost from €1.50 to €2.50.

GARDENS

**Callosa d'
En Sarrià**   Cactus D'Algar, Botanical Garden   ☎ 965-881 095
Over 500 species of cacti set in 50,000m^2 of gardens. Free parking, cafeteria and disabled access to the gardens.

Elche   El Huerto del Cura, Porta de la Morera 49   ☎ 965-451 936
💻 www.huertodelcura.com).
Set in the heart of Elche's palm tree forest, this unique botanical garden houses over 1,000 species of palm including the spectacular Imperial Palm, as well as water features, Mediterranean plants and cacti. Open from 10am daily. Adults €4 (€2 Elche residents), children €2.

Guardamar Paraje Natural El Oasis
del Segura Situated some 3km (nearly 2mi) from San Fulgencio (to the west of
Guardamar del Segura) this recreational park offers a woodland area
with spectacular views of the surrounding countryside, a children's
play area, picnic area with barbecues and a football pitch. More
information is available from San Fulgencio's tourist office (☎ 966-
790 021).

LEISURE COMPLEXES

Alicante   Panoramis   ☎ 965-989 300
⌨ www.panoramis.com
The Panoramis, situated right on the waterfront at Alicante marina,
is a purpose-built leisure complex built in modern glass
architecture and houses numerous bars, cafes, restaurants, shops
and boutiques as well as nightclubs and a ten-screen cinema. The
complex, one of Alicante's most popular night spots, is open daily
from 10am until the small hours. There's ample parking and the
complex can also be reached by night ferryboat from the port area.
For more information visit the website.

Torrevieja   Ozone Leisure Centre   ☎ 965-705 414
Situated on the CV-90 on the way out of Torrevieja, this new centre
offers over 25 restaurants, a bowling alley, casino and eight-screen
cinema. Open daily from late afternoon.

MISCELLANEOUS ATTRACTIONS

Benidorm   Benidorm City Sightseeing Bus Tour   ☎ 965-854 322
✉ benidorm@benidorm.llorentebus.es
The open topped bus takes a circular tour of the city from the
Rincón de Loix to the Hotel Bali with several trips a day from
March to November. Tickets €3.60 (no reduction
for children).

Benidorm Tourist Bus Tour   ☎ 965-280 592
A unique way to see the city by tram, stopping at eight sights of
interest in Benidorm including the beaches, bullring, park, port and
La Cala. Tickets (the price include earphones and an audio guide
to sights along the way) are valid for 24-hours and you can get on
and off the bus as many times as you like in that time. Adults €5,
children €3.

Helicopter Tours   ☎ 965-813 631
⌨ www.helicostablanca.com   ☎ 606-548 296
A unique way to see the Costa Blanca from the air. Flights cost
from €100 and must be pre-booked.

Limón Exprés Train   ☎ 966-803 103
🖳 www.limonexpres.com
The Limón Exprés narrow-gauge train runs from Benidorm to Gata
taking in some of the best views of the coast and mountains. Trains
leave from Benidorm station at 9.40am Tuesdays to Fridays and
return from Gata at 1.45pm. Pre-booking is essential. Adults €22,
children €18.

Marco Polo Expeditions   ☎ 965-863 399
🖳 www.marcopolo-exp.es
Numerous adventure activities for all ages are available from this
company, including guided off-road tours, horse riding, paintball,
jeep and quad safaris, and mountain biking. Activity holidays and
'team building' sessions are also available.

Denia   Benidoleig Caves   ☎ 966-404 235
On the road from Benidoleig to Pedreguer (to the north of
Denia, accessible from the AP-7).
These small prehistoric caves running for some 300m include
spectacular stalactite and stalagmite formations as well as
numerous high domes rising to up to 20m (66ft). The caves are
open daily from 10am to 6pm in winter and from 10am to 8.30pm in
summer. Adults €3.50, children (aged 6 to 12) €2 , seniors €2.50.

Elche   Balloon Flights   ☎ 966-637 401
🖳 www.neresis.com/aeroglobo/
Aero Globo offers trips in a hot air balloon over the
countryside in the southern part of the coast. Standard trips
include 40 minutes flying time and a picnic. Longer flights or
to different areas are also available. Trips require a minimum
number of passengers.

Santa Pola   Tabarca Island
This small island lies 7km (4mi) off the west coast of Santa Pola
and is the only permanently inhabited island in the region. Boat
trips (several daily) leave from Santa Pola and Torrevieja (see page
213). The island has a colourful history and is inhabited by
descendants from Genoa who were granted asylum on the island
by the Spanish in the eighteenth century after they were captured
from their original island home near Tunisia. The island, popular
with day trippers, has a new museum documenting the island's
history, several bars and restaurants, and two hotels. It's also a
marine reserve and provides some excellent opportunities for
snorkelling.

Torrevieja   Torrevieja Submarine
Torrevieja port is home to the Spanish Navy's S-61 submarine, now
a permanent floating museum and exhibition. Open from 9am to
2pm Wednesdays to Sundays. Entrance is free.

MUSEUMS

Alicante   Archaelogy Museum (MARQ), Plaza Dr
Gómez Ulla s/n   ☎ 965-149 000
🖥 www.marqalicante.com
Housed in the interesting San Juan de Dios hospital, the museum
displays a fine selection of archaeological finds from the area.
Open Tuesdays to Saturdays 10am to 2pm and from 4 to 8pm, and
on Sundays from 10am to 2pm. Adults €3, children (7 to 15) and
seniors €1.50.

Calpe   Collector's Museum (*Museo del Coleccionismo*),
Plaza de la Villa s/n.
An interesting selection of collectors' items including cameras and
photographs. Open 10.30am to 1.30pm and from 5pm to 9pm
Tuesdays to Sundays. Entrance is free.

Denia   Ethnological Museum, C/ Cavallers s/n   ☎ 966-420 260
This small museum has an interesting section on the local raisin
industry. Open Tuesdays to Saturdays 10.30am to 1pm and from 4
to 7pm, and on Sunday 10.30am to 1pm. Entrance is free.

Toy Museum, C/ Calderón s/n   ☎ 966-420 260
Numerous displays exhibit toys made locally in the town from 1904
to the '60's. Open 10am to 1pm and from 4pm to 8pm daily.
Entrance is free.

Guadalest   Collection of Old Vehicles, Ctra Callosa-
Guadalest km 7   ☎ 965-882 197
(next to the El Riu Restaurant)
🖥 www.museovehiculosguadalest.com
One of Spain's largest private collections of small cars, motorbikes
and other vehicles from the past. Open everyday except Saturdays
10.30am to 6pm in winter and 10.30am to 8pm in summer. Adults
€3, children €2.

Jávea   Archaeological and Ethnological Museum,
C/ Primicies s/n   ☎ 965-791 098
Interesting displays of local finds, including copies of a magnificent
set of Iberian gold jewellery (the original is displayed in Madrid).
Open March to October on Tuesdays to Fridays 10am to 1pm and
from 6 to 8pm, and 10am to 1pm at weekends. Open November to
February 10am to 1pm on Tuesdays to Sundays. Entrance is free.

Torrevieja   Salt and Sea Museum, C/ Patricio Pérez 10   ☎ 966-706 838
A tribute to Torrevieja's links with the sea including archaeological
finds from the sea and exhibitions on the fishing and salt industries.
Open Tuesdays to Saturdays from 10am to 1.30pm and from 5 to
9pm, and on Sundays and public holidays from 10am to 1.30pm.
Entrance is free.

Valencia   Ciudad de Las Artes y Ciencias (City of Arts
& Sciences), Avda Autopista del Saler 1-7   ☎ 902-100 031
💻 www.cac.es
This largest cultural and educational complex in Europe must be
seen, if only to admire the ultra-modern architecture and includes
L'Oceanogràfic. L'Oceanogràfic is the largest aquarium in Europe
with over 500 species of sea animals. Open daily from 10am to
6pm (8pm in spring and autumn, and midnight in summer). Adults
€20.50, children (under 12) €15.50.

Museu de les Ciències
A hands-on science museum with exhibitions on future technology
and genetics. Open daily from 10am to 8pm (9pm in summer).
Adults €7, children (under 12) €5.50.

L'Hemisfèric
A space-age building with audio-visual presentations (planetarium,
IMAX and laser show). Sessions throughout the day. Adults €7,
children (under 12) €5.50.

L'Umbracle
A garden promenade. Entrance is free.

Palau de les Arts ☎ 902-100 031
A centre for the performing arts (currently under construction). The
complex has ample parking (€1.50 an hour), catering facilities and
shops. Discount combined tickets are available and are valid for
one or two consecutive days. Adults €28, children (under 12) €21.
The complex is very popular so it's best to book in advance.
Booking can also be done via travel agencies and El Corte Inglés
and FNAC stores.

Villajoyosa   Chocolate Museum, Avda Pianista Gonzalo
Soriano 13   ☎ 965-890 950
This museum, run by Valor (Spain's largest cocoa company), gives
an insight into the making and marketing of chocolate. Guided
visits are available by appointment only. Open daily. Entrance is
free.

NATURAL PARKS

The Comunidad Valenciana and neighbouring Murcia have several
natural parks offering the chance to enjoy some spectacular scenery, often
in complete peace and quiet. Many parks are busy at weekends and
holidays, but if you're prepared to walk some distance it's easy to get away
from the crowds. **Natural parks are highly protected areas and some
sections have restricted or prohibited access.** In some areas of the parks
the number of visitors is limited daily and you may have to book

beforehand. Some parks organise guided or semi-guided tours and walks during the year. Information is available from the parks themselves and from the regional environmental authorities at the regional government department (*Consellería de Territorio y Vivienda*) whose website provides comprehensive information about each park as well as downloadable leaflets (🖳 http://parquesnaturales.gva.es).

Natural Parks within the Costa Blanca

The province of Alicante is home to eight natural parks, which can be divided into wetlands and mountainous areas.

Wetlands

Large sections of the coastline south of Valencia are home to extensive areas of salt-pans or marsh wetlands, many of which are now protected areas and home to numerous birds including flamingos, and a rich selection of fish and other waterlife.

Parque de la Albufera

Although this park, situated some 10km (6mi) south of Valencia, lies outside the Costa Blanca it's within easy reach and as one of Europe's largest freshwater lagoons it's well worth a visit. The park with over 21,000 hectares consists of the huge lagoon known as La Albufera and a narrow strip of pine-covered sand dunes, La Devesa, separating the lagoon from the sea. Nearly 100 bird species inhabit the area, which is also visited by some 250 others who stop at the lagoon on migration. Bird watching is the chief activity in the park where there are also guided walks and boat trips. For the visitor centre (situated at Racó de la Olla) or general information contact ☎ 961-627 345 or ✉ raco.olla@terra.es.

Parque de El Fondo

These wetlands, situated to the west of Guardamar del Segura, offer possibilities for walks and bird watching. For the visitors' centre or general information contact ☎ 966-678 515.

Parque Natural de Las Lagunas de La Mata y de Torrevieja

The two huge salt lakes just outside Torrevieja are home to numerous species of birds. Several trails for walkers and/or bikes circle the lakes where extraction of salt for consumption still takes place. For the visitors' centre or general information contact ☎ 966-920 404 or ✉ lamata_eea@gva.es.

Parque Natural de Las Salinas de Santa Pola

This park, to the south of Santa Pola, consists of some 2,500 hectares of salt-pans (home to flamingos throughout most of the year), dunes and unspoilt beaches where there are numerous trails for walkers. For the visitors' centre, situated at the Salt Museum (*Museo de la Sal*), or general information contact ☎ 966-693 546 or ✉ parque.santapola@cma.m400.gva.es.

Parque Natural de Marjal de Pego-Oliva

Situated in the far north of the province, the Marjal wetlands provide good opportunities for bird watching, walking trails and bike rides. For general information contact ☎ 966-400 251 or ✉ parque_pegooliva@gva.es.

Mountainous Areas

Parque Natural de la Sierra Mariola

This newly declared natural park, situated to the north of Alcoy, has attractive limestone peaks including the highest point, Montcabrer (1,389m/4,584ft) with possibilities for walking and hiking.

Parque Natural del Carrascal de la Font Roja

Situated to the south of Alcoy, these attractive pine-covered mountains which are part of the Sistema Bético, offer numerous possibilities for walking and trekking including a trail to the highest peak, Menejador (1,356m/4,475ft). The park authorities offer guided walks and visits to the area. For the visitors' centre or general information contact ☎ 965-337 620 or ✉ parque.fontroja@cma.m400.gva.es.

Parque Natural del Montgó

Situated to the west of Denia, the Montgó massif covers more than 2,000 hectares including dramatic mountain scenery, spectacular cliffs and some of the area's best examples of plant and bird life. Activities include hiking (from the challenging climb to the summit taking around eight hours (!) to easier gentle climbs) and rock climbing. The comprehensive map of the park, *Parque Natural de Montgó – Cap de Sant Antoni* (Institut Cartogràfic de Valencia) shows many trails and is available from local bookshops and tourist offices. For general information contact ☎ 966-423 205 or ✉ parque_montgo@gva.es.

Parque Natural del Peñón de Ifach

The distinctive rocky outcrop of the Peñón de Ifach, situated at Calpe and the symbol of the Costa Blanca, is one of Europe's smallest protected areas. The Peñón is home to a vast array of flora including an orchid unique to the rock and numerous species of birds. The walk to the top (some 330m/1,090ft high) is a popular (and strenuous) one and numbers of walkers are limited in July and August, **so if you plan to walk up then make sure you arrive early**. Rock climbing is also popular and there are 21 designated routes. Information on the routes can be obtained from the visitors' centre and in the leaflet, *Escaladas*, available from local tourist offices. For the visitors' centre or general information contact ☎ 965-972 015 or ✉ ifac_cma@gva.es.

The Costa Blanca is also within relatively short driving distance of numerous other natural parks such as Sierra de Espuña in Murcia (one of Spain's most renowned parks with excellent climbing and walking possibilities. It takes at least three hours to reach these parks so it's best to go for a weekend or longer. Information is available from ☎ 968-431 430 and 🖥 www.sierraespuna.com.

NIGHTLIFE

If you're a night owl (and the Spanish generally are) possibilities on the Costa Blanca are endless and range from theme pubs to some of the most sophisticated nightclubs in Europe. Most localities have a good selection of nightclubs open until the small hours, but the most famous are Ku and Pachá in Benidorm, and Guaracha in Panoramis, Alicante (see below). If you're prepared to travel further afield, the city of Valencia boasts one of Spain's best nightlife scenes and on Friday and Saturday nights its many discos are packed to capacity as thousands of locals live up to Valencia's reputation as one of the best places in Spain to party. Opening hours are usually from 10 or 11pm to 3 or 6am. Many clubs have a dress code and you may be required to show identification on entry. Some clubs open in the summer months only. Entry fees range from nothing to up to €50 – if you have to pay to get in the first drink is usually included in the price. **Drinks are usually very expensive in clubs, e.g. from €10 for a spirit plus a mixer.**

Leisure & Nightclub Complex

Alicante   Panoramis   ☎ 965-989 300
🖥 www.panoramis.com
The Panoramis, situated right on the waterfront at Alicante marina, is a purpose-built leisure complex built in modern glass architecture and houses numerous bars, cafes, restaurants, shops and boutiques as well as nightclubs and a ten-screen cinema. The complex, one of Alicante's most popular night spots, is open daily from 10am until the small hours. There's ample parking and the

complex can also be reached by night ferryboat from the port area. For more information contact the website.

Live Music

You can hear live music of almost any sort on the coast at different venues. Classical music concerts are given regularly by the Murcia Symphonic Orchestra at the Víctor Villegas Auditorium in the city (see **Theatres** on page 234) during the season from October to June, and other national and foreign orchestras also include the Costa Blanca in their tours.

There are numerous bars and clubs that offer live music as part of their nightly entertainment and you can hear live jazz, local bands and singers, and flamenco. Alfaz del Pi has an annual jazz festival in the autumn and San Javier holds its international jazz festival in June and July, for more information visit 💻 www.jazzsanjavier.com. Expatriate crooners singing cover versions are popular entertainment at foreign bars and pubs. Needless to say, some are better than others.

Spanish singers and bands play regularly on the coast and top international soloists and bands occasionally give concerts, particularly during the summer months. Tickets for concerts are usually on sale at local record shops, tourist offices and at El Corte Inglés.

If you're into making your own music, lots of bars and clubs offer karaoke nights or jam sessions.

Habaneras

Habaneras are traditional melodies of nostalgia, love and lament, and were sung by sailors on route to and from the New World, particularly Cuba. The music is a unique mixture of Spanish, Cuban and African traditional song and is sung individually or by a choir. Torrevieja is the heartland of the *Habaneras* and holds a week-long festival in the summer with competitors from all over the world.

SOCIAL CLUBS & ORGANISATIONS

The cosmopolitan nature of the Costa Blanca has spawned a huge variety of clubs catering for just about every activity and nationality, ranging from bridge to square dancing, cycling and football, from the Conservatives abroad to Labour clubs, and from American to South African social clubs. There are also chapters of global social clubs such as the Lions Club, the Inner Wheel and Toastmasters International. Charitable and self-help organisations such as Alcoholics Anonymous, Cáritas (Catholic welfare charity), Help (charity assisting all nationalities with any problem), the British Legion and numerous animal protection societies also operate on the coast.

Many clubs advertise their activities and venues in the local press (both *The Costa Blanca News* and *CB Friday*'s supplement *Friday Freetime* have particularly comprehensive listings) or on local notice boards. Some town councils (e.g. Benidorm) have a database of clubs and associations in their area. Children's activities are often posted on school notice boards.

Spanish speakers also have the option of joining a local club, of which there are many. These clubs are often subsidised by the local council and provide low-cost sports activities and social occasions. Pensioners are particularly well catered for and most towns have a social centre known as the *Hogar del Jubilado* or *del Pensionista*. Local town councils can provide information.

University of the Third Age

Residents of any age who aren't in full-time employment may be interested in the University of the Third Age (U3A), centred in Calpe, which offers courses in English courses (including computer literacy). Spanish classes are also provided throughout the academic year. Information is available from the President (Mary Anderton who can be contacted on ☎ 965-832 081), or from the club's website (🖳 www.u3acalpe.org).

THEATRES

A good choice of plays and concerts is offered at venues around the coast and most towns have an extensive cultural programme, mostly in Spanish, although many events are in English. Productions can be seen in English performed by numerous theatre groups and clubs on the coast who perform regularly at different locations. The largest groups include:

Alfaz del Pi	Alfaz English Theatre Group	☎ 966-868 445
Altea	Alteatro	☎ 965-845 039
Denia	Castle Theatre Group 🖳 www.deniacastletheatre.com	
Jávea	Jávea Players	☎ 966-460 192

See the local press for details of performances and venues.

Theatres are located at the following venues:

Area One– Marina Alta

Denia   Casa Municipal de Cultura, Plaza Jaume 1 ☎ 965-783 656
✉ cultura@ayto-denia.es
Offers a year-round programme of theatre, exhibitions and
concerts.

Area Two – Marina Baja

Altea   Palau Altea Arts Centres   ☎ 902-332 211
🖥 www.palaualtea.com
The modern and architecturally striking Palau Altea arts centre
offers an extensive year-round programme of theatre, dance, jazz
and opera. The centre also doubles up as a conference centre.

Area Three – Alicante

Alicante Sala Arniches, Avda Aguilera 1   ☎ 965-934 784
This theatre has just been extensively refurbished and is now
considered one of the Comunidad Valenciana's most innovative
theatres. The Sala Arniches offers a year-round theatre
programme.

Teatro Principal, Plaza Ruperto Chapí s/n ☎ 965-202 380
🖥 www.teatroprincipalicante.com
The *Teatro Principal* is Alicante's main theatre. It's situated in the
centre of the old quarter and offers a year-round programme of
music, opera, dance and theatre, mostly in Spanish and Valencian,
although occasionally foreign companies perform. **Demand for
seats is high so you should book as early as possible.** Ticket
prices range from €9 to €40 depending on the performance.
Tickets can be booked online or by telephone (ServiCAM ☎ 902-
444 300 – lines are open 8am to 11pm Mondays to Saturdays and
9am to 9pm on Sundays and public holidays).

Area Four – Vega Baja

Elche   Gran Teatro, Pasaje Kursal   ☎ 965-451 403
🖥 www.culturadelx.com
This large theatre offers an extensive year-round cultural
programme including music, opera and theatre as well as an
annual film festival. Tickets can be bought from the theatre box
office which is open from 10am to 1pm and 5 to 8pm Tuesdays to

Saturdays or from ServiCAM (☎ 902-444 300 – lines are open
8am to 11pm Mondays to Saturdays and 9am to 9pm on Sundays
and public holidays).

Orihuela   Teatro Circo   *information* ☎ 966-744 657
                                                box office ☎ 966-740 104
The town's magnificent *Teatro Circo* has a year-round programme
of ballet, theatre and recitals. Entrance is often free.

Rojales   Teatro Capitol, C/ Alberto González
                Vergel s/n   ☎ 966-715 129.
The town's new theatre offers theatre, dance and concerts.

Other Theatres

Murcia   Víctor Villegas Auditorium, Avda Primero
                de Mayo   *information* ☎ 968-341 060
                                                box office ☎ 968-343 080
The city of Murcia has its own symphony orchestra (*Orquesta
Sinfónica de la Ciudad de Murcia*), which offers regular
performances during its 'symphony season' (usually from October
to June) at this auditorium. Discount season tickets are available.

Valencia   The city has a lively theatre scene and its many theatres offer
                a year-round varied cultural programme, usually in Spanish
                or Valencian (see page 188):

                L'Altre Espai, C/ Platero Suárez 11B   ☎ 963-651 446

                Olympia, C/ San Vicente 44   ☎ 963-517 315

                Sala Matilde Salvador, Carrer de la
                Universitat 2   ☎ 963-864 377

                Teatro Círculo, C/ Roger de Flor 17   ☎ 963-922 023

                Teatro El Musical, Plaza del Rosario 3   ☎ 963-242 552

                Teatro Marionetas La Estrella, C/
                Los Angeles 33   ☎ 962-562 292
                🖥 www.teatrolaestrella.com
                Specialises in puppet shows.

                Teatro Principal, C/ Barcas 15 *information* ☎ 963-539 200
                Specialises in opera and music. *box office* ☎ 963-539 260

Teatro Rialto, Plaza del Ayuntamiento 17   ☎ 963-539 300

Teatro Talía, C/ Caballeros 31   ☎ 963-912 920

WATER PARKS

Note that the parks get very crowded in July and August when queues for attractions are very long. It's also advisable (sensible!) to wear plenty of high-factor sunscreen.

Benidorm   Aqualandia, Rincón de Loix   ☎ 965-800 100
💻 www.aqualandia.net
Aqualandia claims to be Europe's biggest water park with numerous water attractions suitable for all ages. Open during the summer months only, from 10am to 6pm (7pm in July and August). Prices are approximate: adults €16, children €11.20.

Aquapark, Ciudad Quesada, C/ del
Norte s/n   ☎ 966-718 612
There are plenty of water attractions for all ages. Open from June to September only, from 10.30am to 7pm. Adults €9, children (under 11) and seniors €7. Discounts are available after 3pm.

Torrevieja   Aquópolis, Finca La Olla Grande   ☎ 902-345 008
💻 www.aquopolis.es/torrevieja
A large water park with plenty of fun attractions. Open from mid-June to mid-September from 11am to 7pm. Adults €14, children €9.50. Discounts are available for season tickets. Transport is available from Torrevieja bus station to the park.

WILDLIFE PARKS & ZOOS

Benidorm   Aqualandia, Rincón de Loix   ☎ 965-800 100
💻 www.aqualandia.net
Benidorm's water park offers a 'Sea Lions Adventure', which includes an educational talk about sea lions followed by a swim with the animals themselves. Prices include use of a wet suit and a towel. Open during the summer months only, from 10am to 6pm (7pm in July and August). Prices are approximate: adults €16, children €11.20.

MundoMar, Sierra Helada s/n   ☎ 965-869 101
(near Benidorm Palace on the eastern side of the Levante beach)
💻 www.mundomar.es

Aquarium, marine life including dolphin shows and display of exotic animals. Open daily from 10am. Adults €18, children and seniors €12.

Guadalest   El Arca, Valle de Guadalest, Ctra
Benimantell – Alicante   ☎ 965-972 359
(300m from Guadalest village)
El Arca is a huge wild animal refuge with an award winning protection programme. Open from 10am to 6pm in winter and from 10am to 8pm in summer. Adults €5, children €3.

Penáguila   Safari Aitana, Ctra Villajoyosa-Sella-
Benasua (CV-770)   ☎ 965-529 273
💻 www.safariaitana.com
Set in some of the Costa Blanca's most spectacular mountain scenery, the safari park includes a children's zoo, birds of prey display, funfair rides and restaurants. Open daily from 11am. Adults €13, children €10.

Santa Pola   Río Safari Elche, Ctra Santa Pola-Elche
(CV-865) km 4   ☎ 966-638 288
💻 www.riosafari.com
Includes safari attractions (seen from a train), aquarium, aviary, plus funfair attractions and catering facilities. Open from 10.30am daily. Adults €13, children €10.

Santa Pola Aquarium, Acuario Municipal,
Pza Francisco Ordóñez s/n   ☎ 965-416 916
Aquariums showing Mediterranean life and different ecosystems. The centre also acts as a hospital for injured marine animals, particularly turtles. Open daily from 16th June to 15th September, from 11am to 1pm and from 6 to 10pm. From 16th September to 15th June the centre is open in the morning, Tuesdays to Sundays, from 10am to 1pm and from 5 to 7pm. Adults €2.40, children (aged 4 to 16) and seniors €1.20.

El Vergel   Safari Park Vergel, Ctra El Vergel-Pego
(CV-700) km 65   ☎ 966-439 808
(west of Denia, AP-7 exit 62)
A safari park with over 1,400 animals, which can be seen along three different routes taken on foot or by car. Open from 10am to 5pm in winter (7pm in summer). Adults €13, children €7.50.

OTHER PLACES TO VISIT

The Costa Blanca is near some beautiful cities and towns, as well as spectacular scenery. Cities within easy reach of most of the Costa Blanca are included in the list below.

All are well worth a visit and can be visited in a day, although Valencia warrants a weekend to make the most of the trip.

Days trips to most of the locations below are available and prices start at around €15 including the coach and tour and entrance fees. Most trips offer lunch for an extra price. Trips usually leave early in the morning and return in the evening. Tickets for day trips can be bought at most travel agents and hotels. Information on the various destinations can be found at tourist offices on the coast or from the Costa Blanca tourist website (💻 www.costa blanca.org). Good guide books to the region are the *AA Essential Guide Costa Blanca & Alicante* (AA Publishing), *Berlitz Costa Blanca Guide* (Berlitz Pocket Guides), *Costa Blanca Insight Guide* (Insight Guides), *Costa Blanca* (Dorling Kindersley) and *Valencia & The Costa Blanca* (Lonely Planet).

Two useful books describing car trips and excursions around the Costa Blanca are *Inland Trips from the Costa Blanca* by Derek Workman (Santana Books) and *Costa Blanca: Car Tours & Walks* by John and Christine Oldfield (Sunflower Books).

Alcoy

Alcoy (56km/35mi from Alicante), an industrial town, that between 22nd and 24th April celebrates one of Spain's most colourful events, the Moors and Christians festival (*Moros y Cristianos*) – see page 222.

Cartagena

Historic Cartagena (125km/78mi from Alicante) is one of Spain's oldest cities with an interesting historic centre including a fine naval port and Roman ruins. Modern Cartagena is widely tipped as one of Spain's most up and coming cities.

Murcia

The city of Murcia (80km/50mi from Alicante) is a typically Spanish city on the banks of the Segura River and is home to some fine architecture and good shopping.

Valencia

The region's capital (177km/111mi from Alicante) is Spain's third largest city with excellent shopping facilities, interesting architecture and Europe's largest aquarium (L'Oceanogràfic – see page 229).

Other Destinations

In addition to local places of interest the Costa Blanca provides easy access to the Balearic Islands.

Balearics

Regular ferries connect Denia and Valencia with the Balearic Islands, although out of season the number of services is much reduced.

Denia   Balearia Lines   ☎ 902-160 180
              🖳 www.balearia.net
              Balearia Lines has a daily service from Denia to Ibiza Town and
              San Antonio (two hours on a superfast ferry, three and a half hours
              on a normal ferry), and to Palma de Mallorca (three and a half
              hours on a superfast ferry, nine hours on a normal ferry). One-way
              tickets cost from €49 (on foot) and €145 (with a car). Balearia
              Lines often has special offer day return tickets (around €50) to
              Ibiza.

              Iscomar   ☎ 902-119 128
              🖳 www.iscomar.com   ☎ 971-437 500
              Iscomar runs services from Denia to Ibiza (four and a half hours)
              and Palma (ten hours) everyday except Saturday. One-way tickets
              cost from €30 (on foot) and €90 (with a car).

Valencia   Trasmediterranea   ☎ 902-454 645
              🖳 www.trasmediterranea.com
              Spain's main ferry company, Trasmediterranea, runs daily ferry
              services from Valencia to Ibiza (crossing takes three hours) and
              Majorca (four hours on a high-speed ferry, over seven hours
              otherwise) throughout the year and a once-weekly service to
              Minorca (crossing takes 15 hours) during the summer months.
              Fares vary depending on the time and day of crossing, and
              time of year.

Moraira

11

Sports

The Costa Blanca's pleasant year-round climate lends itself to a range of sporting activities and you can participate in just about any sport, although golf, sailing and tennis are the most popular. This chapter looks at the different sporting activities on the coast.

MUNICIPAL SPORT

If you speak some Spanish and want the chance to integrate into local society, it's a good idea to join a sports club or group at your local sports centre. Municipal centres also offer the opportunity to join sports federations and to compete at regional and national levels. The cost is usually low (and subsidised for residents in many cases) and annual membership may be available. A wide variety of classes are offered throughout the day (usually 10am to 2pm and 4 to 8pm), Mondays to Saturdays, although evenings are the most popular. **Some activities are very popular and heavily over-subscribed (e.g. football and swimming) so you need to book your place early.** Ask at your local town hall for information on sports venues and activities available in your area. Municipal sports centres typically offer aerobics, athletics, badminton, basketball, football, gymnastics, handball, judo, karate, rhythmic gymnastics, swimming, tai chi, tennis and yoga. Most centres also have a gymnasium and sauna. **Note that all swimmers must wear swimming caps.**

The Alicante Sports Board (Patronato de Deportes de Alicante) can also provide information (C/ Foguerer José Romeu Zarandieta 4, Alicante, ☎ 965-916 012, ✉ patronato.deportes@alicante-ayto.es).

ATHLETICS

Athletics is becoming increasingly popular on the Costa Blanca where there are several athletics tracks, the most important of which is the track in Alicante (C/ Hondón de las Nieves). Running is extremely popular and there are numerous races held at towns all over the coast throughout the year. The Costa Blanca also has a Harriers Hash club.

BOWLS

Numerous bowls clubs play weekly at greens around the Costa Blanca and competitions are held on a regular basis. Comprehensive information about bowling clubs, including contact details as well as forthcoming events and competitions, is published in the local expatriate press.

CRICKET

Cricket whites are worn regularly on the Costa Blanca at the Columbus Oval in Albir where the local team, Sporting Alfás Cricket Club, practise and play during the summer. Further information is available from ☎ 966-866 449 or 🖥 www.tyarth.com/sacc.php.

FOOTBALL

Football is very popular on the Costa Blanca and there are numerous pitches, mostly municipal. Leagues operate at local, provincial and regional level for amateur players of all ages. Children may join the Spanish football federation and play with teams in the federation leagues. 'Football Schools' consisting of several days intensive football training are held at some sporting venues and schools in the school holidays. Check the local press for details.

The La Manga Professional Football Centre in Los Belones (☎ 968-338 066, 🖥 www.lamangaclub.es), where many professional clubs train, also offers a Football Academy suitable for children of all ages and abilities. Programmes usually last a week.

Football Teams

Valencia CF is one of Spain's top football teams and was the champion of the 2003-4 Spanish league and also the UEFA champion in 2004. Valencia CF's home matches offer the chance to see some of the best footballers in the world (concentrated in Real Madrid and FC Barcelona) in action at the club's La Mestalla stadium (☎ 963-372 626, 🖥 www.valenciacf.es). Valencia's second team, Levante, was promoted to the first division at the start of the 2004-5 season and started well – in late 2004 they were near the top of the table! Football teams in the Costa Blanca area include Elche and Hercules (the Alicante team), both of which now play in the second division after moments of glory in first division football.

Local teams play in provincial and regional leagues with varying degrees of success!

GOLF

The Costa Blanca is home to numerous golf courses, some of which rank among the best in Spain and the pleasant golf-playing conditions all-year round have led to a boom in the demand, particularly from Northern European golfers – rained (or frozen!) off the courses in their home countries during the winter months.

Below is a directory of the main golf courses on the coast together with contact information and an approximate idea of green fees. **Bear in mind that winter is high-season on the golf courses and prices are often lower in July and August.** Some prices may include buggy fees. Most golf courses offer 'pay and play' facilities, although some may have 'members-only' playing times or sessions. It's advisable to check before going to play.

Area One – Marina Alta

Benissa   Club de Golf Ifach, Urb San Jaime, Ctra
Moraira-Calpe km 3   ☎ 966-497 114
🖳 www.clubgolfifach.com
A 9-hole course designed by Javier Arana. The course is open
daily from 7.30am to 6pm (8pm in summer) and green fees cost
around €30.

Denia   Club de Golf La Sella, Ctra Xara-Jesús Pobre   ☎ 966-454 252
✉ lasella@arrakis.es
An 18-hole course designed by Juan de la Cuadra Oyanguren. The
course is open daily from 8am to nightfall and green fees cost
around €60.

Jávea   Club de Golf Jávea, Ctra Jávea-Benitachell
km 45   ☎ 965-792 1584
🖳 www.javeagolf.com
A 9-hole course designed by Francisco Moreno. The course is
open daily from 8am to nightfall and green fees cost around €50.

Area Two – Marina Baja

Altea   Club de Golf Don Cayo, Urb Sierra de Altea   ☎ 965-848 046
✉ doncayo@ctv.es
A 9-hole course designed by Gregorio Sanz and Pedro Barber. The
course, one of the first to be opened on the Costa Blanca, is open
daily from 8am to nightfall and green fees cost around €36.

Area Three – Alicante

Alicante   Alicante Golf, Avda Locutor Vicente Hipólito
37, Playa de San Juan   ☎ 965-152 043

An 18-hole course designed by Severiano Ballesteros. The course is open daily from 8am to 6pm (9pm in summer) and green fees cost around €60.

Club de Golf Bonalba, Partida de Bonalba,
Muchamiel   ☎ 965-955 955
🖳 www.golf-bonalba.com
An 18-hole course designed by Ramón Espinosa. The course is open daily from 8am to 8pm and green fees cost around €55.

Club de Golf El Plantío, Ctra Alicante-Elche
km 3   ☎ 965-189 115
🖳 www.elplantio.com.
An 18-hole course designed by Manuel Ferry Ruiz. The course is open daily from 8am to nightfall and green fees cost around €70.

Golf Alenda, Ctra Alicante-Madrid km 15,
Monforte del Cid   ☎ 965-620 521
✉ alendaclub@retemail.es
An 18-hole course designed by Roland Farrat. The course is open daily from 8am to 8pm (10pm in summer) and green fees cost around €50.

Area Four – Vega Baja

Algorfa   La Finca Algorfa Golf, Ctra Algorfa-
Los Montesinos km 3   ☎ 965-967 058
🖳 www.golflafinca.com
An 18-hole course designed by José Gancedo. The course is open daily from 8am to nightfall and green fees cost around €75.

Cartagena   Campo de Golf Villamartín, Ctra Alicante-
Cartagena km 50, Urb Villamartín   ☎ 966-765 170
🖳 www.golfvillamartin.com
An 18-hole course designed by Paul Putman. The course is open daily from 8am to nightfall and green fees cost around €55.

Club de Golf Las Ramblas de Orihuela, Ctra
Alicante- Cartagena km 48, Urb Las Ramblas ☎ 965-323 011
🖳 www.golframblas.com
An 18-hole course designed by José Gancedo. The course is open daily from 8am to nightfall and green fees cost around €45.

Real Club de Golf Campoamor, Ctra
Alicante- Cartagena km 48, Orihuela Costa   ☎ 965-320 410
🖳 www.lomasdecampoamor.com

An 18-hole course designed by Carmelo Gracia Caselles. The course is open daily from 8am to nightfall and green fees cost around €45.

Rojales   Golf & Country Club La Marquesa, Avda
Justo Quesada, Rojales   ☎ 966-714 258
✉ golflamarquesa@ctv.es
An 18-hole course designed by Justo Quesada. The course is open daily from 8am to nightfall and green fees cost around €45.

Area Five – Mar Menor

Los Belones La Manga Club, La Manga Club   ☎ 968-175 000
💻 www.lamangaclub.com
Three championship 18-hole courses, designed by Robert Putnam. The course is open daily from 8am to nightfall and green fees cost around €80 for resort guests and €170 for the public.

Torre   Club de Golf Torre Pacheco, C/ Gregory
Pacheco   Peter s/n, Torre Pacheco   ☎ 968-585 111
💻 www.golftorrepacheco.com
A 9-hole municipal course designed by David Thomas. The course is open daily from 8am to nightfall and green fees cost around €30.

Several more golf courses are currently under construction in the Mar Menor area.

HORSE RIDING

There are numerous riding stables (*picaderos* or *establos*) situated on the Costa Blanca and riding lessons and guided rides in the country are available. Horse riding is expensive and costs around €20 for adult beginners in a group (€40 individually) and €15 for children. Some stables organise horse rides in the surrounding countryside at weekends. **Check the stables has adequate third-party insurance.**

ICE SKATING

Perhaps surprisingly, given the area's high temperatures, there are two ice-skating rinks in the Costa Blanca, offering a refreshing way to cool off in the summer. Puerta de Alicante shopping centre has a large new rink where you can skate all year round (information is available from ☎ 965-112 169). The rink is open afternoons and evenings, and offers discounts on

Wednesdays. The town of Elche also has an ice rink situated at Elche Squash Club (C/ Mallorca 37, ☎ 965-453 446).

KARTING

Benidorm   Karting La Cala, Ctra N-332 km 143,
Benidorm – Villajoyosa   ☎ 965-894 676
This circuit offers karting for children (from the age of 4) and adults as well as specially adapted karts for disabled drivers. Open all year and from 10am to 1am in July and August. Sale of karts and accessories.

Finestrat   Karting Club Finestrat: Exit 65A on the
AP-7, Terra Mítica Oeste   ☎ 965-972 227
One of the area's largest karting circuits with over 1,200m of track offering karts for children (from 5), adults and formula competitors. The club regularly organises competitions. Open all year. Bar and cafeteria facilities. Amusements and a roller-skating rink are also available.

Torrevieja   Go-Karts, Ctra de Cartagena km 5.7   ☎ 965-328 069
Separate karting tracks for children (from the age of 5), juniors, adults and high-speed competition. Open every day throughout the year. Bar and restaurant facilities. Quad circuits are also available.

QUAD BIKING

Quad biking is very popular on the Costa Blanca and several companies offer rental of bikes and excursions:

Benidorm   Beniquads   ☎ 650-744 441
💻 www.beniquads.com
Beniquads provide guided off-road quad trips in the countryside behind Benidorm.

Denia   Fun & Quads, Consolát del Mar 8   ☎ 965-787 228
💻 www.funquads.com
Fun & Quads offer quad rental and guided excursions plus a quad circuit in Gandía.

La Manga   Bikes & Quads, Gran Vía km 0   ☎ 968-145 109
✉ bikes.quads@wanadoo.es
Bikes & Quads offer rental of quads and bicycles plus accessories.

Quad Explorers   ☎ 609-739 146
Quad Explorers run guided quad tours around the Mar Menor area leaving from La Manga Golf Club.

San Pedro de Pinatar	Turkana, Puerto de San Pedro de Pinatar ☎ 968-537 327

💻 www.turkana.org
Turkana run guided jeep and quad trips around the Mar Menor area. Suitable for over 12s only.

TENNIS

Tennis is extremely popular on the Costa Blanca where there are numerous tennis clubs and the annual tennis tournament (*Circuito Alicantino*), for young tennis hopefuls with some 1,500 participants, is one of the most important in Spain. Alicante hosted the Davis Cup semi-finals between France and Spain in September 2004. Clay, hard and fast courts are available and prices for court hire vary tremendously, e.g. from €4 to €30 an hour. Most municipal sports centres offer tennis lessons for adults and children – prices are very reasonable (e.g. €15 a month for three one hour classes a week), but classes are often large. Private clubs charge from around €6 to €30 an hour for classes.

Tennis clubs organise regular tournaments for all ages and standards, and there are also several provincial and regional competitions. Many urbanisations have private tennis courts for residents' use. The main private tennis clubs on the Costa Blanca are listed below. Municipal tennis courts are usually located at Municipal Sports Centres. The Spanish Tennis Federation (Real Federación Española de Tenis) has an office in Valencia and can provide information on classes, clubs and events (Avda del Cid 35, 1º, ☎ 963-849 354, 💻 www.rfet.es)

Area One – Marina Alta

Benissa	Tenis Buenavista, Urb Buenavista 36	☎ 965-747 867
Calpe	Club de Tenis, Gargasindi 1-J, Calpe	☎ 965-830 820
Denia	Club de Tenis, Partida Marjal s/n	☎ 965-784 451
Jávea	Club de Tenis Jávea, Partida Saladar s/n	☎ 965-790 289
La Sella	Club de Tenis La Sella, Residencial La Sella, Pedreguer	☎ 966-456 351

Area Two – Marina Baja

Alfaz del Pi	Club de Tenis La Marina-Benidorm, Sendero de la Barrina s/n	☎ 966-866 233

Altea	Club de Tenis	☎ 965-840 482
Benidorm	Pista Central, Partida Pla de Cuartel 21	☎ 966-864 538

Area Three – Alicante

Alicante	Club Atlético Montemar, C/ Padre Esplá 40 ▣ www.camontemar.com	☎ 965-202 570
	Club de Tenis de Alicante, Camino Ferrándiz 1, Muchamiel	☎ 965-950 845
	Pascual Luis Club de Tenis, Fonde Sala s/n	☎ 965-662 252
	QM Sport, Coralos 3, Playa de San Juan ▣ www.qmsportclub.com	☎ 965-157 790

Area Four – Vega Baja

Elche	Club Ilicitano de Tenis, Avda Ferrocarril Este s/n	☎ 965-457 074
Orihuela	Club Social Orcelis, C/ Escorratel s/n	☎ 965-306 900
Santa Pola	Club de Tenis Taula, C/ Marqués de Molins 32	☎ 966-690 175
Torrevieja	Club de Tenis Torrevieja	☎ 966-722 167

Other Racket Sports

Badminton and squash are both played on the Costa Blanca, although neither is as popular as in other countries, e.g. the UK. There are badminton and squash courts at some tennis clubs (see above). Paddle tennis, played on a smaller court with wooden rackets, is a popular sport and many hotels have courts.

WALKING & RAMBLING

Walking is a popular pastime in the Costa Blanca, particularly in the north where there are numerous walking clubs and groups who regularly walk in the countryside in the area. Consult the local press for contact details and further information. There are also several walking routes round the Mar Menor, including an almost complete circuit of the lake and a route through the nearby mining areas. Most routes can also be covered by bicycle. Contact a tourist office on the Mar Menor for details. Two useful books for keen walkers in the area are *Costa Blanca Walks* and *Mountain Walks on the Costa Blanca*, both by Bob Stansfield (Cicerone Guides).

WATERSPORTS

You can do just about every imaginable watersport on the Costa Blanca where there are numerous marinas with sailing clubs as well as other clubs specialising in watersports. Conditions for watersports are usually excellent all-year round. The following provides a guide to some activities on or in the water.

The America's Cup

The port and waters of Valencia have been chosen as the venue for the 32nd edition of the America's Cup in 2007 when yachts from participating countries (including landlocked Switzerland, the defending champion!) will vie for yachting's most prized possession. In preparation for the event, there are numerous projects underway in the city, including an ambitious plan to convert some of the commercial port area into a leisure precinct and seafront walk, and completion of the metro line from the airport to the port. Further information in English and Spanish is available from 💻 www.valencia2007.com.

Boating & Sailing

The Costa Blanca's stunning coastline as well as its proximity to the Balearics offers wonderful opportunities for sailors and for those who can afford it. Sailing and boating along the coast are popular pastimes and possibilities range from luxury power boats to a more modest outboard-powered dinghy. You can hire a boat by the hour, day or week.

The coast has numerous marinas (see below) where you must moor your boat and most marinas have excellent facilities, including fuel pumps, shops, cafes, restaurants and often, a social club. In preparation for the America's Cup in 2007 many marinas have plans for expansion, although most projects may not be approved by the authorities on environmental grounds. Note that legally you can only keep fishing boats on beaches and then only in designated areas. Alternatively you can hire a boat (for larger vessels you may need a licence and/or experience) from most marinas. Fishing trips (short and deep sea) are also available from most fishing ports and marinas. For information on boat trips and marine life watching see page 213.

Sailing clubs at most marinas (see below) offer tuition for all levels and ages. The following companies also offer boating classes:

Alicante	Escuela Mediterránea de Vela, Puerto de Alicante 🖳 www.escueladevela.com	☎ 965-211 955
Altea	Fuerza 6 🖳 www.fuerzaseis.com	☎ 965-845 582
Denia	Club Náutico Denia, Ctra Denia-Jávea 1 🖳 www.cndenia.es Offers sailing, canoeing and rowing courses for all ages and levels, plus numerous competitions throughout the year.	☎ 965-780 989
	Denia Maritime Training Centre 🖳 www.deniarya.com Offers all RYA courses	☎ 628-120 158
Jávea	Escuela de Vela Chambergas 🖳 www.chambergas.com	☎ 963-715 856
Mar Menor	Los Urrutias Charter, Club de Regatas, Los Urrutias 1° 🖳 www.losurrutiascharter.com Boat hire (including yachts). Sailing classes.	☎ 968-134 319
Santa Pola	Ocio Náutico Santa Pola 🖳 www.santapola.com/ocionautico	☎ 966-693 076

An excellent publication in Spanish for keen sailors in the Costa Blanca and Murcia areas is the *AeroGuía del Litoral: Alicante y Murcia* (Geo Planeta), which has detailed aerial photographs of the coastline from Aguilas in Murcia to Oliva (north of Denia) showing ports, marinas, suitable mooring areas and navigational hazards plus useful information about places to visit and a comprehensive road map of the area. A useful publication for sailors in the Marina Alta area is *Carta Blanca*, published twice a year and available from tourist offices, and includes nautical events and a comprehensive map of the coast and waters from Moraira to Denia.

Marinas

Area One – Marina Alta

Benissa	Les Bassettes 💻 www.cnlesbasetes.com) 80 berths	☎ 965-831 213
Calpe	Calpe Marina 💻 www.cncalpe.es 276 berths	☎ 965-831 809
	Puerto Blanca 106 berths	☎ 965-831 337
Denia	Denia Marina 💻 www.cndenia.es 601 berths. There are plans for a further 275 berths to be built in preparation for the America's Cup. This marina is one of the most prestigious in the area and the headquarters of several international sailing events.	☎ 965-780 989
	Denia Port 580 berths	☎ 965-780 067
Jávea	Jávea Sailing Club 💻 wwwcnjavea.com 352 berths	☎ 965-791 025
	Jávea Port 89 berths	☎ 966-460 555
Moraira	Moraira Marina 💻 www.cnmoraira.com This marina is one of the most attractive on the Costa Blanca and also one of the largest with moorings for some 620 boats, including depth of up to 6m (20ft) for large vessels.	☎ 965-744 461

Area Two – Marina Baja

Altea	Altea Marina 💻 www.cnaltea.com Situated within the town itself has 375 berths.	☎ 965-841 579
	Altea Port 487 berths	☎ 966-880 105
	Marina Greenwich 💻 www.marinagreenwich.com	☎ 965-842 200

Has 542 berths, is one of the Costa Blanca's most exclusive marinas and is situated in Urb Mascarat, north of Altea. The marina has shops, cafes and restaurants.

Villajoyosa   Villajoyosa Marina   ☎ 965-893 606
💻 www.cnlavila.org
325 berths

Area Three – Alicante

Alicante is an important Mediterranean port and also has several marinas:

Alicante   Alicante Sailing Club   ☎ 965-921 250
💻 www.rcra.es
Has 400 berths and is one of Spain's oldest clubs and organises numerous sailing events and competitions.

Marina Alicante   ☎ 965-213 600
💻 www.magicalicante.com
Located in the city centre with 748 berth, and has numerous shops and restaurants along the quays.

Nautical Club   ☎ 965-154 491
💻 www.costablanca.org/cnalicante
Is situated between San Juan and the city centre, and has 230 berths.

El Campello Sailing Club   ☎ 965-631 748
💻 www.cncampello.com
474 berths

Area Four – Vega Baja

Guardamar   Marina de las Dunas   ☎ 965-971 938
del Segura   Has 328 berths and is situated at the mouth of the Segura River in unspoilt natural surroundings.

Orihuela   Cabo Roig   ☎ 966-760 176
Costa   207 berths

Dehesa de Campoamor   ☎ 965-320 386
💻 www.cncampoamor.com
349 berths

Pilar de   Torre de la Horadada Marina   ☎ 966-769 087
la Horadada 500 berths

Santa Pola   Santa Pola Marina   ☎ 965-412 403
💻 www.cnauticosantapola.com

Currently has 545 berths, which are planned to be increased by another 283 in preparation for the America's Cup.

Torrevieja   International Marina   ☎ 965-713 650
859 berths

Sailing Club ☎ 965-710 108
🖥 www.rcnt.com
600 berths. The town has major expansion plans for its marina and port area, which will be greatly enlarged in preparation for the America's Cup when it will house a further 813 berths.

Diving & Snorkelling

The Mediterranean waters around the Costa Blanca provide excellent conditions for diving and snorkelling, for both beginners and more advanced divers. The waters around Denia, particularly the Cabo San Antonio protected marine reserve, are generally considered to provide the best and most interesting conditions. Tabarca island's waters are also of interest and the *Islas Hormigas* off the Cabo de Palos marine reserve to the south of La Manga provide some unique diving opportunities. To dive in Spanish waters you need a permit (around €7), available from diving clubs and schools (see below).

Hunting with spears or harpoons is prohibited. If you want to learn to dive, most diving clubs and schools on the coast offer tuition leading to the world-recognised PADI qualification.

> **Even if you're an experienced diver, never dive alone and make sure you have above water support when diving.**

Diving clubs are found at the following locations:

Area One – Marina Alta

Calpe   Peñón Divers-Buceo, Aquagym Esmeralda,
Ponent 1   ☎ 966-836 101

Denia   Diving Center Costa Blanca, Edif Mare
Nostrum II, Ctra Las Rotas 38   ☎ 965-781 079

Dive Center Denia, Marina de Denia,
Dique Sur I   ☎ 607-600 900

Jávea   Buceo Pelicar, C/Sertorio 2, Local 9   ☎ 966-462 183

Buceo La Nao, Comercial Jávea, Park 71   ☎ 965-794 653
🖳 www.cabolanao.com

Area Two – Marina Baja

Benidorm   Costa Blanca Sub, C/Santander 20   ☎ 966-801 784

Poseidon Club, C/Santander 9   ☎ 965-853 227

Scuba Diving Benidorm, Avda Otto de
Habsburgo 10   ☎ 966-809 712
✉ buceobenidorm@wanadoo.es

Area Four – Vega Baja

Santa Pola   Diving Center Mares, Pasaje de Granada 5   ☎ 966-692 986
🖳 www.natural.es/scubaelx

Torrevieja   Diving Mediterraneo, Rambla Juan Mateo 37   ☎ 965-704 309
🖳 divingmediterraneo.com

Tevere, C/San Policarpo 8   ☎ 965-716 555

Scubatribe   ☎ 966-719 936
🖳 www.scubatribe.freeservers.com

Torrevieja Sub, C/ Huerto 22   ☎ 607-451 794
✉ torreviejasub@fowof.es.

Area Five – Mar Menor

San Pedro Club de Buceo, Puerto Deportivo de
de Pinatar San Pedro   ☎ 676-745 022
🖳 www.buceosanpedro.com

Surfing & Windsurfing

When the wind blows conditions are ideal for surfing and windsurfing, and there are several surfing clubs on the coast, although the waves can hardly ever be classed as 'rollers', but some beaches (e.g. those at Calpe and Gandía) make good practice grounds for beginners. The tranquil (and warm) waters of the Mar Menor at the southern end of the Costa Blanca also provide ideal conditions for windsurfing beginners.

Windsurfing schools can be found at:

Area One –Marina Alta

Calpe   Escuela de Windsurf Waikiki, Playa
             de Levante   ☎ 965-832 856

Denia   Windsurfing Center, Ctra Marines-Racons
             km 12   ☎ 965-755 307
             💻 www.windcenterdenia.com

Area Four – Vega Baja

Santa Pola Ocio Náutico, Playa de Levante   ☎ 689-596 067
             💻 www.ociomas.com

             Windsurf Santa Pola   ☎ 689-596 067
             💻 www.ociomas.com

Area Five – Mar Menor

La Manga   Mangasurf   ☎ 968-145 331
             💻 www.mangasurf.com

             Cavanna Wind   ☎ 968-563 506

Other Watersports

Numerous other watersports can also be done around the Costa Blanca. Waterskiing, rides on inflatables and jet ski rides are offered by beach bars, beach clubs and sports stands on beaches. **Make sure the owner has a licence and adequate insurance for all sports and particularly for jet skis** – in the summer of 2002 several people were killed or badly injured in jet ski accidents and legislation has since been tightened up.

Altea   Kayaking Costa Blanca   ☎ 605-884 420
             💻 www.palesimar.com
             Kayaking Costa Blanca offers excursions and kayak courses based
             around Altea.

Denia   MareMoto   ☎ 966-422 765
             💻 www.maremotojets.com
             The MareMoto boat company offers excursions and the hire of jet
             skis and speed boats around the coast.

For those who like to stay firmly on dry land or get seasick even in the calmest waters, watching watersports or strolling round the marinas is a good substitute!

Golf club, Murcia

12

Shopping

Shopping facilities on the Costa Blanca have improved beyond all recognition over the last few years and there's now an excellent choice of both large and small shops, national chainstores, hypermarkets and supermarkets. Imported goods, including an excellent range of foreign food, are also available in most areas. This chapter looks at where to shop on the Costa Blanca for specific items and includes a list of markets and shopping centres.

BOOKS

There are some good bookshops on the coast, particularly in Alicante, and most large towns boast at least one good bookstore. Hypermarkets also stock a selection of books. English-language books are available at specialist shops (see below) and a limited selection (usually paperback bestsellers) can be found at some large supermarkets and newsagents. Otherwise you can buy online from one of the many internet bookshops such as Amazon (🖳 www.amazon.co.uk), The Book Place (🖳 www.the bookplace.com) or WH Smith (🖳 www.whsmith.co.uk) and have the books delivered by post. There are also second-hand bookshops in most towns where you can purchase or exchange English-language books.

Main bookshops on the coast are listed below:

Area One – Marina Alta

Calpe   Bookworld España, C/ Gabriel Miró 15,
Edif Perla Mar   ☎ 965-831 751
🖳 www.bookworldespana.com
A large selection of English-language books as well as cards and
wrapping paper. An ordering is service is available.

Librería Europa, C/ Oscar Esplá 2   ☎ 965 835 824
A selection of foreign languages books is available, including
English.

Denia   Denia Bookshop, C/ Patricio Fernández 33   ☎ 965-785 329
A large selection of English-language books is available. An
ordering is service available.

Denia Librería Exlibris, Plaza Jorge Juan 7   ☎ 966-851 501
General selection, including some English-language titles.

Jávea   Bookworld España, Avda Amanecer de
España   ☎ 966-462 253
🖳 www.bookworldespana.com

A large selection of English-language books as well as cards and
wrapping paper. An ordering service is available.

Area Two – Marina Baja

Benidorm   Books & Books, C/ Sant Roc 17
A good selection of new and second-hand English-language books
as well as cards.

Librería Francés, C/ Ruzafa, Edif París 4   ☎ 965-851 501
General selection.

Librería Ulises, Avda Almendros 16   ☎ 965-864 499
General selection.

Villajoyosa   Vila Llibres, C/ Ciudad de Valencia 14   ☎ 965-891 266
General selection. An ordering service is available.

Area Three – Alicante

Alicante has several good bookshops, usually offering a limited selection
of English-language books.

Alicante   Arce Libros, C/ Arquitecto Morell 19   ☎ 965-131 271
General selection.

Bestseller Librerías, Avda Blasco Ibañez 33 ☎ 966-673 780
General selection. A telephone ordering service is available.

El Corte Inglés, Avda Federico Soto
The ground floor section of the shop has a wide range of books,
including an excellent selection for children.

FNAC Boulevar, Avda la Estación   ☎ 966-010 131
🖳 www.fnac.es
Excellent range of books, including English-language ones. An
online ordering service is available.

Librería CILSA, C/ Italia 6   ☎ 965-122 355
🖳 www.libreriacilsa.com
Travel and scientific books. An online ordering service is available.

Librería Internacional, C/ Rafael
Altamira 6   ☎ 965-217 925
General selection. A telephone ordering service is available.

Librería Lux, C/ Poeta Quintana 12   ☎ 965-205 357
General selection. A telephone ordering service is available.

Area Four – Vega Baja

Elche   Ali I Truc, Paseo de las Heras de Santa
                 Lucía 5-7   ☎ 965-453 864
                 General selection. A telephone ordering service is available.

                 Librería Séneca, C/ Capitán Lagier 4   ☎ 965-453 920
                 🖥 www.senecalibros.com
                 General selection. A telephone ordering service is available.

Torrevieja   Librería Papiro, C/ Joaquín Chapaprieta 24 ☎ 965-705 629
                 General selection.

CLOTHING & FOOTWEAR

Chain Stores

Numerous fashion chain stores operate on the Costa Blanca and the following is a list of the main stores you can expect to find in most high streets and shopping centres.

Clothing for Adults

- **Benetton –** Italian fashion for women. Good for knitwear. Note that some Benetton stores are franchise shops and it may be difficult to return or exchange an item if you bought it in a different store.

- **Berska –** Mainly women's fashion, although there are a few lines for men. Casual wear aimed at the young and teenage market.

- **Cortefiel –** Men and women's fashion. Casual and smart. Good for quality knitwear, coats and suits. Generally better quality and more upmarket than Zara and Mango.

- **Mango –** Women's fashion. You have to pretty slim to get into most of the garments.

- **Massimo Dutti –** Men and women's fashion. Casual and smart. Good quality and more expensive than Zara.

- **Pull & Bear** – Mainly men's fashion, although there's a small women's section. Casual wear predominates. Inexpensive and good for basics such as T-shirts and sweaters.

- **Springfield** – Men's fashion. Good value average quality casual and smart wear.

- **Women's Secret** – Women's nightwear, swimwear and underwear at reasonable prices.

- **Zara** – Men and women's fashion. Spain's flagship fashion store where lines change frequently. Good value casual and smart wear, although quality can be poor and clothes usually only last for a season. Note that the women's clothes are designed for those on the slim side and the men's clothes don't fit tall men.

Children's Clothes

- **Benetton** – Most Benetton stores stock clothes for children aged 0 to 12 years. Clothes are expensive, but the quality is generally good.

- **El Corte Inglés** – A good choice for children aged 0 to 16 years. Good brand as well as designer labels. Prices range from reasonable to very expensive. Quality is generally good.

- **Hypermarkets** – Hypermarkets such as Alcampo, Carrefour and Hypercor sell good basics such as trousers, tracksuits and underwear at very reasonable prices.

- **Mayoral** – Mayoral is a Spanish company with several stores on the coast stocking clothes for children aged 0 to 16 years. Good quality and reasonable prices.

- **Zara** – Clothes and footwear for children aged 0 to 16 years. Reasonable prices, but quality is average.

Department Stores

El Corte Inglés is the main department store on the Costa Blanca, in addition to being Spain's largest department store company and one of the country's most profitable. Branches can be found in Alicante and Valencia. The store offers a good choice of fashion, including own name lines (Easywear and Gold Coast) and national and international designers such as Burberry, Dior, DKNY, Episode and Tommy Hilfiger. It is good for knitwear and basics, and there are real bargains in the sales.

Footwear

Home to a large section of the Spanish shoe manufacturing industry, the Costa Blanca has plenty of shoe shops (*zapaterías*) and there's an excellent choice of casual and smart footwear to suit all tastes and budgets. It's worth shopping around and comparing prices, but bear in mind that not all shoes are leather, and it's worth stocking up on several pairs during the sales when many shoe shops have huge discounts (up to 50 per cent). Note that it's difficult for women with a foot size of 41 (7) or over to find a good choice of shoes.

Children's Shoes

Unlike shoe shops in some other countries, shoe shops in Spain don't generally stock children's shoes as well as adults'. Children's shoes are usually sold in a specialist shop, of which there aren't many. The El Corte Inglés has a good selection of children's footwear and Zara also sells some children's footwear. Most towns have one or two shops where you can buy children's shoes. Note that shops usually don't measure children's feet (you will be asked their size) and there's usually only one width fitting.

DIY MATERIALS

There are numerous places where you can buy DIY materials on the Costa Blanca and although many people favour the large specialist stores, it may be worth asking at your local ironmongers (*ferretería*) or household supplies shop (*droguería*) for the item you need – it's often cheaper and much more convenient.

Builders' Merchants

Large orders of building materials can be made through builders' yards, although you might get a better discount if you order through a builder rather than in person. Delivery is usually extra.

Chain Stores

The Costa Blanca has several large DIY stores, including Akí in San Juan (Ctra de Valencia km 89), Leroy Merlín in Alicante (CC Vistahermosa) and Brico House with branches at Denia, Finestrat, Orihuela Costa, Santa Pola and Torrevieja. They all offer a comprehensive range of DIY and gardening equipment, including items of furniture and machinery. **Although these** stores have a good choice, they aren't always the cheapest and it's worth shopping around.

Local Shops

Ferretería sell a wide range of DIY materials as well as numerous other items for the home. You can usually buy small objects such as nails or bolts by weight or number rather than having to buy a whole packet. *Droguerías* sell paint and brushes (etc.). Some larger shops may deliver and most will offer a discount on a large order.

Warehouses

Most towns have several warehouses (*almacén*) specialising in building material, tiles or plumbing and electrical goods. Stores are generally situated on the outskirts of towns or in industrial areas (*polígono industrial*). Most usually have a good selection of products on display and in stock; other items can be ordered within a week. Delivery is usually extra unless you have a very large order and most warehouses will offer a discount if you ask. Prices vary greatly and it's worth shopping around and comparing prices – especially if you plan to buy a lot.

FOOD

Fresh Produce

Spain has a fantastic variety of fresh produce produced nationally and available all year round, although many fruit and vegetables are seasonal and out of season produce tends to be imported. A large proportion of Spain's fruit and vegetables are grown in the regions of Valencia and Murcia, where you can see vast areas under market garden cultivation, particularly citrus fruits. Some tropical fruits are also grown on the Costa Blanca such as avocados and mangoes.

Fish and shellfish are available in abundance, much of which is caught locally–you can go to the daily fresh fish auctions in several towns in the area (e.g. Denia, Santa Pola, Torrevieja and Villajoyosa). Note that fresh fish isn't usually for sale on Mondays since fishermen don't usually go out on Sundays. Fresh meat tends to be Spanish and of excellent quality. Pork and veal are particularly good.

The best place to buy fresh produce is at an indoor market – most towns have one – open Mondays to Saturdays from around 8.30am to 2pm. The best produce is available first thing, although bargains may be available at closing time. Shop around the different stalls – some sell top-quality produce at top prices and others sell cheaper inferior quality produce. A good guide to the best stalls is to look at the queues. Haggling is acceptable, although not for individual items but rather as a reduction of the final price (stall holders often round down to the nearest euro) or a special price if you buy more. Shopping in indoor markets is an enjoyable experience and not one to be done in a hurry since everyone wants to discuss local and national affairs!

Fresh produce can also be bought in shops in towns where there are butchers (*carnicerías*), greengrocers (*fruterías*), bakers (*panaderías*) and grocery stores (*ultramarinos*). Produce in these shops is usually good quality and value. Supermarkets also sell fresh produce, although the quality may be inferior. A recent survey of foodstores in Spain found that the best fruit and vegetables, and fish are found in small shops, and meat in both small shops and supermarkets.

Foreign Food

There's generally a good variety of foreign food available at supermarkets on the Costa Blanca and many 'foreign' products, e.g. cereals and biscuits, are actually produced in Spain. British and German products are the easiest to find, although there may not be much choice, particularly between brands. Not all supermarkets stock foreign foods, although you can usually find what you need at local supermarkets, hypermarkets and at specialist foreign food shops, e.g. Islandia or foreign-run supermarkets.

Bear in mind that foreign food, particularly if imported, is expensive and there may be a cheaper Spanish equivalent, although there are no Spanish baked beans!

Britbuys is a company specialising in British foodstuffs which you can buy online. Post and packaging is extra, and the minimum order is €30. The company has a huge range of products (more than you find in most supermarkets here) and does specialist lines in Christmas and Easter goodies. **Note that it's not cheap**, but if you're craving a bar of Turkish delight or need some wholemeal flour maybe it's worth taking a look at the website 🖥 www.britbuys.com.

Markets

Markets (*mercadillos* or *rastros*) are an essential part of life on the Costa Blanca and at the larger ones (Torrevieja's Friday market claims to be one of the biggest) you can buy just about everything, usually very cheaply, especially if you haggle. Markets are usually open from 9am to 2pm. If a public holiday coincides with market day or it's raining the market probably won't take place. Markets are popular and can get very crowded – **keep your belongings safe and your money well protected since pickpockets may be about**. The following is a list of the general markets that take place on the Costa Blanca during the week.

* Denotes markets selling crafts and second hand goods (known as *rastros*) or car boot sales.

Mondays	Callosa d'en Sarrià
	Denia
	Elche
	La Nucia
	San Pedro del Pinatar
Tuesdays	Altea
	Jalón
	Los Alcázares
	Orihuela
Wednesdays	Benidorm
	Benitachell
	Guardamar
	Orba
	Polop de la Marina
	Teulada
	Torrevieja (La Mata)
Thursdays	Jávea
	Pego

	Rojales
	San Javier
	Urb Marina
	Villajoyosa
Fridays	Alfaz del Pi
	Cala de Finestrat
	Denia
	Finestrat
	Gata
	Moraira
	Pilar de la Horadada
	Torrevieja
Saturdays	*Benissa
	Calpe
	Elche
	*Elche (Plaza de Raval)
	*Jalón
	Orihuela Costa (Playa Flamenca)
	Pedreguer
Sundays	Benidorm (antiques)
	*Ciudad Quesada
	*Guardamar

* La Nucia (antiques)

*Teulada

*Villajoyosa

Local Stores

There are numerous small shops in localities on the coast selling food and, although prices at these shops are generally higher than supermarkets, the quality and service is better. They also give you a good chance to practise your Spanish! Local shops are generally open from around 9.30am to around 2pm and from around 4.30 to around 8pm Mondays to Fridays. They are also usually open on Saturday mornings.

Supermarkets

There are several supermarket chains on the coast. Opening hours are usually from around 9.30am to around 8.30pm Mondays to Saturdays. Some supermarkets open on Sundays in the summer and during the Christmas and Easter holidays. The main supermarkets are:

● **Caprabo** – Reasonably priced produce with many own brand products plus some foreign produce. There are several large stores around the Costa Blanca, all offer home delivery, parking and several also have petrol stations with reasonably priced petrol. Further information is available from ☎ 902-116 060, 🖥 www.caprabo.es.

● **El Corte Inglés** – There's an El Corte Inglés supermarket at the Avda Federico Soto store in Alicante. Food here is generally good quality and more expensive than other supermarkets. There are many good quality own brand products. Some foreign produce is available. Further information is available from ☎ 901-122 122 and 🖥 www.el corteingles.es (online shopping available to certain areas).

● **MasyMas** – A regionally based supermarket chain with branches throughout central and northern Costa Blanca. They offer a good range of fresh produce at reasonable prices. Further information is available from 🖥 www.fornes.masymas.es.

● **Mercadona** – Mercadona, based in Valencia, offers inexpensive reasonable quality products, with many own brand products instead of other brands. Stores, open from 9am to 9.30pm, often have their own parking facilities (free if you make a purchase). There are numerous stores around the Costa Blanca. Further information is available from ☎ 902-113 177 and 💻 www.mercadona.es (online shopping is available to certain areas).

Foreign Supermarkets

The Costa Blanca has a good selection of foreign supermarkets around the area specialising in foreign brand products, particularly British. The southern part of the coast is particularly well-catered for and some stores will even order foreign goods for you.

Discount Stores

There are numerous so-called discount stores on the Costa Blanca where products are sold at cheaper prices than in supermarkets. Discount stores tend to display produce in boxes rather than on shelves and there's little choice of brands. They are, however, inexpensive and offer good value for money in basics such as pasta, flour and cleaning products. **Note that you have to pay for plastic bags in most discount stores (€0.05 each) and queues for the check-out can be very long.**

Discount stores on the coast are:

● **Día** – Discount supermarkets with many own brand products. There are stores in Alicante (several), Calpe, Denia, Santa Pola and Torrevieja (several). Free parking is provided. Further information is available from ☎ 902-453 453 and 💻 www.dia.es.

● **Lidl** – Discount supermarket with mainly German produce. They also sell clothing and household goods. There are numerous stores around the coast open from 9am to 9.30pm. Free parking is provided. Further information is available from ☎ 902-243 222 and 💻 www.lidl.es.

● **Makro** – Wholesale only and you need to have a card to buy here, although cards are easy to obtain if you have a business or are self-employed. There are stores situated in Alicante (Avda Mare Nostrum 13, ☎ 965-282 211, open from 8am to 9.30pm Mondays to Saturdays) and Finestrat (C/ Calpe 4, ☎ 966-889 098, open from 8am to 9pm Mondays to Saturdays). Further information is available from 💻 www.makro.es.

● **Plus** – Discount supermarkets with many own brand products. There are stores in Alicante (3), Benidorm, Elche, Orihuela, San Juan and Torrevieja (2). Free parking is provided. Further information is available from ☎ 901-102 202 and 💻 www.plus-supermercados.es.

Hypermarkets

The large shopping centres on the Costa Blanca usually include a hypermarket selling just about everything for the home (the choice of furniture is usually limited) as well as food, clothes and footwear, books and music, and toys. Hypermarkets also offer a range of services such as home delivery and discount cards. Most hypermarkets have in-store cafeterias or restaurants and travel agents. Hypermarkets are generally open from 10am to 10pm Mondays to Saturdays and are open on Sundays in the summer (July and August) and during the Christmas and Easter holidays. **Note that you need a €0.50 or €1 coin for trolleys.**

- **Alcampo** – CC Plaza Mar, Alicante. Part of the French company, Auchan with many own brand products. Open from 9am to 10pm Mondays to Saturdays. Home delivery is available to those who live in the Alicante area only and supervised childcare is available for the under 10s. Parking is free. Further information is available from 🖥 www.alcampo.es.

- **Carrefour** – A French company with a huge presence throughout Spain usually with excellent special offers. Parking is free. Further information is available from ☎ 902-202 000 and 🖥 www.carre four.es. Online shopping is available to certain areas. Carrefour has branches in:

  - **Alicante** (CC Gran Vía, open from 10am to 10pm Mondays to Saturdays);

  - **Alicante** (CC Plaza Mar, open from 10am to 10pm Mondays to Saturdays);

  - **Elche** (Ctra Alicante-Murcia km 53, open from 9am to 10pm Mondays to Saturdays);

  - **Finestrat** (next to CC La Marina, open from 9am to 10pm Mondays to Saturdays);

  - **San Juan** (Ctra Valencia km 89, open 9am to 10pm Mondays to Saturdays);

  - **Torrevieja** (Ctra Crevillente, open 9am to 10pm Mondays to Saturdays).

- **Eroski** – There are hypermarkets situated in Elche (C/ Jacarilla s/n) and Orihuela (Ctra Orihuela-Bigastro km 1), both have free parking.

Eroski belongs to a Basque company and is the only fully Spanish hypermarket chain in the country. Special emphasis is placed on consumer rights and the company also offers an excellent online magazine (💻 www.consumer.es) free to email subscribers. Further information is available from ☎ 902-540 340 and 💻 www.eroski.es. Online shopping is available to certain areas.

- **Hipercor** – The Costa Blanca's only Hipercor branch can be found at CC Puerta de Alicante, open from 9am to 10pm Mondays to Saturdays. Hipercor is part of the El Corte Inglés giant and offers quality food and products at higher prices than other hypermarkets. Further information is available from ☎ 901-122 122 and 💻 www.hipercor.es. Online shopping is available to certain areas.

Hypermarkets and supermarkets are popular places for pickpockets and thieves. Don't leave your bag or wallet unattended, especially when you're at the checkout or packing your car. Women on their own or with children are favourite targets.

HOUSEHOLD GOODS

A list of the main stores selling household goods is given below.

- **Casa** – Several branches on the coast specialise in inexpensive items for the home, including decorative products, linen, kitchenwear and small pieces of furniture.

- **El Corte Inglés** – Everything you need for the home and catering for all tastes and budgets.

- **Zara Home** – The recently created home section of the fashion store Zara sells mainly household linen and accessories at reasonable prices.

Furniture

Furniture stores (*tiendas de muebles*) are everywhere on the coast and most have a good selection of furniture at a range of prices. Some stores cater for budget furnishings only and offer to furnish a two-bedroom apartment for €3,000. Most have frequent special offers and discounts, and these are advertised in the local press. Some self-assembly furniture is available from hypermarkets and DIY stores (see pages 273 and 266).

Household Appliances

Generally most household appliances from another European country will work on the Costa Blanca with just a change of plug, but you should check with an electrician beforehand. **Televisions and videos from the UK don't usually work in Spain** (you can get a picture but no sound) and if you bring a washing machine from the UK you will need to block off the hot water pipe since washing machines in Spain heat their own water rather than taking it from the house hot water supply.

Appliances can be bought from specialist shops, department stores and hypermarkets. Special offers and discounts are frequent and most outlets offer credit facilities. Note that some shops don't include installation of the new appliance or the removal of the old appliance in the price.

MUSIC

The best selection of CDs and tapes of all types of music can be found at the El Corte Inglés department store and at FNAC in the Boulevar shopping centre in Alicante, although many small music shops offer good selections. Hypermarkets also sell music but usually only pop or with a very limited choice of other types of music. At most shops you can order CDs or tapes and buy tickets for local concerts. Music shops on the coast are listed below.

Area One – Marina Alta

Denia	Discos Marsal: C/ Diana 18	☎ 965-780 255
Jávea	Clave de Sol, Pje Pío X, 3	☎ 965-792 043
	Todo Música, Avda Lepanto 6	☎ 966-460 022

Area Two – Marina Baja

Benidorm	Fun Record, C/ Buen Retiro 7	☎ 966-811 059
	Maci Rock, C/ Tomás Ortuño 84	☎ 965-853 961
	Wild West Music, C/ Roma 2 🖳 www.djone.com Online shopping is available	☎ 966-803 167

| **Finestrat** | Maci Rock, Avda Marina Baja s/n | ☎ 966-889 228 |

Area Three – Alicante

| **Alicante** | Discos Merlin, C/ Portugal 26 | ☎ 965-126 517 |
| | Tip, C/ Arquitecto Morell 19 | ☎ 965-121 464 |

Area Four – Vega Baja

Elche	Musical 2000, Avda Juan Carlos I, 12	☎ 965-453 381
	Oky Discos, C/ Hospital 16	☎ 965-421 936
Orihuela	Cara B Bits, C/ Pintor Agrassol 48	☎ 965-305 290

Pirate copies of CDs is **big** business in Spain and it's common to be approached by someone selling pirate CDs on the beach or while you're sitting in a bar. Pirate CDs are cheap at around €3 compared to at least €10 in the shops, but the quality is poor (the sound deteriorates rapidly) and it's illegal. Don't feel you're helping out the seller by buying one – most proceeds go to the big fish at the top running the piracy operation and exploiting the sellers.

SHOPPING CENTRES

Until relatively recently there were no shopping centres (*Centros Comerciales*/CC) on the Costa Blanca, but over the last few years, however, shopping centres have started to spring up round the coast. Centres are generally open from 10am to 10pm Mondays to Saturdays and open on Sundays during July and August and during the Christmas holidays. Parking is usually free or you have a number of free hours (e.g. three).

Shopping centres are very popular, especially in the evenings and at weekends. Christmas is particularly crowded and queues to get in and out of car parks can be extremely long.

Thieves and pickpockets love shopping centres and people are victims of theft everyday. A favourite trick is to distract you as you're loading your car while an accomplice takes your bag or money. Keep your car doors locked while you're unloading shopping and when returning your trolley. Don't leave belongings unattended even for a few seconds and watch out for pickpockets in the crowds. Women on their own or with children are favourite targets.

The main shopping centres on the Costa Blanca are listed below.

Area Two – Marina Baja

Benidorm/   CC La Marina   ☎ 966-889 733
Finestrat   🖥 www.cclamarina.com)
CC La Marina is located near the AP-7 (exit 65A) on the N-332 to the west of Benidorm. A train station (Hiper Finestrat stop) is also nearby. This new centre houses a multi-screen cinema, numerous chain stores (mainly clothes) as well as other shops selling accessories, sportswear or household products. There's a good choice of eateries and cafes. Free parking for 1,300 cars is available on site. Next to the centre is the Carrefour hypermarket. La Marina has proved to be one of the coast's most popular centres and gets very crowded in the afternoons and on Saturdays. The centre is open from 10am to 11pm Mondays to Fridays, from 10am to 1am on Saturdays and from 1pm to 11pm on Sundays and public holidays.

Area Three – Alicante

Alicante   CC Puerta de Alicante
Situated to the west of the city in Avda Alcalde Carbonell, with numerous fashion shops and restaurants and cafes as well as a Hypercor hypermarket and 13-screen cinema. The centre is open from 10am to 11pm Mondays to Fridays, from 10am to 1am on Saturdays and from 1pm to 11pm on Sundays and public holidays.

CC Boulevard Plaza   ☎ 965-928 440
Centrally situated in the Avda de la Estación this centre includes the large music and book store, FNAC, plus fashion stores, cafes and restaurants.

CC Gran Vía
A large modern shopping centre situated in the north of Alicante at the end of the Gran Vía. There are numerous fashion and household goods stores, along with cafes and eateries, as well as a bowling alley and fitness centre. Open 10am to 10pm Mondays to Saturdays.

CC Plaza Mar 2
The city's newest shopping centre is centrally located near Playa Postiguet on Avda Denida. There are numerous fashion, music and household goods stores, as well as Alcampo hypermarket.

CC Vistahermosa
Situated on the Avda Ramos Carratalá to the north of Alicante this huge centre includes PC World, Leroy Merlin (DIY), Media-Markt (electrical goods) and a sportswear store as well as numerous

other fashion and household goods shops. The centre also houses a 12-screen cinema and a large canopy-covered central square where events and shows take place. Free parking is available for 2,000 cars.

Future Shopping Centres

Elche   CC Elx Plaza
Situated on Elche's southern ring-road this huge shopping and leisure complex will open shortly, housing numerous shops and restaurants as well as a Cinebox cinema.

La Marina   CC Bahía de las Dunas   ☎ 966-726 197
Situated on the N-332 km 74.4 near La Marina, this centre is currently under construction and expected to be finished in late 2005. It will house some 100 stores and eateries, and will provide ample parking.

La Zenia   Complejo Supercor
Situated on the N-332 at La Zenia, this large complex, opening in spring 2005, will house a Supercor hypermarket as well as numerous other shops and banks.

Santo Domingo, Orihuela

13

Miscellaneous Matters

This chapter includes miscellaneous information, of all which is useful to anyone living or staying on the Costa Blanca, namely (in alphabetical order) information on church services, climate, consulates, crime, geography, libraries, pets, registering as a resident and residence permits, refuse collection, services, telephone (fixed and mobile, and internet connections and cafes), television and radio, and utilities (electricity, gas and water).

CHURCHES

There are numerous churches on the Costa Blanca that hold services in English. The following is an alphabetical list of churches and services.

Baptist & Evangelical

Alfaz del Pi   New Life Evangelical Church, C/ Joaquín Turina 1
Sundays at 6.30pm.

Benidorm   Evangelical Community Church, C/ La
Garita 22   ☎ 965-870 911
Sundays at 6pm.

Calpe   Evangelical Community Church, Avda
Diputación 38   ☎ 965-870 911
Sundays at 10am.

Jávea   Evangelical Community Church, L'Ancora
Tennis Club   ☎ 965-870 911
Sundays at noon.

International Baptist Church, Jávea
International College   ☎ 966-470 303
Sundays at 11am.

Torrevieja   Evangelical Community Church, Hotel
Fontana   ☎ 965-870 911
Tuesdays at 5pm.

La Siesta Evangelical Church, Urb La Siesta   ☎ 966-760 620
Sundays at 11.15am.

Catholic

Catholic churches in large towns usually hold daily services and several at weekends in Spanish only. The following churches hold services in English.

Els Poblets   San José church, Miraflor
First and third Saturday of the month at 7pm.

Torrevieja   Main church in Urb La Siesta
Sundays at 10am.

Christian Fellowship

Calpe   Avda Gabriel Miró, Edif Perlamar 1-7   ☎ 965-832 607
Sundays at 11am.

Torrevieja   Christian Centre, C/San Luis 20   ☎ 966-700 391
Sundays at 9.30am and 11.30am.

Church of England

Benidorm   Nuestra Señora de la Almudena church   ☎ 966-868 180
Sundays at 9.45am.

Calpe   La Merced church   ☎ 965-831 089
Sundays at 5pm.

Campello   Chapel in Los Salesianos   ☎ 965-952 788
Sundays at noon.

Denia   Chapel on Las Rotas road   ☎ 965-783 176
Sundays at 11.45am.

Jávea   Ermita del Popul, C/ Jesús el Pobre   ☎ 965-770 632
Sunday mornings.

Mar Menor   St Teresa church   ☎ 968-338 292
Second and fourth Sundays of the month at 6pm.

Orba   La Ermita in Orbeta   ☎ 965-587 108
Sundays at 9.45am.

**San
Fulgencio**   Urb La Marina main church   ☎ 966-797 368
Sundays at 11am.

Urb La Siesta main church   ☎ 966-762 715
First and third Sundays of the month at 6pm.

Torrevieja   Urb Lago Jardín main church   ☎ 966-722 100
Saturdays (except July and August) at 6pm.

Urb Los Balcones main church ☎ 965-719 216
Sundays at 10.30am (11am in July and August).

Further information on churches in the Torrevieja area is available from ☎ 965-971 045 and 💻 www.c-of-etorrevieja.com.

Church of the Good Shepherd

San Juan   C/ Francisco Seva 3, bajo ☎ 965-950 231
Sundays at 11am.

Dutch Evangelical

Benidorm   Evangelical Centre, Avda Ametla de Mar s/n
Sundays at 10am.

Skandinaviksa Turistkyrkan, Avda Madrid
26, Torre Principado ☎ 966-830 715
Sundays at 11.15am.

Jehovah's Witnesses

Benidorm   Salón de Asambleas, C/ Yugoslavia s/n ☎ 966-802 222
Tuesdays at 7pm, Fridays at 7pm and Sundays at 11am.

Jávea   Cron Figueras, C/ Pacheco 18 ☎ 962-856 041
Wednesdays at 7.30pm and Sundays at 5pm.

Torrevieja   C/ Hermanos Bazán 86 ☎ 965-715 530
Thursdays at 7pm and Sundays at 11am.

Jewish

Benidorm   International Synagogue ☎ 965-855 418
Friday evenings.

Salvation Army

Denia   C/ San José 14
Sundays at 10am.

Port Denia Hotel
Sundays at 5.45pm.

Seventh Day Adventist Church

Calpe   ☎ 630-723 963

Denia   ☎ 965-893 834

Villajoyosa   ☎ 965-893 834

CLIMATE

With more than 325 days of sunshine a year, the Costa Blanca is considered by the World Health Organisation to have one of the world's best climates. Seasonal weather is generally as follows:

Spring

Very pleasant, with average temperatures of around 20°C to 24°C (68°F to 75°F) during the day. April, May and June are often the best months. Rainfall is occasional and it usually doesn't after the end of May.

Summer

Hot and sunny. The temperature rises in July and August when it's often over 30°C (86°F). Note that some areas of the Costa Blanca are often several degrees warmer, particularly Alicante and the southern part of the coast. It rarely rains in summer. The northern part of the coast is generally cooler than the rest of the region, as the Montgó mountain generates its own cooler micro-climate.

Autumn

Warm and sunny, although rainfall can be frequent and may be torrential. The phenomenon known as the *Gota Fría* (high cold air mixing with warm air below) affects the area and causes torrential rainfall along much of the eastern coast. September and October are usually pleasant months.

Winter

The lowest temperatures are around 12°C (54°F), although in an exceptional year they may be lower and occasionally there's snow on the highest mountains. In the day the temperature often rises to 20°C (68°F).

Note that even though day-time temperatures may be high, you need some form of heating at home. Rainfall can be frequent and is often torrential, but bad weather rarely lasts for more than three or four days at a time.

> **Flooding and flash floods are common during torrential rain, when dry river or stream beds can turn into fast flowing currents within a matter of minutes. If it's raining, don't attempt to cross a river or stream on foot or by car (even in a four-wheel drive vehicle), as you can easily be swept away. Flooding is common in low-lying areas in southern Costa Blanca, although floods may occur anywhere; for example, extensive areas of the Marina Alta were flooded in spring 2004.**

Local Variations

Most of the Costa Blanca enjoys much the same pleasant climate, although there are slight variations depending on the location. All localities claim to have the best climate and many also claim a particular micro-climate, but it's generally agreed by the experts that Jávea has the best climate in the area. Local variations are as follows:

Northern Coast

The area around Denia and Jávea is generally cooler in summer and warmer in winter than the average on the Costa Blanca.

Southern Coast

This section of the Costa Blanca is generally warmer than the rest of the coast, both in winter and summer (often several degrees). This is an advantage in winter, but less so in the summer. Rainfall is also lower and drought often threatens the area. Alicante itself can be particularly hot in July and August.

Inland

All towns and villages inland are colder in the winter and, due to the lack of sea breezes, hotter in the summer than the coast. The difference can be more than five degrees. In mountain villages frosts are common in the winter and in some villages (e.g. Tárbena) snows falls occasionally. Humidity is also higher than on the coast.

CONSULATES

Consulates of numerous countries are represented on the Costa Blanca and most have their offices in Alicante. Consulates provide useful services for foreigners in Spain, including passport renewal and information. Consulate hours are usually 9am to 2pm Mondays to Fridays and consulates close on public holidays – both those of Spain and those of their home country.

Belgium	Avda Catedrático Soler 8, Alicante	☎ 965-929147
Denmark	Plaza de Calvo Sotelo 3, 7º, Alicante	☎ 965-207 938
Finland	C/ Vikingos 4, Benidorm	☎ 965-853 599
France	C/ Arquitecto Morel 8, Alicante	☎ 965-921 836
Germany	Plaza de Calvo Sotelo 1, 2º, Alicante	☎ 965-217 060
Iceland	Avda Mediterráneo, Casa Las Flores 13, Benidorm	☎ 965-850 863
Italy	C/ Reyes Católicos 24, Alicante	☎ 965-221 945
Luxembourg	Avda Juan Bautista Lafora 3, 4ºC, Alicante	☎ 965-205 333
Netherlands	C/ Castaños 29, 1º, Alicante	☎ 965-212 175
Norway	Avda Ramón y Cajal 3, Alicante	☎ 965-218 412
Switzerland	Esplanada de España 29, Alicante	☎ 965-218 300
UK	Plaza de Calvo Sotelo 1, 2º, Alicante	☎ 965-216 022

CRIME

In general, the crime rate on the Costa Blanca is low for Spain, although petty theft from property and cars is common in the summer, and some areas, such as Alicante city and Torrevieja, are more susceptible to crime than others. Alicante province crime statistics are among the worse in the country and second only to Madrid in the number of murders committed. Police statistics for 2003, however, show that the crime rate decreased by at least 8 per cent in the region as a whole, mainly as a result of increased police presence.

Violent crime isn't uncommon and the Costa Blanca has a reputation for 'mafia' crime, which is highly publicised and dramatised by the media. One of the worst areas is Torrevieja, where the vast majority of violent crime takes place, although most is committed by organised crime groups, mainly Eastern Europeans. There are occasional shootings between rival gangs, but most people are completely unaffected by mafia violence, which rarely intrudes on everyday life.

To prevent petty crime, you should do the following:

Property

- Always lock your property when you're out, even if you just pop to the swimming pool. This is particularly important if the property is on a holiday complex –groups of gypsy women operate on the coast and 'specialise' in entering holiday property.

- Fit your property with an alarm connected to a security company (don't bother with just an alarm, as no one takes any notice of ringing alarms). Fit your windows with grilles or other security devices.

- Leave cash and valuables locked in a safe when you go out; don't carry large amounts of cash around (most insurance companies will only refund up to €100 in cash) and don't leave your handbag unattended, even next to your feet while you're having coffee.

Cars

- Never leave valuables in a car, particularly a hired car.

- Fit your car with an alarm and, better still, a steering wheel lock. This is especially important if you have an expensive or rare model, as many cars on the Costa Blanca are stolen to order.

- Lock your car at petrol stations when you're filling up or paying.

- At petrol stations, shopping centres and car parks, watch out for someone asking for directions or claiming you've got a flat tyre. While you're distracted, an accomplice could be helping himself to your belongings.

Reporting a Crime

If you're the victim of a crime on the Costa Blanca, you should report it to the police, not least in order to make a claim on your insurance. You can report a crime in the following ways:

- **In Person** – At the local national police (*Policía Nacional* – see page 302) station at any time. There are interpreter services at most police stations on the coast, but these may not be available when you wish to make your claim, which must be made in Spanish. Queues can be long.

- **By Telephone** – A relatively easy and quick way of reporting a crime is by phoning ☎ 902-102 112 (cost of a local call). Some staff speak English (although you may have to wait until one's available). You report the crime and are given a reference number. You then go to your local police station after 10am the following day and within 72 hours of making the report with the reference number you've been given to sign and collect the report.

- **By Internet** – Crime report forms are available on the internet (🖥 www.policia.es) in Spanish only. You fill in the form online and, when you send it, you receive a reference number. You then go to your local police station after 10am the following day and within 72 hours of making the report with the reference number to sign and collect the report.

If you're reporting a violent crime or can identify a criminal by name, you cannot make a report by telephone or internet.

Neighbourhood Watch

In some areas of the Costa Blanca (mainly the Vega Baja), neighbourhood watch groups have been formed and crime against property has decreased greatly in the areas where they operate. For information about groups in your area, contact your local police station.

EMERGENCY NUMBERS

- **Ambulance & Medical Emergency** ☎ 061

- **Fire Brigade** ☎ 080

- **General Emergency Number** ☎ 112

- **Police**

  - **Civil Guard** ☎ 062

  - **Local Police** ☎ 092
    (individual police station numbers are listed in **Chapter 4**)

- **National Police**   ☎ 091
  (see also **National Police Stations** on page 302)

● **Sea Rescue**   ☎ 900-202 202

GEOGRAPHY

The Costa Blanca can be divided into two main geographical areas: the south and the north. The southern area stretches from the Mar Menor to Alicante and is characterised by its low-lying flat fertile plains, punctuated by numerous salt-pans and marshes – the saline lagoon at Torrevieja is particularly large. Vegetation here is mainly scrub with pines on the coast and palm plantations rising up as if near oases. The coastline consists of long sandy stretches, some of which are almost totally undeveloped.

North of Alicante the landscape becomes much more dramatic with jagged limestone mountain ranges (e.g. Sierra Aitana, Sierra de Bernia and Sierra Helada), some of which boast peaks rising to over 1,500m (4,950ft). The northern coastline is abrupt with plunging cliffs and rocky coves, which around the Cabo de la Nao (mainland Spain's most easterly point) are reminiscent of the nearby Balearic Islands. Vegetation in this part is typically Mediterranean with pines, almond trees and citrus groves.

LIBRARIES

Spain generally has one of the poorest provisions for libraries in the EU and you shouldn't expect to find the range of books and lending facilities you may be used to in your home country, particularly if you come from the UK. Provisions on the Costa Blanca are, however, quite good and libraries on the coast are well stocked and user friendly. There are public libraries in all towns – in dedicated buildings in larger towns or within the *Casa de la Cultura* in smaller places. Numerous districts and small villages have *Agencias* or *Puntos de Lectura* (similar to mobile libraries in the UK), open in the mornings or afternoons, where you can borrow or order books. Three beaches in the area (Benidorm, San Juan de Alicante and Villajoyosa) have 'beach libraries' (*Biblioplaya*), usually open during the summer months (Benidorm's are open all year) and offering books, magazines and daily newspapers in Spanish and English.

Public libraries stock Spanish-language books and offer a selection of newspapers and magazines, CDs and DVDs. Most also offer private study facilities and internet access (you can usually use the internet for an hour at a time, although you may have to book). Some libraries on the Costa Blanca stock a limited selection of foreign-language books.

Public libraries make no charge for borrowing books; you simply register at your local library (you need a passport photograph and some form of identification) and are issued with a card, with which you can take out up to six books for around two weeks. Library cards issued by any library within the Comunidad Valenicana are valid at all other libraries in the region.

Most libraries open from 9 or 10am to 1.30pm and from 4 to 8pm Mondays to Fridays. Opening times are different in the summer months, when many are open in the morning only from 9am to 2pm. Many libraries close on Saturdays or open from 10am to 2pm only.

Public libraries can be found at the following places:

Area One – Marina Alta

Benissa C/ Purísima 28, 1º   ☎ 965-731 313
Open 9am to 1.30pm and 3 to 8.30pm Mondays to Fridays.

Calpe Avda Masnou 1, 1º   ☎ 965-839 905
Open 9.30am to 1.30pm and 4.30 to 8.30pm Mondays to Fridays.

Denia Plaza Jaime I, s/n   ☎ 965-783 665
Open 10am to 2pm and 5.30 to 9pm Mondays to Fridays.

Jávea C/ Major 9, 2º   ☎ 965-793 938
Open 9am to 2pm and 4 to 8pm Mondays to Fridays.

Teulada Avda Sta Caterina 39   ☎ 965-740 158
Open 10.30am to 1.30pm and 5 to 8pm Mondays to Fridays.

Area Two – Marina Baja

Altea C/ Pont de Moncau 14   ☎ 965-842 853
Open 9.30am to 2pm and 4.30 to 8.30pm Mondays to Fridays.

Benidorm Plaza de los Reyes de España 3   ☎ 965-855 098
Open 10am to 8pm Mondays to Fridays.

Callosa d' En Sarrià Plaza Reina Sofía 11   ☎ 966-756 659
Open 9am to 2pm and 4 to 8pm Mondays to Fridays.

La Nucia Avda Carretera 15   ☎ 966-896 496
Open 10.30am to 2pm and 4.30 to 8pm Mondays to Fridays.

Area Three – Alicante

The city of Alicante has numerous libraries, including specialist and university libraries and archives. The main libraries are listed below:

Alicante   C/ García Andreu 35–37   ☎ 965-124 676
Open 9am to 1pm and 4 to 7pm Mondays to Fridays.

C/ Paseíto de Ramiro 15   ☎ 965-206 600
Open 9am to 8.30pm Mondays to Fridays.

C/ Serra de Cavalls 2/n   ☎ 965-179 594
Open 10.30am to 1pm and 4 to 7pm Mondays to Fridays.

Parque lo Morant s/n   ☎ 965-181 438
Open 9am to 1pm and 4 to 7pm Mondays to Fridays.

Campello   Plaza de Canalejas 6   ☎ 965-632 124
Open 9.30am to 1.30pm Mondays to Fridays.

San Juan   C/ La Mar s/n   ☎ 965-941 129
Open 8am to 1pm and 5 to 8pm Mondays to Fridays.

Area Four – Vega Baja

Elche   C/ Antonio Brotons Pastor 72   ☎ 965-460 511
Open 9am to 9pm Mondays to Fridays.

C/ Bernabé del Campo 26   ☎ 966-612 596
Open 10am to 1.30pm and 4.30 to 8pm Mondays to Fridays.

C/ Mario Pastro Sempere 43   ☎ 965-439 453
Open 10am to 1.30pm and 4.30 to 8pm Mondays to Fridays.

Guardamar   C/ Colón 60   ☎ 965-728 610
del Segura   Open 9am to 1.30pm and 4.30 to 8pm Mondays to Fridays.

Orihuela   Plaza Marqués de Rafal 1   ☎ 965-302 497
Open 10.30am to 2pm and 5 to 8pm Mondays to Fridays.

Pilar de   C/ Carretillas 19   ☎ 965-351 124
la Horadada   Open 9am to 2pm and 5 to 9pm Mondays to Fridays.

Rojales   C/ Zulaida 20   ☎ 966-712 038
Open 11.30am to 1pm and 5 to 8pm Mondays to Fridays.

Santa Pola   C/ Elche 26   ☎ 966-692 773
Open 9.30am to 1.30pm and 4.30 to 8pm Mondays to Fridays.

Torrevieja   C/ Joaquín Chapaprieta 39   ☎ 965-706 164
Open 9am to 3pm and 4 to 9pm Mondays to Fridays.

Area Five – Mar Menor

San Javier   Plaza Gardá Alix s/n
Open 10am to 1.30pm and 5 to 8pm Mondays to Fridays.

Santiago de   C/ Padre Juan s/n
la Ribera   Open 9am to 1.30pm and 5 to 8pm Mondays to Fridays.

English-language Libraries

Several English-language libraries operate around the coast, often run by
volunteers. There's usually an annual subscription fee.

Area One – Marina Alta

Denia   English Lending Library, Passeig del Saladar

Area Two – Marina Baja

Altea   Altea English Library, Bar Miramar 1°   ☎ 965-844 707

Benidorm   European Library, C/ Juan Fuster, Edif
Aquarium 3, 3°   ☎ 966-804 781
This municipal library has books in Dutch, English, French,
German and Italian as well as a good selection of Spanish books
for foreigners. Open 10.15am to 1.30pm and 5 to 8pm (closed in
July).

Area Three – Alicante

Campello   International Library, Club Centro, C/ Castilla

Other ways of borrowing English-language books include the following:

● Some expatriate clubs and associations have lending library facilities,
  usually small (but better than nothing!) and there may be a small
  charge or lending facilities may be limited to members.

● Most international schools have good libraries and parents may be
  allowed to borrow books.

● Get together with friends and start your own library or reading circle!

PETS

Importing a Pet

If you plan to bring your pet to the Costa Blanca (and many people do), you should check the latest regulations, particularly if you're bringing a pet from the UK or another country with strict quarantine regulations. Bear in mind that you may have to return to the UK at short notice and need to take your pet with you.

Spanish Regulations

Travellers to Spain may bring a maximum of two pets with them and a rabies vaccination is usually compulsory, although accompanied pets entering Spain directly from the UK (i.e. by air or sea) and pets under three months old are exempt. If a rabies vaccination is given, it must be administered not more than a month and no more than 12 months before the pet enters Spain. **If you come to Spain via France (e.g. if you drive to Spain), a rabies vaccination is compulsory.**

You also need two official certificates: one signed and stamped by a registered vet declaring that the animal has been vaccinated against rabies, and the other signed by the owner declaring that the animal has been under his supervision for at least three months before entering Spain. Both certificates are in Spanish and English, and are valid for 15 days **only** after signing. You can obtain the certificates from Spanish consulates abroad (they're downloadable from some consulate websites).

Pets other than dogs, cats, hamsters and rabbits may require a special import licence, and the importation of 'exotic' animals is generally prohibited. All international airports and sea ports in Spain accept entry by animals, but you should inform the carrier beforehand.

British Regulations

In 2000, the UK introduced a pilot 'Pet Travel Scheme (PETS)', which replaced quarantine for qualifying cats and dogs. Under the scheme, now included under the EU Pet Passport scheme, pets must be microchipped (they have a microchip inserted in their neck) and vaccinated against rabies and undergo a blood test and they're issued with an EU pet passport. **Note, however, that the EU pet passport isn't issued until six months AFTER all the above have been carried out!** In the UK EU pet passports are issued by Local Veterinary Inspectors (LVI) only. In other EU countries passports are issued by all registered vets.

The scheme is restricted to animals imported from rabies-free countries and countries where rabies is under control – initially 22 European countries, but if successful it's expected to be extended to other countries, including North America. However, the current quarantine laws will remain in place for pets coming from Eastern Europe, Africa, Asia and South America. To qualify, pets must travel by sea via Dover, Newhaven, Plymouth, Poole or Portsmouth, by train via the Channel Tunnel or via Gatwick, Heathrow or Manchester airports. Only certain carriers are licensed to carry animals and these are listed on the Department for Environment, Food and Rural Affairs (DEFRA) website (💻 www.defra. gov.uk/animalh/quarantine). Additional information is available from DEFRA (☎ UK 0870-241 1710, ✉ pets.helpline@defra.gsi.gov.uk).

The new regulations cost pet owners around GB£200 (for a microchip, rabies vaccination and blood test), plus GB£60 per year for annual booster vaccinations and around GB£20 for a border check. Shop around and compare fees charged by a number of veterinary surgeons.

British owners must complete an Application for a Ministry Export Certificate for dogs, cats and rabies susceptible animals (form EXA1), available from DEFRA at the above address. DEFRA will contact a vet you've named on the form and he will perform a health inspection. You will then receive an export health certificate, which must be issued no more than 30 days before your entry into another EU country with your pet.

Further information is available from DEFRA (☎ UK 020-7904 6000 or ☎ 020-7238 6951, ✉ pets.helpline@defra.gsi.gov.uk).

Cats

Cats should be vaccinated against feline gastro-enteritis, typhus, feline leukaemia virus and feline enteritis. Cats also need regular treatment against fleas – powder or collars are effective.

You should have your cat neutered, unless you plan to breed from it, as there's a plague of stray and unwanted cats on the Costa Blanca, and there's little point in adding to the already overlarge population.

Dogs

When you arrive on the Costa Blanca, you must register your dog and have it microchipped – most vets provide this service, which costs from €30. The microchip contains the owner's name and address, so don't forget to change it if you move. Dogs should be kept on a lead at all times and are generally not allowed in public parks, on beaches (some permit dogs from October to April) or in restaurants, cafes or shops. Bear in mind that the Spanish aren't generally enthusiastic about dogs in public places and it's probably best to leave them at home.

If you bring your dog to the Costa Blanca, the following information may be useful:

● **Cleaning Up** – Many streets on the Costa Blanca are a minefield of dog excrement. **Always clean up after your dog.** It's illegal not to and you can be fined in many towns.

● **Leishmaniasis** – Leishmaniasis (also called Mediterranean or sandfly disease), which is carried by a type of mosquito and is almost always fatal, is common on the Costa Blanca. There are some special collars on the market, which claim to provide protection, but the only sure way of preventing this disease in your dog is to keep him inside from dusk to dawn and fit windows and doors with fly screens. For most dog owners, this isn't practical, particularly during the summer when everyone's outside. However, according to experts, this is the only effective way to protect your dog.

● **Poison** – If you walk your dog in rural areas, beware of poisoned bait (usually meat laced with strychnine) left by hunters and poachers to control predators such as foxes (an illegal practice), as many dogs have died as a result. Fit your dog with a muzzle to prevent it eating while out in a rural area.

● **Processionary Caterpillars** – Certain pine trees in many areas on the Costa Blanca are favoured by the processionary caterpillar moth, which lays its eggs in the branches. The caterpillars hatch in the early spring and descend in procession to the ground, where they bury themselves. Their hairs are extremely toxic to animals (fatal in many cases) and cause intense irritation in humans. The caterpillars are easy to identify from their striped, hairy bodies (about 6cm long) and by the fact that they attach themselves to each other and 'parade' (hence their name). If you have these caterpillars in trees on your property, you can have the trees treated. Pine trees in many public areas are treated and it's hoped that the caterpillar will eventually be exterminated. However, many tree owners don't treat their pines, so you should be vigilant.

● **Summer Temperatures** – Bear in mind that the Costa Blanca is very hot from June to October and dogs need plenty of fresh water and shade. **Never leave your dog in a car in the summer, even in the shade.**

- **Ticks & Leeches** – Ticks infest rural areas on the Costa Blanca (mainly from sheep and goat herds) and are particularly virulent in early spring. You can buy tick collars or capsules to prevent these. Treatment takes about a week to become effective and needs repeating every three to six months. Leeches are common in water (fresh or stagnant) – the best prevention is to not allow your dog to go in water and especially not to drink from it. Leeches can only be removed by vets.

- **Vaccinations – Vaccinate your dog against rabies (preferably before arrival), leptospirosis, parvovirus, hepatitis, distemper and kennel cough.** Vaccinations must be renewed every year.

Dangerous Dogs

Spain has strict regulations on ownership of certain breeds of dog regarded as dangerous, namely the Akita, American Staffordshire Terrier, Dogo Argentino, Fila Brasileirso, Japanese Tosa, Pit Bull, Rottweiler and Staffordshire Bull Terrier. 'Dangerous' breeds also include dogs that have all or most of the following characteristics: a strong and powerful appearance; a strong character; short hair; shoulder height between 50 and 70cm and weight over 20kg (44lb); square and robust head with large jaws; wide and short neck; broad and deep chest; robust fore legs and muscular hind legs. If you aren't sure whether your dog has most of these 'monster' characteristics, you should consult your vet. Owners of such dogs must be over 18, have no criminal record, undergo psychological and physical tests, have compulsory third party insurance for €120,000 and have a special licence (available only from local councils). Dangerous dogs must be muzzled and kept on a lead no longer than 2m in public places.

> **Pet thieves operate on the Costa Blanca and often steal to order. If you have an unusual and/or expensive breed of dog or cat, look after it and don't let it roam free.**

Kennels & Catteries

There's a reasonable choice of kennels and catteries on the Costa Blanca, many of which are located on the outskirts of towns or in the country. Services and facilities vary greatly and you may wish to check these before you leave your dog or cat there. Check also that the establishment is registered with the local authorities – ask to see a current opening licence (*licencia de apertura*). Fees start at around €4 per day for a cat and €6 for a small dog. Many kennels offer discounts for long stays. Pets must be vaccinated in order to stay at a kennels. Kennels and catteries advertise in the English-language press and at vet clinics.

If you cannot bear the thought of your dog or cat being cooped up, alternatives are a house- and dog-sitter (this service is quite common on the Costa Blanca, but check the sitter's references) or a private residence – some people look after dogs or cats in their own homes (again you should ask for references). These services are considerably more expensive than kennels, but your pet should receive better care and attention.

Vets

There are plenty of vets on the Costa Blanca – most large urbanisations have one and there are several in towns – and most of them speak English. Vets are generally highly trained and offer an excellent (if expensive) service as well as invaluable advice about looking after your pet. Clinics usually have a 24-hour emergency service. Ask around for recommendations or look in the English-language press, where many advertise, or the yellow pages. Vets also sell animal food and accessories, although cheaper dog and cat food is sold at supermarkets and hypermarkets.

REFUSE

Refuse is collected daily in most localities on the Costa Blanca and usually at night (don't be surprised to hear the clang of bins at 2am), although the service in some urbanisations, villages and remote areas may be less frequent. There may be large bins at various points on streets, or complexes may have a refuse point or small shed where bins are kept. For hygienic reasons you're supposed to put rubbish out after a certain time (usually 9pm) and some areas impose a fine for not respecting this. If a bin is full, put your rubbish in another – don't be tempted to leave your rubbish outside a bin, as local dogs and cats will shred bags and scatter the contents everywhere, and the refuse collectors won't clear it up.

Some areas have installed innovative 'ecological islands', which consist of silver funnels on the pavement leading to underground containers, which are emptied daily. These improve the appearance of the area and don't smell.

Recycling

Recycling has improved a lot on the coast in recent years and you can now recycle a substantial part of household waste reasonably easily. It's worth getting into the habit of recycling, as it will be compulsory by 2007, when Spain will be obliged to comply with the EU directive of separating household rubbish for recycling. Recycling containers can be found all over the coast, often next to general rubbish bins, and are colour-coded as follows:

- **Dark Blue** – Paper (including newspapers and cardboard);

- **Green** – Glass (any colour) but no corks or bottle tops;

- **Yellow** – Plastics (such as water bottles, margarine, yoghurt and egg cartons, cellophane, string bags from fruit), tins (drink and food) and cartons (milk and juice, e.g. Tetra-Brik);

- **Yellow Metal** – Clothes, shoes and household fabrics. You should put items in bags before putting them into the bin and only recycle items in a good state of repair.

Batteries

Most areas have battery collection points. If you cannot find one, ask at your council. It's worth making the effort, as batteries are one of the most contaminating objects in household rubbish.

Household Goods

Refuse collectors don't usually take household goods (furniture, appliances, etc.), but all councils and many urbanisations provide a household goods collection service, which is usually made once a week. The service will generally take anything, but it's best to check beforehand. The usual procedure is to phone and enquire which day collections are made in your area and arrange where to leave your unwanted goods.

When you buy a new household appliance, many large shops include the removal of the old appliance in their price. Smaller shops may offer this service but at extra cost.

Car Waste

Just about any waste from a car (e.g. oil, batteries, tyres) can be disposed of safely at a reputable garage, many of which have 'green points' where you can leave potentially contaminating material.

Garden Waste

Many towns and urbanisations have disposal points for garden waste (e.g. grass cuttings and branches). If you cannot find a point, ask at your local council or community office. Don't leave garden rubbish anywhere else, as it's a serious fire hazard and also attracts rats and other vermin.

REGISTRATION

Many foreign residents live on the Costa Blanca without registering with their local council. Registration (*empadronamiento*) – a process similar to registering on the electoral roll in the UK – isn't compulsory, but it provides benefits for both you and the council. Local councils in Spain receive money (from €60 per person) from the central and regional governments based on the number of registered inhabitants in the locality. Regional governments also provide education, police and health services based on the population figures. If residents don't register, the amount of money paid to the local council is less than it should be, meaning that local services are under-funded and over-stretched, and some additional services (e.g. extra classrooms or police) aren't provided.

Other benefits of registering include:

● Better access to local sports facilities and leisure activities – subsidies are often available for registered residents, and local residents are given priority;

● Inclusion on the electoral roll, which allows EU nationals to vote in local elections.

Note that *empadronamiento* is a different process from obtaining a residence permit and doesn't necessarily mean you're liable for Spanish taxes, although if you're a resident you may have to pay income tax and all property owners are liable for property taxes. In some cases you must register, e.g. if you want to enrol your child at a local state school.

Registering is a straightforward process: you simply go to your local council offices, fill in a form, and show some form of identification and proof that you're living in a property in the area (e.g. title deeds, rental contract, utility bill in your name). Many councils claim that if all foreign residents were registered, provisions and facilities would improve markedly.

RESIDENCE PERMITS

EEA Nationals

EEA nationals in full-time employment (as an employee or self-employed) **and** paying Spanish taxes (income tax and social security) or in full-time education don't require a residence permit. Many residents have found, however, that it's useful to have one if you need to prove your identity (its credit card size is handier than a passport) and some banks require a residence permit for transactions such as opening a resident's bank account or taking out a resident's mortgage. Residence permits can usually be obtained quite quickly from a national police station once you've presented proof of identity, three photographs and evidence that you're employed or studying in Spain.

Retirees

If you're retired, you must apply for official resident status. Once you've arrived in Spain, you should go to your nearest national police station within 15 days of arrival and apply for a residence permit. At the police station you should go to the foreigners' department, where there may be someone who speaks English, French or German, although at locations inland this is less likely.

Information about what's required (although not necessarily the definitive details!) is available online (in Spanish only) from the Ministry of the Interior website (⌨ www.mir.es), which also includes downloadable forms. The Ministry runs a free telephone helpline (☎ 900-150 000) during office hours.

You will need to fill in the required form and take along the following documents:

● Your passport and a photocopy of the pages showing your particulars;

● Three photographs (passport size);

● Proof you have sufficient funds to support yourself (e.g. bank statements);

● Proof of private medical insurance or that you're entitled to medical treatment under the Spanish public health system.

Once you've presented the correct documentation, your application is processed and the authorities contact you when your permit is ready (this takes from one to six months). In the meantime you're given a receipt for your application and this serves as proof that you've applied for residence. Once you've been notified, you must go to the police station in Alicante to collect your permit and have your fingerprints taken for police records. **Note that fingerprints can only be taken at the Alicante national police station.**

Family Members

The applicant's family members, including spouse and children under 21, may also apply for residence with the main application. Children are included on one of their parents' residence permit. Each family member needs to fill in the required form and take along the following documents:

● Passport and a photocopy of the pages showing the particulars;

● Three photographs (passport size);

● A certificate of good health (not always required);

● A document proving the family link (e.g. marriage certificate, birth certificate, family book).

If family members don't plan to work, the main applicant must prove that sufficient funds are available to support the whole family and that each family member has medical insurance.

Documents that aren't in Spanish (e.g. marriage certificate, birth certificate) must be translated by an official translator (*traductor oficial*). The processing procedure is the same as for retirees (see above).

Non-EEA Nationals

Obtaining a residence permit is considerably more difficult for non-EEA nationals and the documentation required more complicated. First you must usually obtain a residence visa from a Spanish consulate in your home country **before** you arrive in Spain. Regulations often change and, before applying, you should check the latest requirements with a Spanish consulate or embassy in your home country. **Don't be tempted to come to Spain with a tourist visa and stay on; if you're caught, you will be deported home and possibly not allowed back.**

Once you've arrived in Spain, you should go to Alicante national police station to apply for a residence and work permit. Owing to a recent backlog in applications and subsequent lengthy queues, the authorities have introduced an appointment system for non-EU nationals. To arrange an appointment you should ring ☎ 965-019 315, 965-019 325 or 965-019 32 between 9am and 2pm Mondays to Fridays.

National Police Stations

National police stations with a foreigners' office on the Costa Blanca can be found at the following locations:

Area One – Marina Alta

Denia	C/ Castell d'Olimbroi 5 Open 9am to 2pm Mondays to Fridays.	☎ 966-420 555

Area Two – Marina Baja

Benidorm	C/ Apolo XI 36 Open 9am to 2pm Mondays to Fridays.	☎ 965-855 308

Area Three – Alicante

Alicante	C/ Ebanistería 4–6 Open 9am to 2pm Mondays to Fridays.	☎ 965-019 300

Area Four – Vega Baja

Orihuela	C/ Sol 34 Open 9am to 2pm Mondays to Fridays.	☎ 965-303 204

SERVICES

A full range of services is available on the Costa Blanca, including building, carpentry, electrical installation and maintenance, and plumbing, and numerous companies, both Spanish and foreign, offer a wide range of services. Many companies provide services throughout the coast, although those located in Alicante may be reluctant to travel far along the coast, those centred at the north or south end may only serve areas on that part of the coast, and some companies may not travel to inland locations.

Most companies and businesses on the coast are bona fide and have a good reputation (and wish to keep it), offering a full guarantee for both goods and services and providing an official bill. Some companies and individuals, however, are little more than 'cowboy' outfits, operating illegally in order to pocket as much cash as possible before doing a vanishing act. Be very wary of companies or individuals with the following characteristics – they're usually foreign (mostly British) and, if they do a bad job or provide faulty goods, you have no means of tracing them to complain and no legal redress:

● Their only means of contact is a mobile phone (mobiles with cards aren't registered and their owners cannot be traced);

● They cannot provide a fiscal number (a *CIF* in the case of a company, *NIF* or *NIE* in the case of an individual), which should be printed on their quotes, receipts, etc;

- They will accept cash payment only. **It's tempting to pay in cash, as you save 16 per cent VAT, but without a bill you have no guarantee, no means of complaining and no proof that you've paid!**

Finding a Company

- Word-of-mouth and references are the best ways of finding a reputable company that does a good job. Ask neighbours and friends, and ask to see examples of goods and/or services.

- A comprehensive list of companies in Alicante province is provided in the yellow pages (💻 www.paginasamarillas.es). An index in Spanish and English can be found at the front of the directory.

- Local press, both Spanish and English, include advertisements for goods and services. *Costa Blanca News* has a good selection.

With the current boom in construction and related industries on the coast it can be difficult to obtain many services quickly. Practically all builders, carpenters, electricians and plumbers are snowed under, so you must book their services several weeks in advance, and many often don't turn up at the arranged time. If you need any work done, arm yourself with patience!

TELEPHONE

Telephone technology on the Costa Blanca is as good as anywhere in Western Europe and phone lines are available almost everywhere except the most remote rural areas. Telephone lines are provided only by Telefónica (the monopoly holder), but calls are provided by numerous companies and there are some good deals available.

Line Installation & Registration

If you require a phone line, go to a Telefónica office, phone ☎ 1004 or fill in a form online (💻 www.telefonica.net). You must submit or send proof of identity and a copy of your title deeds or rental contract. Installation of a new line costs around €110 plus 16 per cent VAT and, if the infrastructure is already in place, takes around a week. Installation in remote areas (if possible) takes considerably longer and costs are far higher. Note that, if you live in a house without an existing line, you're responsible for laying the phone line from the house to the road.

If you move into a house with a phone line already installed, you can arrange with the previous owner or occupant to have the account transferred to your name when you move in. Don't forget to check that previous bills have been paid.

Telefónica has just introduced a telephone helpline service in English in response to demand from foreign residents. The service (☎ 952-449 020) includes phone and internet connection and a number of other products and services as well as tariff information. The service cannot yet deal with billing and technical problems, which must be referred to the usual Telefónica number (☎ 1004).

Costs

Line rental costs around €13 plus VAT per month. Call charges vary with the service provider, and there are numerous companies offering good deals. You should shop around for the best prices and consider registering with several companies. Registration usually costs nothing and many companies don't make a monthly charge.

The main companies operating on the Costa Blanca are:

● **Auna** – ☎ 015, 🖳 www.auna.es;

● **Spantel** – ☎ 902-020 202, 🖳 www.span-tel.com;

● **Tele2** – ☎ 900-760 772, 🖳 www.tele2.es;

● **TeleConnect** – ☎ 900-902 122, 🖳 www.teleconnect.es;

● **Telefónica** – ☎ 1004, 🖳 www.telefonica.es.

Mobile Phones

You can buy mobile phones from numerous outlets on the Costa Blanca, including supermarkets, hypermarkets, department stores and specialist shops. Prices vary tremendously according to the type and make of phone, the cheapest model costing around €60 (including €30 in calls).

There are three mobile phone companies in Spain:

● **Amena** – ☎ 1474, 🖳 www.amena.es;

- **Movistar** – ☎ 1485 (from a fixed line), ☎ 609 (from a mobile), 💻 www. movistar.net;

- **Vodafone** – ☎ 1444 (from a fixed line), ☎ 123 (from a mobile), 💻 www.vodafone.es.

There are two options when it comes to choosing a mobile, and it's wise to weigh up the advantages and disadvantages before you make a purchase:

- **Card Phone** – You buy a phone (which may be expensive) and pay for calls as you make them. New phones usually come with a fixed amount in calls already in the card (e.g. €30) and you top up the card when it runs out. Cards can be topped up for €5, €10, €20, €30 and €50 at some cash machines and in numerous establishments, including supermarkets, petrol stations, newsagents and specialist shops.

- **Contract Phone** – You pay a certain amount each month, irrespective of the number of calls you make, but may pay little or nothing for the phone itself. You must usually provide proof of accommodation and have a bank account, as payment must be made by direct debit.

If you plan to use a mobile phone a lot, you're usually better off with a contract than a card phone.

Rates for calls depend on where and when you're calling, and it's worth shopping around for the best deal, as prices can vary more than 100 per cent between companies. However, it's almost always more expensive to phone anywhere by mobile phone than by fixed phone and usually costs more to call another mobile than a fixed line number.

Mobile phone theft is rife on the Costa Blanca. Don't leave your phone unattended anywhere, even for a second, and if you have an expensive phone, don't flash it around.

Internet

Internet access is widely available on the Costa Blanca from many companies, including most telephone companies (see **Telephone** above). Rates and deals vary greatly according to when you use the internet and how often. Most companies offer special deals and prices, and it's worth shopping around to get the best rates for your usage.

Broadband

Broadband (ADSL) technology is available on the Costa Blanca, but not yet in all areas. As a general rule, it's available in the main towns (e.g. Alicante,

Denia and Torrevieja) and some large urbanisations but not in rural areas. To find out if broadband is available in a certain area, phone Telefónica (☎ 1004) and provide your telephone number or, if you haven't bought or rented a property and need to find out before you commit yourself, a neighbour's number. Make sure it's an immediate neighbour, as a connection may be available in one street but not in an adjacent one.

There are numerous broadband providers and competition is intense. Shop around, as prices and conditions vary considerably, although 24-hour access usually costs around €40 per month.

As with all services, it's best to use a reputable operator (and preferably one that invests in the service) with good customer service. Complaints about broadband services are common – usually because the speed of the connection is slow or it's difficult to terminate a contract.

There are around 50 broadband providers in Spain, but the main ones are:

● **Telefónica** – The largest, with over 1 million clients (☎1004 and 🖥 www.telefonica.net);

● **Terra** – An affiliate of Telefónica, with around 160,000 clients (☎ 902-152 025, 🖥 www.terra.es);

● **Tiscali** – The smallest but fastest growing, with 70,000 clients (☎ 902-765 657, 🖥 www.tiscali.es);

● **Wanadoo** – The second-largest, with over 180,000 clients (☎ 902-011 902, 🖥 www.wanadoo.es);

● **Ya.Com** – Has over 100,000 clients (🖥 www.ya.com).

Internet Cafes

All towns on the Costa Blanca have internet cafes (*cibercafés*) or premises where you can surf the internet and check your emails. Some (but by no means all) offer broadband connection. Prices are around €3 per hour. You can also use the internet at public libraries, although use is usually limited to an hour and you may have to wait for a computer. Telephone kiosks (*locutorios telefónicos*) may also provide internet services. Some of the many internet cafes are situated at the following venues:

Area One – Marina Alta

Calpe	Cybercenter, C/ Portalet 18	☎ 965-839 035
Denia	Cibercafé CB, C/ Senija 5	☎ 966-420 321

Jávea	Café Internet Group, Rda Norte 9	☎ 965-794 796
	E Place, Arenal de Jávea 66	☎ 965-795 210
Teulada	C/ Búho 7	☎ 965-744 616

Area Two – Marina Baja

Alfaz del Pi	Albir Internet Café, C/ Narciso Yepes 4, Albir	☎ 966-864 492
Altea	Red Attack, C/ Zubeldia 9	☎ 966-881 291
Benidorm	Bermay 22, C/ Lepanto 9, Rincón de Loix	☎ 965-855 229
	Moes, C/ Ruzafa 6, Rincón de Loix	☎ 966-804 719

Area Three – Alicante

Alicante	CBR Ciber, C/ Tte Alvarez Soto 8	☎ 965-141 425
	Nohayhuevos, C/ Padre Mariana 22	☎ 965-205 085.

Area Four – Vega Baja

Elche	Aldea Digital, Avda Joan Carlos I 61	☎ 965-427 927
Orihuela Costa	Jan Wallin, Ctra Alicante-Cartagena 23	☎ 966-730 605
	Torpling Intenational, Urb Zenia s/n	☎ 966-761 185
Santa Pola	El Paseo de la Iglesia, C/ Iglesia 8	☎ 966-694 246
Torrevieja	Urb El Limonar 3	☎ 966-786 793

TELEVISION & RADIO

Television and radio reception is excellent in most areas of the coast, but there are no local English-language television (TV) channels. Spanish television broadcasts in Spanish with occasional original version films shown on La 2 channel, but to watch English-language TV regularly you must install satellite TV (see below). Note that there's no TV or radio licence.

Television Standards

Televisions and video recorders operating on the British (PAL-I), French (SECAM) or North American (NTSC) systems won't work in Spain, which, along with most other continental European countries, uses the PAL B/G standard. You can buy a multi-standard European TV (and VCR) containing automatic circuitry that switches between different systems. Some multi-standard TVs also include the North American NTSC standard and have an NTSC-in jack plus connection allowing you to play back American videos. A standard British, French or US TV can be modified. The same applies to foreign video recorders, which won't operate with a Spanish TV unless they're dual-standard.

Satellite TV

There are generally two options for English-language satellite TV and both are widely available on the Costa Blanca: a basic satellite package with BBC and ITV channels (no Sky) plus many European channels, costing from around €500 per year; or a Sky satellite package with Sky, BBC and ITV channels costing from around €550. Installation is usually straightforward and numerous specialist companies operate on the coast, where competition is keen. Many advertise in the expatriate press (e.g. *Costa Blanca News*), but shop around and compare prices (which vary greatly), and ask friends and neighbours for recommendations. **Be wary of companies offering cut-price offers and check a company's credentials – satellite companies are notorious for 'disappearing', leaving customers with systems that don't work.**

Before installing a satellite dish, you must check whether you need permission from your landlord or the local authorities. Some towns and buildings (such as apartment blocks) have strict laws regarding the positioning of antennae, although generally owners can mount a dish almost anywhere without receiving complaints.

Radio

There are now several English-language radio stations broadcasting on the Costa Blanca. Most offer a similar pattern of chat shows and music with news, sports and traffic bulletins. Some offer coverage of local sporting events.

- **Costa Blanca FM** – Broadcasts in the southern section only on 106FM;

- **Holiday FM** – Broadcasts on 102.6 and 102.8FM (🖳 www.holiday fm.co.uk);

- **Onda Cero International (OCI)** – Broadcasts on 94.6FM (☎ 966-882 830);

- **Radio Altea** – Broadcasts in English on Saturdays from 3 to 4pm on 107.6FM (☎ 965-845 706, 🖳 www.radioaltea.com);

- **Spectrum FM** – Broadcasts on 88.2FM in the Benidorm area, 96.9FM around Elche and 105.1FM around Torrevieja (☎ 902-105 551, 🖳 www.spectrumfm.net);

- **Sunshine FM** – Broadcasts on 102.6FM in La Manga and on 102.8FM in the rest of the Costa Blanca (☎ 966-761 291, 🖳 www.holiday fmradio.com).

UTILITIES

Electricity

The electricity supply in Spain has been liberalised and, in theory, you can now choose who supplies your electricity, but in practice on the Costa Blanca there's only one supplier, Iberdrola (☎ 901-202 020, 🖳 www. iberdrola.es), one of Spain's largest electricity companies, and no other companies currently show any interest in providing an alternative. The service is generally reasonable, although power cuts are common, particularly during storms, and some areas are prone to occasional power surges. Consumer protection groups claim that in 2003 each Iberdrola client was without power for an average of three hours, and power cuts were common in summer 2004, mainly due to poor infrastructure. Iberdrola claims to be investing vast sums of money in improvements to the supply.

Most communications to do with electricity (except paying the bill) can be made by telephone or online and you shouldn't have to go to an office in person. Note that when you contact Iberdrola you must provide your supply number (*contrato de suministro*), found at the top left of your bill. Staff who answer the phone don't usually speak English.

Iberdrola has offices (known as *Agencia Iberdrola*) or agencies (known as *Punto Iberdrola* and located within a shop) in the main towns on the coast (take plenty to read – queues are **very** long). There may be staff who speak English, but don't count on it. Offices, generally open from 9am to 2pm and from 4 or 5pm to 7 or 8pm Mondays to Fridays, are situated at the following locations:

Area One – Marina Alta

Denia   Agencia Iberdrola, C/ Valencia 36

Jávea   Punto Iberdrola, Gabrial Sapena, C/ Sant Pere Martir 2

Area Two – Marina Baja

Altea   Punto Iberdrola, Master Cadena, C/ Vora la Via 1, Edif Llimera

Benidorm   Agencia Iberdrola, C/ Antonio Ramos Carratala 18

Area Three – Alicante

Alicante   Agencia Iberdrola, C/ Calderón de la Barca 16

San Juan   Agencia Iberdrola, C/ Mar 50

Area Four – Vega Baja

Orihuela   Punto Iberdrola, Electrovisión Orihuela, C/ Duque de
               Tamamés 18

Pilar de   Punto Iberdrola, Ondagua, C/ Escultor Rivera Girona 42
la Horadada

Torrevieja Agencia Iberdrola, C/ Orihuela 13

Area Five – Mar Menor

Murcia   Agencia Iberdrola, C/ de los Pinos 7

San Javier Punto Iberdrola, Master Cadena Establecimiento Cortado,
               C/ Dr Pardo López 11

Costs

Electricity currently costs €0.08 per kwh. In addition you pay a monthly standing charge, including electricity tax (around 5 per cent) and VAT at 16 per cent.

Bills

Bills can be paid by direct debit, in most banks or at electricity offices. Bills are issued every two months and if you pay by direct debit there's usually a week between the bill being sent and the bank paying for it.

Moving In

When you move into a property, you should immediately make sure that the electricity supply hasn't been cut off and that bills will be sent to you. The procedure to follow depends on the type of property:

Resale Properties

If you're taking over the electricity supply from the previous owner, there are two possible procedures, described below:

1. Telephone Iberdrola and give the electricity supply number, your details and a bank account number. The next bill should then be sent to you and paid by your bank. Although this method is simpler, the electricity contract remains in the previous owner's name and he might cancel the contract in the future, with the result that your supply could be cut off without warning!

2. Arrange with the previous owner to change the electricity contract into your name as soon as you move in. This is done by means of a simple document signed by the previous owner giving his authorisation. This document, which costs around €30, is sent with copies of the identity papers (passport or residence permit) of both previous and new owners to Iberdrola. A *gestor* can do the paperwork for you for a small charge.

New Properties

In order to obtain an electricity supply to a newly built property, you will need an electricity certificate (*boletín de electricidad*) from the developer. This certificate must be sent to Iberdrola, who then send an electrician to the property to connect the supply, which costs from €90 to €110 depending on the power of the supply. Note that it takes at least ten days to be connected and in some areas new owners are currently having to wait much longer, simply because Iberdrola cannot keep up with the demand.

Rental Properties

Under most rental contracts you're responsible for the electricity charges. You can either pay the electricity bills at a bank or telephone Iberdrola with your bank details and arrange for bills to be paid by direct debit.

GAS

Mains Gas

Mains gas is currently available only in Alicante and Elche and is provided by Gas Natural (Customer Service ☎ 900-760 760, Repairs and Emergencies ☎ 900-750 750). Gas Natural provides online services (🖳 www.gasnatural.com), including meter reading, which can also be done by phone (☎ 900-770 770).

Bottled Gas

Bottled gas (*butano*) provides a popular and economical means of heating and cooking and is widely available. Bottles are available in 12.5kg and 35kg sizes, costing around €8.50 and €24 respectively, and can be delivered to your home or collected from an authorised point. Small (camping size) bottles can be bought at Repsol service stations. Repsol Butano is the official distributor on the Costa Blanca and has representatives in all main towns, as follows:

Area One – Marina Alta

Benissa	Gas Benissa, Avda País Valenciano 89	☎ 965-733 273
Benitachell	Gasante SL, Ctra Jávea s/n	☎ 966-494 013
Calpe	Butano Candela, C/ Benissa 2 🖥 www.butano-altea.com.	☎ 965-830 789
Denia	Such y Peris SL, C/ Colóm 69	☎ 965-781 111
Jávea	Gasante SL, C/ Virgen de los Angeles 7	☎ 965-791 566

Area Two – Marina Baja

Alfaz del Pi	Butano Candela, C/ La Mar 32, Altea 🖥 www.butano-altea.com	☎ 965-842 730
Altea	Butano Candela, C/ La Mar 32 🖥 www.butano-altea.com	☎ 965-842 730
Benidorm	Benigás SL, C/ Tomñsa Ortuño 6, Rincón de Loix	☎ 965-855 091
Callosa d' En Sarrià	Gas Callosa, C/ Azorín 1 🖥 www.gascallosa.com	☎ 965-820 213
La Nucia	José Mª Pérez Fernández, C/ L'Ermita 101	☎ 966-895 312
Villajoyosa	Hontehijos, C/ Ciudad de Valencia 37	☎ 965-890 609

Area Three – Alicante

Alicante	Repsol Butano, C/ Churruca 2-4	☎ 965-125 276
San Juan	Bernagás SA, Avda Rambla 8	☎ 965-655 714

Area Four – Vega Baja

Elche	Vicente Covés e Hijos, Ctra Aspe s/n	☎ 966-672 222
Guardamar del Segura	Hermanos Martí Pomares, C/ Ingeniero Mira 2	☎ 965-729 701

Orihuela	Eurogas Vegabaja SL, Avda La Vega 16	☎ 966-744 171
Santa Pola	Gas Butano Vicente Covés, C/ Virgen del Carmen 14	☎ 965-413 473
Torrevieja	Butano Repsol, C/ Gabriel Miró 6	☎ 965-710 937

Area Five – Mar Menor

La Manga	Repsol YPF SA, Urb Villas Romanas 33	☎ 968-337 064
Los Alcázares	López y Soto, C/ Meseguer 127	☎ 968-171 203
San Pedro del Pinatar	Establecimientos Sánchez SA, Bda Tárragas s/n	☎ 968-180 977

WATER

Water is supplied from the various reservoirs in the area and is provided by numerous private companies. For information on the water supplier in your area contact the local council or your community of owners' office. Water is inexpensive in most localities, although prices have risen in recent years.

The quality and taste of water vary, although tap water is safe to drink everywhere on the coast and it isn't necessary for hygiene reasons to buy bottled water. Some residents fill water bottles and containers from springs along the coast. Water from drinking fountains and springs is safe to drink unless there's a sign saying '*Agua No Potable*'.

In spite of the abundance of green areas and extensive irrigation, water is in short supply on the Costa Blanca, where rainfall is erratic – there may be not a drop of rain for months at a time and then downpours for several weeks – and droughts aren't uncommon. In autumn 2004 the Vega Baja area suffered from drought after months without rain, a situation that frequently repeats itself. There are currently desalination plants at Jávea, Pilar de la Horadada and on the Canal de Taibilla (north-west of Orihuela) and there are government plans to build new desalination plants in the Marina Alta, Marina Baja and in the Alicante area within the next few years.

Use every drop of water carefully!

Vilafamés

Appendices

Appendix A: PUBLICATIONS

English-language Newspapers & Magazines

CB Friday, C/ Sandunga 52, Denia (☎ 966-425 313, 🖳 www.think spain.com). Weekly newspaper published on Fridays, price €1.

The Broadsheet (☎ 915-237 480, 🖳 www.thebroadsheet.com). Monthly magazine about Spain in general with listings and articles about the Costa Blanca.

Costa Blanca News, CC Las Moriscas Local 10, Avda Juan Luís Peralta, 29629 Benalmadena Pueblo (☎ 952-448 730, 🖳 www.costablanca-news.com). Weekly newspaper (news, events and small ads) published on Fridays, price €1.

Everything Spain, Medway House, Lower Road, Forest Row, East Sussex RH18 5HE, UK (☎ 01342-828 700, 🖳 www.everythingSpainmag.co.uk). Bi-monthly lifestyle and property magazine.

Leader, Edif Centro Zenia 1º, Avda de Villamartín, Urb La Zenia, Orihuela Costa (☎ 966-730 057). Free weekly newspaper published on Tuesdays with news and events in southern Costa Blanca.

Living Spain, Albany Publishing Ltd, 9 High Street, Olney, Bucks MK46 4EB, UK (☎ 01234-710 992, 🖳 www.livingspain.co.uk). Bi-monthly lifestyle and property magazine.

Round Town News, Emilio Ortuño 6, 3º1, Benidorm (☎ 966-813 583 (Benidorm office), ☎ 965-705 204). Free weekly newspaper published on Tuesdays.

Spanish Magazine, Cambridge House South, Henry Street, Bath BA1 1JT, UK (☎ 01225-786 844). Bi-monthly lifestyle and property magazine.

Spanish Property Ads, Paseo de Almería 3, 2ª, Almería (☎ 902-195 880, ✉ info@vivaspain.com). Free monthly property magazine with property for sale on several Spanish *Costas* including the Costa Blanca and Mar Menor.

Villas &..., SKR Española, Apdo Correos 453, San Pedro de Alcántara (☎ 952-884 994, 🖳 www.villas.com). Monthly property magazine with articles in English, French, German and Spanish.

Books

The books listed below are just a selection of the hundreds written about Spain and the Costa Blanca. The publication title is followed by the author's name and the publisher's name (in brackets). Note that some titles may be out of print, but may still be obtainable from book shops or libraries. Books prefixed with an asterisk are recommended by the author.

Food & Wine

*AA Essential Food and Drink Spain (AA)

*The Best of Spanish Cooking, Janet Mendel (Santana)

The Complete Spanish Cookbook, Jacki Passmore (MacDonald)

A Flavour of Andalucía, Pepita Aris (Chartwell)

*Floyd on Spain, Keith Floyd (Michael Joseph)

The Food and Wine of Spain, Penelope Casas

Great Dishes of Spain, Robert Carrier (Boxtree)

*The 'La Ina' Book of Tapas, Elisabeth Luard (Schuster)

Mediterranean Seafood, Alan Davidson (Penguin)

**Rioja and its Wines, Ron Scarborough (Survival Books)

Shopping for Food and Wine in Spain (Santana)

*Spanish Cooking, Pepita Aris (Apple Press)

*The Spanish Kitchen, Pepita Aris (Wardlock)

The Spanish Table, Marimar Torres (Ebury Press)

*Spanish Wines, Jan Read (Mitchell Beazley)

The Tapas Book, Adrian Linssen & Sara Cleary (Apple Press)

*The Wine and Food of Spain, Jan Read & Maite Manjón (Wedenfeld & Nicolson)

The Wine Roads of Spain, M&K Millon (Santana)

**The Wines of Spain, Graeme Chesters (Survival Books)

Living & Working in Spain

**The Best Places to Buy a Home in Spain, Joanna Styles (Survival Books)

Choose Spain, John Howells & Bettie Magee (Gateway)

Introducing Spain, B.A. McCullagh & S. Wood (Harrap)

Life in a Spanish Town, M. Newton (Harrap)

**Living and Working in Spain, David Hampshire (Survival Books)

Simple Etiquette in Spain, Victoria Miranda McGuiness (Simple Books)

Spain: Business & Finance (Euromoney Books)

*You and the Law in Spain, David Searl (Santana)

Tourist Guides

AA Essential Explorer Spain (AA)

AA Essential Guide Costa Blanca & Alicante, Sally Roy (AA Publishing)

*Baedeker's Spain (Baedeker)

Berlitz Blueprint: Spain (Berlitz)

Berlitz Costa Blanca Guide (Berlitz Pocket Guides)

*Blue Guide to Spain: The Mainland, Ian Robertson (Ernest Benn)

*Cadogan Guides: Spain, Dana Facaros & Michael Pauls (Cadogan)

Costa Blanca, Mary Ann Gallagher (Dorling Kindersley)

Costa Blanca Insight Guide (Insight Guides)

Daytrips Spain & Portugal, Norman Renouf (Hastings House Pub)

Excursions in Eastern Spain, Nick Inman & Clara Villanueva (Santana)

*Eyewitness Travel Guide: Spain, Deni Bown (Dorling Kindersly)

Fielding's Paradors in Spain & Portugal, A. Hobbs (Fielding Worldwide)

*Fodor's Spain (Fodor's Travel Publications)

*Fodor's Exploring Spain (Fodor's Travel Publications)

*Frommer's Spain's Best-Loved Driving Tours, Mona King (IDG Books)

Guide to the Best of Spain (Turespaña)

The Insider's Guide to Spain, John de St. Jorre (Moorland)

*Insight Guides: Spain (APA Publications)

*Let's Go: Spain & Portugal (Macmillan)

*Lonely Planet Spain (Lonely Planet)

*Michelin Green Guide Spain (Michelin)

*Michelin Red Guide to Spain and Portugal (Michelin)

Off the Beaten Track: Spain, Barbara Mandell & Roger Penn (Moorland)

Rick Steves' Spain & Portugal, Rick Steves (John Muir Pubns)

Spain: A Phaidon Cultural Guide (Phaidon)

Spain at its Best, Robert Kane (Passport)

Spain: Everything Under the Sun, Tom Burns (Harrap Columbus)

Spain on Backroads (Duncan Petersen)

*Spain: The Rough Guide, Mark Ellingham & John Fisher (Rough Guides)

Special Places to Stay in Spain, Alistair Sawday (ASP)

Time Off in Spain and Portugal, Teresa Tinsley (Horizon)

Valencia & the Costa Blanca, Miles Roddis (Lonely Planet)

*Which? Guide to Spain (Consumers' Association and Hodder & Stoughton)

Travel Literature

*As I Walked Out One Midsummer Morning, Laurie Lee (Penguin)

*Between Hopes and Memories: A Spanish Journey, Michael Jacobs (Picador)

*The Bible in Spain, George Borrow (Century Travellers Series)

*The Bottlebrush Tree, Hugh Seymour-Davis (Black Swan)

*Cider With Rosie, Laurie Lee (Penguin)

*The Face of Spain, Gerald Brenan (Penguin)

Gatherings in Spain, Richard Ford (Dent Everyman)

*Handbook for Travellers in Spain, Richard Ford (Centaur Press)

Iberia, James A. Michener (Secker & Warburg)

*A Rose for Winter, Laurie Lee (Penguin)

*In Spain, Ted Walker (Corgi)

*Spain, Jan Morris (Penguin)

*Spanish Journeys: A Portrait of Spain, Adam Hopkins (Penguin)

*A Stranger in Spain, H.V. Morton (Methuen)

Miscellaneous

*Blood Sport: A History of Spanish Bullfighting, Timothy Mitchell

Cities of Spain, David Gilmour (Pimlico)

Dali: A Biography, Meredith Etheringon-Smith (Sinclair-Stevenson)

*A Day in the Life of Spain (Collins)

*Death in the Afternoon, Ernest Hemingway (Grafton)

Gardening in Spain, Marcelle Pitt (Santana)

The Gardens of Spain, Consuela M Correcher (Abrams)

*In Search of the Firedance, James Woodall (Sinclair-Stevenson)

The King, Jose Luis de Vilallonga (Weidenfeld)

Liz Parry's Spanish Phrase Book, Liz Parry (Santana Books)

Moorish Spain, Richard Fletcher (Phoenix)

*Nord Riley's Spain, Nord Riley (Lookout)

*On Foot Through Europe: A Trail Guide to Spain and Portugal, Craig Evans (Quill)

*Or I'll Dress You in Mourning, Larry Collins & Dominique Lapierre (Simon & Schuster)

*The New Spaniards, John Hooper (Penguin)

Selection of Wildflowers in Southern Spain, Betty Molesworth Allen (Santana)

Spain: A Literary Companion, Jimmy Burns (John Murray)

Spain's Wildlife, Eric Robins (Mirador)

The Story of Spain, Mark Williams (Santana)

*A Traveller's History (Phoenix)

Trekking in Spain, Marc S. Dubin (Lonely Planet)

*Walking Through Spain, Robin Nellands

*Wild Spain, Frederic Grunfeld & Teresa Farino (Ebury)

Wildlife Travelling Companion Spain, John Measures (Crowood Press)

*Xenophobe's Guide to the Spanish (Ravette)

Appendix B: Property Exhibitions

Property Exhibitions are commonplace in the UK and Ireland, and are popular with prospective property buyers who can get a good idea of what's available in Spain in general and make contact with estate agents and developers. The Costa Blanca is usually well-represented at property exhibitions and most large estate agents on the coast exhibit there. Below is a list of the main exhibitions organisers in the UK and Ireland. Note that you may be charged a small admission fee.

Homes Overseas (☎ 020-7939 9852, 💻 www.blendoncommunications. co.uk). Homes Overseas are the largest organisers of international property exhibitions and there are several exhibitions annually at a range of venues in both the UK and Ireland.

International Property Show (☎ 01962-736712, 💻 www.international propertyshow.com). The International Property Show is held several times a year in London and Manchester.

Spain on Show (UK only ☎ 0500-780878, 💻 www.spainonshow.com). Spain on Show specialises in property on the Costa Blanca and organises several annual property exhibitions at venues around the UK.

Town & Country (UK only ☎ 0845-230 6000, 💻 www.spanish property.uk.com). This large estate agency organises small Spanish property exhibitions at venues around the UK twice a month.

World Class Homes (☎ 0800-731 4713, 💻 www.worldclasshomes.co.uk). Exhibitions organised by World Class Homes show mainly UK property developers in small venues around the UK.

World of Property (☎ 01323-726040, 💻 www.outboundpublishing.com). The World of Property magazine publishers also organise three large property exhibitions a year, two in the south of the UK and one in the north.

APPENDIX C: USEFUL WEBSITES

The following list contains some of the many websites dedicated to the Costa Blanca and Spain in general. Town council and tourist board sites are included in the relevant chapters of this book, in addition to sites about particular aspects of the Costa Blanca.

Costa Blanca Websites

Comunitat Valenciana (💻 www.comunitatvalenciana.com). Official tourist guide to the whole region of the Comunidad Valenciana including the Costa Blanca.

Costa Blanca (💻 www.costablanca.org). The official tourist website for the area.

Costa Blanca.com (💻 www.info-costablanca.com). A general guide to the area.

This is Costa Blanca (💻 www.thisiscostablanca.com). General relocation information plus news and views.

Spanish Websites

About Spain (💻 www.aboutspain.net). Information about specific regions in Spain.

All About Spain (💻 www.red2000.com). General tourist information about Spain.

Escape to Spain (💻 www.escapetospain.co.uk). General information and a property guide to the Costa Blanca.

Ideal Spain (💻 www.idealspain.com). Information about many aspects of living in Spain.

Spain Alive (💻 www.spainalive.com). Information about specific areas of Spain as well as general information.

Spain Expat (💻 www.spainexpat.com). Information about living in Spain, including an 'ask the legal expert' facility. The site has particularly good links.

Spain For Visitors (⌨ http://spainforvisitors.com). Good general information about visiting Spain.

Spanish Forum (⌨ www.spanishforum.org). A wealth of useful and continually updated information about all aspects of living and working in Spain, including a free monthly 'e-newsletter'.

Survival Books (⌨ www.survivalbooks.net). Survival Books are the publishers of this book and *Buying a Home in Spain, Costa del Sol Lifeline, Living & Working in Spain, The Best Places to Buy a Home in Spain,* and *The Wines of Spain*. The website includes useful tips for anyone planning to buy a home, live, work, retire or do business in Spain.

TurEspaña/Spanish National Tourist Office (⌨ www.tourspain.co.uk or ⌨ www.spain.info).

Travelling in Spain (⌨ http://travelinginspain.com). Information about Spanish cities.

TuSpain (⌨ www.tuspain.com). General information about Spain with the emphasis on buying property and residential matters.

Typically Spanish (⌨ www.typicallyspanish.com). Information about a wide range of Spanish topics and listing of services.ide range of Spanish topics and listing of services.

INDEX

D

E

SURVIVAL BOOKS ON SPAIN

Buying a Home in Spain is essential reading for anyone planning to purchase property in Spain and is designed to guide you through the property jungle and make it a pleasant and enjoyable experience. Most importantly, it's packed with vital information to help you **avoid the sort of disasters that can turn your dream home into a nightmare!**

Living and Working in Spain is essential reading for anyone planning to live or work in Spain, including retirees, visitors, business people, migrants and students. It's packed with important and useful information designed to help you **avoid costly mistakes and save both time and money.**

The Best Places to Buy a Home in Spain is the most comprehensive and up-to-date homebuying guide to Spain, containing detailed regional guides to help you choose the ideal location for your home.

Costa del Sol Lifeline is the essential guide to the most popular region of Spain, containing everything you need to know about local life. Other titles in the series include Dordogne/Lot, and Poitou-Charentes.

Foreigners in Spain: Triumphs & Disasters is a collection of real-life experiences of people who have emigrated to Spain, providing a 'warts and all' picture of everyday life in the country.

Order your copies today by phone, fax, post or email from: Survival Books, PO Box 3780, YEOVIL, BA21 5WX, United Kingdom (☎/🖷 +44 (0)1935-700060, ✉ sales@survivalbooks.net, 🖥 www.survivalbooks.net).

Qty.	Title	Price (incl. p&p)			Total
		UK	Europe	World	
	The Alien's Guide to Britain	£6.95	£8.95	£12.45	
	The Alien's Guide to France	£6.95	£8.95	£12.45	
	The Best Places to Buy a Home in France	£13.95	£15.95	£19.45	
	The Best Places to Buy a Home in Spain	£13.95	£15.95	£19.45	
	Buying a Home Abroad	£13.95	£15.95	£19.45	
	Buying a Home in Florida	£13.95	£15.95	£19.45	
	Buying a Home in France	£13.95	£15.95	£19.45	
	Buying a Home in Greece & Cyprus	£13.95	£15.95	£19.45	
	Buying a Home in Ireland	£11.95	£13.95	£17.45	
	Buying a Home in Italy	£13.95	£15.95	£19.45	
	Buying a Home in Portugal	£13.95	£15.95	£19.45	
	Buying a Home in South Africa	£13.95	£15.95	£19.45	
	Buying a Home in Spain	£13.95	£15.95	£19.45	
	Buying, Letting & Selling Property	£11.95	£13.95	£17.45	
	Foreigners in France: Triumphs & Disasters	£11.95	£13.95	£17.45	
	Foreigners in Spain: Triumphs & Disasters	£11.95	£13.95	£17.45	
	Costa Blanca Lifeline	£11.95	£13.95	£17.45	
	Costa del Sol Lifeline	£11.95	£13.95	£17.45	
	Dordogne/Lot Lifeline	£11.95	£13.95	£17.45	
	Poitou-Charentes Lifeline	£11.95	£13.95	£17.45	
	Living & Working Abroad	£14.95	£16.95	£20.45	
	Living & Working in America	£14.95	£16.95	£20.45	
	Living & Working in Australia	£14.95	£16.95	£20.45	
	Living & Working in Britain	£14.95	£16.95	£20.45	
	Living & Working in Canada	£16.95	£18.95	£22.45	
	Living & Working in the European Union	£16.95	£18.95	£22.45	
	Living & Working in the Far East	£16.95	£18.95	£22.45	
	Living & Working in France	£14.95	£16.95	£20.45	
	Living & Working in Germany	£16.95	£18.95	£22.45	
Total carried forward (see over)					

ORDER FORM

Qty.	Title	Price (incl. p&p)			Total
				Total brought forward	
			Price (incl. p&p)		
		UK	Europe	World	
	L&W in the Gulf States & Saudi Arabia	£16.95	£18.95	£22.45	
	L&W in Holland, Belgium & Luxembourg	£14.95	£16.95	£20.45	
	Living & Working in Ireland	£14.95	£16.95	£20.45	
	Living & Working in Italy	£16.95	£18.95	£22.45	
	Living & Working in London	£13.95	£15.95	£19.45	
	Living & Working in New Zealand	£14.95	£16.95	£20.45	
	Living & Working in Spain	£14.95	£16.95	£20.45	
	Living & Working in Switzerland	£16.95	£18.95	£22.45	
	Normandy Lifeline	£11.95	£13.95	£17.45	
	Renovating & Maintaining Your French Home	£16.95	£18.95	£22.45	
	Retiring Abroad	£14.95	£16.95	£20.45	
				Grand Total	

Order your copies today by phone, fax, post or email from: Survival Books, PO Box 3780, YEOVIL, BA21 5WX, United Kingdom (☎/🖷 +44 (0)1935-700060, ✉ sales@ survivalbooks.net, 🖳 www.survivalbooks.net). If you aren't entirely satisfied, simply return them to us within 14 days for a full and unconditional refund.

I enclose a cheque for the grand total/Please charge my Amex/Delta/Maestro (Switch)/MasterCard/Visa card as follows. (delete as applicable)

Card No. _ _ _ _   _ _ _ _   _ _ _ _   _ _ _ _   Security Code* _ _ _

Expiry date _____   Issue number (Maestro/Switch only) _____

Signature _____   Tel. No. _____

NAME _____

ADDRESS _____

_____

_____

* The security code is the last three digits on the signature strip.